Paul D'Anieri and Taras Kuzio (Eds.)

ASPECTS OF THE ORANGE REVOLUTION I

Democratization and Elections in Post-Communist Ukraine

ibidem-Verlag
Stuttgart

Bibliografische Information der Deutschen Nationalbibliothek
Die Deutsche Nationalbibliothek verzeichnet diese Publikation in der Deutschen Nationalbibliografie; detaillierte bibliografische Daten sind im Internet über http://dnb.d-nb.de abrufbar.

Bibliographic information published by the Deutsche Nationalbibliothek
Die Deutsche Nationalbibliothek lists this publication in the Deutsche Nationalbibliografie; detailed bibliographic data are available in the Internet at http://dnb.d-nb.de.

Except for the introduction to volumes I-VI, the contributions in this book were originally published in © *Communist and Post-Communist Studies*, vol. 38, no. 1, June 2005, pp. 131-292. We gratefully acknowledge the journal editors' kind permission to reprint these papers here.

Formatting assistance: Olena Sivuda

Frontcover Picture: Poster on Kyiv's *Maidan Nezalezhnosti* (Independence Square) during the Orange Revolution saying: "Tak [Yes]! Yushchenko". © Tammy Lynch, 2004.

∞

Gedruckt auf alterungsbeständigem, säurefreien Papier
Printed on acid-free paper

ISSN: 1614-3515

ISBN-10: 3-89821-698-5
ISBN-13: 978-3-89821-698-2

© *ibidem*-Verlag
Stuttgart 2007

Alle Rechte vorbehalten

Das Werk einschließlich aller seiner Teile ist urheberrechtlich geschützt. Jede Verwertung außerhalb der engen Grenzen des Urheberrechtsgesetzes ist ohne Zustimmung des Verlages unzulässig und strafbar. Dies gilt insbesondere für Vervielfältigungen, Übersetzungen, Mikroverfilmungen und elektronische Speicherformen sowie die Einspeicherung und Verarbeitung in elektronischen Systemen.

All rights reserved. No part of this publication may be reproduced, stored in or introduced into a retrieval system, or transmitted, in any form, or by any means (electronic, mechanical, photocopying, recording or otherwise) without the prior written permission of the publisher. Any person who does any unauthorized act in relation to this publication may be liable to criminal prosecution and civil claims for damages.

Printed in Germany

Soviet and Post-Soviet Politics and Society (SPPS) Vol. 63
ISSN 1614-3515

General Editor: Andreas Umland, *Shevchenko University of Kyiv*, umland@stanfordalumni.org

Editorial Assistant: Olena Sivuda, *Dragomanov Pedagogical University of Kyiv*, sivuda@ukrcognita.com.ua

EDITORIAL COMMITTEE*

DOMESTIC & COMPARATIVE POLITICS
Prof. **Ellen Bos**, *Andrássy University of Budapest*
Dr. **Ingmar Bredies**, *Kyiv-Mohyla Academy*
Dr. **Andrey Kazantsev**, *MGIMO (U) MID RF, Moscow*
Dr. **Heiko Pleines**, *University of Bremen*
Prof. **Richard Sakwa**, *University of Kent at Canterbury*
Dr. **Sarah Whitmore**, *Oxford Brookes University*
Dr. **Harald Wydra**, *University of Cambridge*

SOCIETY, CLASS & ETHNICITY
Col. **David Glantz**, *"Journal of Slavic Military Studies"*
Dr. **Rashid Kaplanov**, *Russian Academy of Sciences*
Dr. **Marlène Laruelle**, *EHESS, Paris*
Dr. **Stephen Shulman**, *Southern Illinois University*
Prof. **Stefan Troebst**, *University of Leipzig*

POLITICAL ECONOMY & PUBLIC POLICY
Prof. em. **Marshall Goldman**, *Wellesley College, Mass.*
Dr. **Andreas Goldthau**, *Stiftung Wissenschaft und Politik*
Dr. **Robert Kravchuk**, *University of North Carolina*
Dr. **David Lane**, *University of Cambridge*
Dr. **Carol Leonard**, *University of Oxford*

Dr. **Maria Popova**, *McGill University, Montreal*

FOREIGN POLICY & INTERNATIONAL AFFAIRS
Dr. **Peter Duncan**, *University College London*
Dr. **Taras Kuzio**, *George Washington University, DC*
Prof. **Gerhard Mangott**, *University of Innsbruck*
Dr. **Diana Schmidt**, *University of Bremen*
Dr. **Lisbeth Tarlow**, *Harvard University, Cambridge*
Dr. **Christian Wipperfürth**, *N-Ost Network, Berlin*
Dr. **William Zimmerman**, *University of Michigan*

HISTORY, CULTURE & THOUGHT
Dr. **Catherine Andreyev**, *University of Oxford*
Prof. **Mark Bassin**, *University of Birmingham*
Dr. **Alexander Etkind**, *University of Cambridge*
Dr. **Gasan Gusejnov**, *University of Bremen*
Prof. em. **Walter Laqueur**, *Georgetown University*
Prof. **Leonid Luks**, *Catholic University of Eichstaett*
Dr. **Olga Malinova**, *Russian Academy of Sciences*
Dr. **Andrei Rogatchevski**, *University of Glasgow*
Dr. **Mark Tauger**, *West Virginia University*
Dr. **Stefan Wiederkehr**, *DHI, Warsaw*

ADVISORY BOARD*

Prof. **Dominique Arel**, *University of Ottawa*
Prof. **Jörg Baberowski**, *Humboldt University of Berlin*
Prof. **Margarita Balmaceda**, *Seton Hall University*
Dr. **John Barber**, *University of Cambridge*
Prof. **Timm Beichelt**, *European University Viadrina*
Prof. **Archie Brown**, *University of Oxford*
Dr. **Vyacheslav Bryukhovetsky**, *Kyiv-Mohyla Academy*
Prof. **Timothy Colton**, *Harvard University, Cambridge*
Prof. **Paul D'Anieri**, *University of Kansas, Lawrence*
Dr. **Heike Dörrenbächer**, *DGO, Berlin*
Dr. **John Dunlop**, *Hoover Institution, Stanford, California*
Dr. **Sabine Fischer**, *EU Institute for Security Studies*
Dr. **Geir Flikke**, *NUPI, Oslo*
Prof. **Alexander Galkin**, *Russian Academy of Sciences*
Prof. **Frank Golczewski**, *University of Hamburg*
Dr. **Nikolas Gvosdev**, *"The National Interest," DC*
Prof. **Mark von Hagen**, *Arizona State University*
Dr. **Guido Hausmann**, *Trinity College Dublin*
Prof. **Dale Herspring**, *Kansas State University*
Dr. **Stefani Hoffman**, *Hebrew University of Jerusalem*
Prof. **Mikhail Ilyin**, *MGIMO (U) MID RF, Moscow*
Prof. **Vladimir Kantor**, *Higher School of Economics*
Dr. **Ivan Katchanovski**, *University of Toronto*
Prof. em. **Andrzej Korbonski**, *University of California*
Dr. **Iris Kempe**, *Center for Applied Policy Research*
Prof. **Herbert Küpper**, *Institut für Ostrecht München*
Dr. **Rainer Lindner**, *Stiftung Wissenschaft und Politik*
Dr. **Vladimir Malakhov**, *Russian Academy of Sciences*
Dr. **Luke March**, *University of Edinburgh*

Dr. **Michael McFaul**, *Stanford University, California*
Prof. **Birgit Menzel**, *University of Mainz-Germersheim*
Prof. **Valery Mikhailenko**, *The Urals State University*
Dr. **Emil Pain**, *Higher School of Economics, Moscow*
Dr. **Oleg Podvintsev**, *Russian Academy of Sciences*
Prof. **Olga Popova**, *St. Petersburg State University*
Dr. **Alex Pravda**, *University of Oxford*
Dr. **Erik van Ree**, *University of Amsterdam*
Dr. **Joachim Rogall**, *Robert Bosch Foundation, Stuttgart*
Prof. **Peter Rutland**, *Wesleyan University, Middletown*
Dr. **Sergei Ryabov**, *Kyiv-Mohyla Academy*
Prof. **Marat Salikov**, *The Urals State Law Academy*
Dr. **Gwendolyn Sasse**, *University of Oxford*
Prof. **Jutta Scherrer**, *EHESS, Paris*
Prof. **Robert Service**, *University of Oxford*
Mr. **James Sherr**, *Defence Academy of the UK, Swindon*
Dr. **Oxana Shevel**, *Tufts University, Medford*
Prof. **Eberhard Schneider**, *University of Siegen*
Prof. **Olexander Shnyrkov**, *Shevchenko University, Kyiv*
Prof. **Hans-Henning Schröder**, *University of Bremen*
Prof. **Viktor Shnirelman**, *Russian Academy of Sciences*
Dr. **Lisa Sundstrom**, *University of British Columbia*
Dr. **Philip Walters**, *"Religion, State and Society," Leeds*
Dr. **Zenon Wasyliw**, *Ithaca College, New York State*
Dr. **Lucan Way**, *University of Toronto*
Dr. **Markus Wehner**, *"Frankfurter Allgemeine Zeitung"*
Dr. **Andrew Wilson**, *University College London*
Prof. **Jan Zielonka**, *University of Oxford*
Prof. **Andrei Zorin**, *University of Oxford*

* While the Editorial Committee and Advisory Board support the General Editor in the choice and improvement of manuscripts for publication, responsibility for remaining errors and misinterpretations in the series' volumes lies with the books' authors.

Soviet and Post-Soviet Politics and Society (SPPS)
ISSN 1614-3515

Founded in 2004 and refereed since 2007, SPPS makes available affordable English-, German- and Russian-language studies on the history of the countries of the former Soviet bloc from the late Tsarist period to today. It publishes approximately 20 volumes per year, and focuses on issues in transitions to and from democracy such as economic crisis, identity formation, civil society development, and constitutional reform in CEE and the NIS. SPPS also aims to highlight so far understudied themes in East European studies such as right-wing radicalism, religious life, higher education, or human rights protection. The authors and titles of previously published and forthcoming manuscripts are listed at the end of this book. For a full description of the series and reviews of its books, see http://www.ibidem-verlag.de/red/spps.

Note for authors (as of 2007): After successful review, fully formatted and carefully edited electronic master copies of up to 250 pages will be published as b/w A5 paperbacks and marketed in Germany (e.g. vlb.de, buchkatalog.de, amazon.de). English-language books will, in addition, be marketed internationally (e.g. amazon.com). For longer books, formatting/editorial assistance, different binding, oversize maps, coloured illustrations and other special arrangements, authors' fees between €100 and €1500 apply. Publication of German doctoral dissertations follows a separate procedure. Authors are asked to provide a high-quality electronic picture on the object of their study for the book's front-cover. Younger authors may add a foreword from an established scholar. Monograph authors and collected volume editors receive two free as well as further copies for a reduced authors' price, and will be asked to contribute to marketing their book as well as finding reviewers and review journals for them. These conditions are subject to yearly review, and to be modified, in the future. Further details at www.ibidem-verlag.de/red/spps-authors.

Editorial correspondence & manuscripts should, until 2008, be sent to: Dr. Andreas Umland, DAAD, German Embassy, vul. Bohdana Khmelnitskoho 25, UA-01901 Kiev, Ukraine; umland@stanfordalumni.org.

Business correspondence & review copy requests should be sent to: *ibidem*-Verlag, Julius-Leber-Weg 11, D-30457 Hannover, Germany; tel.: +49(0)511-2622200; fax: +49(0)511-2622201; spps@ibidem-verlag.de.

Book orders & payments should be made via the publisher's electronic book shop at: http://www.ibidem-verlag.de/red/SPPS_EN/

Recent Volumes

54   Галина Кожевникова и Владимир Прибыловский
Российская власть в биографиях II
Члены Правительства РФ в 2004 г.
ISBN 978-3-89821-797-2

55   Галина Кожевникова и Владимир Прибыловский
Российская власть в биографиях III
Руководители федеральных служб и агентств РФ в 2004 г.
ISBN 978-3-89821-798-9

56   *Ileana Petroniu*
Privatisierung in Transformationsökonomien
Determinanten der Restrukturierungs-Bereitschaft am Beispiel Polens, Rumäniens und der Ukraine
Mit einem Vorwort von Rainer W. Schäfer
ISBN 978-3-89821-790-3

57   *Christian Wipperfürth*
Russland und seine GUS-Nachbarn
Hintergründe, aktuelle Entwicklungen und Konflikte in einer ressourcenreichen Region
ISBN 978-3-89821-801-6

58   *Togzhan Kassenova*
From Antagonism to Partnership
The Uneasy Path of the U.S.-Russian Cooperative Threat Reduction
With a foreword by Christoph Bluth
ISBN 978-3-89821-707-1

59   *Alexander Höllwerth*
Das sakrale eurasische Imperium des Aleksandr Dugin
Eine Diskursanalyse zum postsowjetischen russischen Rechtsextremismus
Mit einem Vorwort von Dirk Uffelmann
ISBN 978-3-89821-813-9

60   Олег Рябов
«Россия-Матушка»
Национализм, гендер и война в России XX века
С предисловием Елены Гощило
ISBN 978-3-89821-487-2

61   *Ivan Maistrenko*
Borot'bism
A Chapter in the History of the Ukrainian Revolution
With a new introduction by Chris Ford
Translated by George S. N. Luckyj with the assistance of Ivan L. Rudnytsky
ISBN 978-3-89821-697-5

62   *Maryna Romanets*
Anamorphosic Texts and Reconfigured Visions
Improvised Traditions in Contemporary Ukrainian and Irish Literature
ISBN 978-3-89821-576-3

Contents

Introduction to *Aspects of the Orange Revolution I-VI:*
Ukraine's Second Transition in the Russian Mirror
Andreas Umland — 7

Democratization and Elections in Post-Communist Ukraine

Ukraine's 1994 Elections as an Economic Event
Robert S. Kravchuk and *Victor Chudowsky* — 19

Regime Type and Politics in Ukraine under Kuchma
Taras Kuzio — 63

Rapacious Individualism and Political Competition
in Ukraine, 1992-2004
Lucan A. Way — 95

The Ukrainian Orange Revolution Brought More than
a New President: What Kind of Democracy Will the
Institutional Changes Bring?
Robert K. Christensen, Edward R. Rakhimkulov, and
Charles R. Wise — 117

The Last Hurrah: The 2004 Ukrainian Presidential Elections
and the Limits of Machine Politics
Paul D'Anieri — 149

Ukrainian Political Parties and Foreign Policy in Election
Campaigns: The Parliamentary Elections of 1998 and 2002
Anna Makhorkina — 175

The European Union and Democratization in Ukraine
Paul Kubicek — 199

Introduction to *Aspects of the Orange Revolution I-VI*: Ukraine's Second Transition in the Russian Mirror

Andreas Umland, National Taras Shevchenko University of Kyiv

The completion of this project – assembling and editing six collections of previously published and unpublished research papers, election reports, opinion pieces, and official documents ranging from musicology to advanced statistics – took more than two years. What could justify the considerable effort to bring together and, for the reader, hefty costs to buy within one set all of these books? Arguably, the event that has become known as the Orange Revolution will, whatever may happen to Ukraine in the future, remain an important reference point in the international study of democratic transition and consolidation. It is certainly the major event in post-Soviet Ukrainian studies,[1] and will function as – what might be called – a "crucial case" within comparative research into post-communist politics.[2]

These circumstances are in discord with the view of the Orange Revolution held by a surprisingly large number of powerful politicians, influential "political technologists" and even some politologists in Moscow[3] where *oranzhevyi* (orange) has become a swear-word used to label all sorts of supposedly "anti-Russian," "pro-American" actors and activities in- and outside

---
1. Valentin Yakushik, "Politicheskie i tsivilizatsionnye aspekty ukrainiskoi revoliutsii 2004-2005 gg.," *Politicheskaia ekspertiza*, no. 2 (2006): 289-298, http://politex.info/content/view/196/40/.
2. Harry Eckstein, "Case Study and Theory in Political Science," in: Fred I. Greenstein and Nelson W. Polsby, eds., *Handbook of Political Science* (Reading, MA: Addison-Wesley 1975).
3. Obviously, the following critique does not apply to Russia's considerable community of serious political scientists who mostly have a balanced approach to recent Ukrainian history and critical view of current Russian affairs. See, for instance, Vladimir Ya. Gel'man, "Iz ognia da v polymia? Dinamika postsovetskikh rezhimov v sravnitel'noi perspektive," *Politicheskie issledovaniia*, no. 2 (2007): 81-108; Igor' Kliamkin and Tat'iana Kutkovets, "Kremlevskaia shkola politologii: Dekonstruktsiia kremlevskogo diskursa," *Kontinent*, no. 131 (2007): 145-175.

Russia.[4] The currently dominant Russian interpretation of the events in Ukraine in 2004-2005 is documented by the, in Russian terms, relatively moderate text of the Moscow analyst Vladimir Frolov in volume IV.[5] It is conspirological in so far as it portrays the various activities of millions of Ukrainians as well as of hundreds of civic and political Ukrainian organizations during this period as masterminded by the United States government and its various puppets in Ukraine's civil society, mass media, party politics and state apparatus.[6] If one holds such a view of the Orange Revolution, then the interdisciplinary, multi-author, polymethodological and public study of this event – as attempted here – is ridiculous. Instead, the Orange Revolution would be in need of investigation by able, no-nonsense security service officers (to whom

---

[4] I – like other contributors to this project probably too – have been repeatedly identified as an *oranzhevyi* by Russian "patriotic" or Ukrainian pro-Russian commentators. E.g. Ivan Burtsev, "Politicheskii antifashistkii ekstaz?" *Obratnaia storona*, 23 July 2007, http://stolin1969.narod.ru/230707.html. While I would not call myself this way, I am prepared to bear this badge. However, one of my few publications on Ukrainian high politics was not exactly an advertisement for Viktor Yushchenko's "Orange" team, but rather portrayed the political managers of *Nasha Ukraina* in 2005-2007 as a bunch of loosers. See Andreas Umland, "Yushchenko's Big Gamble," *The Moscow Times*, 10 April 2007, p. 10, http://sptimesrussia.com/index.php?action_id=2&story_id=21310. The article became the subject of an attack by the notorious webcampaigner *La Russophobe* who reported that, in it, I had "spewed forth a disgusting torrent of anti-Yuschenko propaganda" – a characterization that would seem to tarnish my reputation as an *oranzhevyi*. See N.N., "Annals of Russophile Gibberish," *La Russophobe*, 11 April 2007, http://larussophobe.wordpress.com/2007/04/11/annals-of-russophile-gibberish/.

[5] Vladimir Frolov, "Democracy by Remote Control," *Russia in Global Affairs*, no. 4 (2005), http://eng.globalaffairs.ru/numbers/13/976.html, reprinted, with kind permission by the copyright holder, in: Ingmar Bredies, Andreas Umland and Valentin Yakushik, eds., *Aspects of the Orange Revolution IV: Foreign Assistance and Civic Action in the 2004 Ukrainian Presidential Elections*. Soviet and Post-Soviet Politics and Society 66 (Stuttgart: *ibidem*-Verlag 2007): 81-86.

[6] See, for instance, the monograph by a Doctor of Science in Chemistry who has, like a whole number of similar publicists, made himself a name, in Russia in recent years, by publishing pamphlets devoted to uncovering the West's "true" intentions on the territory of the former USSR: Sergei Kara-Murza, *Revoliutsii na eksport* (Moskva: Algoritm 2005). Or, see the collected volume edited by a Russian politician who had, for a period of time, been declared *persona non grata* by the Ukrainian government: Konstantin F. Zatulin, ed., *Na fone "oranzhevoi revoliutsii." Ukraina mezhdu Vostokom i Zapadom: vchera, segodnia, zavtra* (Moskva: Institut stran SNG 2005). See also Mikhail Pogrebinsky, ed., *Oranzhevaia revoliutsiia: Versii, khronika, dokumenty* (Kiev: Optima 2005).

Frolov apparently once belonged[7]) disclosing the "hidden forces" behind these events – and not by naïve or/and (under-)paid book worms who, consciously or not, are on the service of the well-known puppeteers at the White House or/and Wall Street. Perhaps, this publication too is an "American plot" – though, of course, an as futile attempt as the Orange Revolution itself! – to undermine Russia's recently established "sovereign democracy"? Clearly, so one hears from disturbingly many well-educated Russians today, the Orange Revolution was, after the bombing of Serbia, occupation of Iraq, or coup in Georgia, yet another exercise of what Washington would like – but thanks to Putin's firm leadership is unable – to do with Russia.

One might add that, during the Orange Revolution, Frolov apparently worked for Gleb Pavlovskii's so-called Effective Policy Foundation, i.e. a Moscow political technology firm involved in the various activities of the outgoing Kuchma administration, and in Yanukovych's campaign for the presidential elections.[8] The various Russian actors with a personal stake in the outcome of the 2004 confrontation underestimated the weight of democratic inclinations, strength of pluralistic traditions, and tenacity of civic actors in Ukrainian society.[9] That, in the aftermath, they have been trying to present the Orange Revolution as an event initiated and manipulated by the West is not surprising, and could be interpreted as a form of rationalization of their own professional failure. The paranoid conspiracy theorizing that still dominates Russian public discourse on the Orange Revolution (as well as many other events) might thus not only be related to the authorities' overblown fear of a democratic revolution in Russia. It might also be the result of Moscow's political technologists' need to explain to their godfathers in the Kremlin why, for instance, the Effective Policy Foundation was ineffective in Ukraine, and failed to prevent Yushchenko's presidency – the Moscow spin-doctors' obvious mission at Kyiv. Frolov's idea of "democracy by remote control" serves as a convenient deflection from the circumstance that, arguably, Pavlovskii and Co., with their

---

7   As indicated in the official biographical note on Frolov at his company's website: http://www.leffgroup.ru/about/experts1.
8   Taras Kuzio, "Russian Policy toward Ukraine during the Elections," *Demokratizatsiya*, 13, 4 (2005): 491-517.
9   Andreas Umland and Ingmar Bredies, "Postsovetskii paradoks: demokratiia v Ukraine, avtokratiia v Rossii," *Zerkalo nedeli*, no. 8(687) (2008), http://www.zn.ua/1000/1600/62203/.

heavy-handed approach, themselves helped the Orange Revolution to succeed, and thus to strengthen those political dynamics that, especially in comparison to concurrent Russian trends,[10] changed the nature of Ukrainian domestic politics and foreign affairs.

The conspirological explanation of the Orange Revolution is also useful in drawing away attention from the fact that the repercussions of Moscow's political technologists' behavior in Kyiv and of the one-sided reporting of Russian television, widely watched in Ukraine, during and after the Orange Revolution did and still do damage to Russian-Ukrainian relations. The arrogant attitude of many journalists and commentators of Russia's government-controlled TV channels to Ukrainian politics and policies (admitted even by the Russian Ambassador to Ukraine Viktor Chernomyrdin) might meet the demands of the Russian elite and public. However, once watched in Ukraine by the objects of such reporting, it tends to make Ukrainians less sympathetic towards Russia, increasingly skeptical about the future of Russian-Ukrainian relations, and more interested in such institutions as the WTO, EU or NATO than they would otherwise be.[11] Here too, alleged machinations of the West and its "fifth column" in Kyiv serve as an excuse for the growing estrangement between Russia's and Ukraine's elites and people – an unfortunate development that is more related to Moscow's continuing play with Russian anti-Ukrainian stereotypes than to any activities of Western governmental and non-governmental organizations at Kyiv.[12]

---

10 For an interesting facet of this difference – youth activism in both countries – see Viktoriya Topalova, "In Search of Heroes: Cultural Politics and Political Mobilization of Youths in Contemporary Russia and Ukraine," *Demokratizatsiya*, vol. 14, no. 1 (2006): 23-41, and Taras Kuzio, "Ukraine is not Russia: Comparing Youth Political Activism," *SAIS Review*, vol. 26, no. 2 (2006): 67-83;.

11 Although, for instance, the acceptance of Ukraine's future membership in NATO among the Ukrainian population was still below 50% in 2007, it has been constantly rising ever since the Orange Revolution – one suspects – not the least because of Russian TV's peculiar style of reporting and commenting on Ukraine's politics and society.

12 For a German language survey of the various Western democracy promotion programs in Ukraine, see the relevant contributions in volumes III and IV of this project as well as my paper, "Westliche Förderprogramme in der Ukraine: Einblicke in die europäisch-nordamerikanische Unterstützung ukrainischer Reformbestrebungen seit 1991. Mit einem Nachwort von Astrid Sahm," *Forschungsstelle Osteuropa Bremen: Arbeitspapiere und Materialien*, no. 63 (2004), http://se2.isn.ch/serviceengine/FileContent?serviceID=10&fileid=D092944E-F352-DC1A-CF4E-3CEFBC401E94&lng=de.

ASPECTS OF THE ORANGE REVOLUTION I 11

This long-winded reference to Moscow's interpretation of the events in Kyiv in 2004 is meant to lead to the two books that I would recommend first of all as complementary reading to the present collection. While not dealing directly with the Orange Revolution, a recent edited volume on comparative regime typology by Andreas Schedler,[13] and an acclaimed monograph on the nature of post-Soviet politics by Andrew Wilson[14] seem to identify most vividly the core of the issue at hand in the following papers. To be sure, there are now a number of further scholarly monographs, collected volumes and research papers specifically on the Ukrainian presidential elections in 2004 that rival the present project and can be recommended too as additional reading.[15] This concerns, for instance, Wilson's other recent important book on the Orange Revolution (a kind of standard reference to the event),[16] Strasser's investigation into the role of civil society in it,[17] as well as paper collections edited by Kurth/Kempe, Bredies, McFaul/Aslund, Kuzio and Shapoval.[18] In addition, there are now numerous individual journal articles that would have been worth re-publication, but, for one reason or another, could not be included in the present project.[19]

---

13   Andreas Schedler, *Electoral Authoritarianism: The Dynamics of Unfree Competition* (Boulder, CO: Lynne Rienner 2006).
14   Andrew Wilson, *Virtual Politics: Faking Democracy in the Post-Soviet World* (New Haven/London: Yale University Press 2005). See also idem, "Ukraine's New Virtual Politics," *East European Constitutional Review*, vol. 10, nos. 2-3 (2001): 60-66.
15   Taras Kuzio, "Ukraine's Orange Revolution: Rush to Judgement?" *Journal of Communist Studies and Transition Politics*, vol. 23, no. 2 (2007): 320-326.
16   Andrew Wilson, *Ukraine's Orange Revolution* (New Haven, CT: Yale University Press 2005).
17   Florian Strasser, *Zivilgesellschaftliche Einflüsse auf die Orange Revolution: Die gewaltlose Massenbewegung und die ukrainische Wahlkrise 2004*. Soviet and Post-Soviet Politics and Society 29 (Stuttgart: *ibidem*-Verlag 2006).
18   Helmut Kurth and Iris Kempe, eds., *Presidential Election and Orange Revolution: Implications for Ukraine's Transition* (Kyiv: Friedrich-Ebert-Stiftung 2005); Ingmar Bredies, ed., *Zur Anatomie der Orange Revolution in der Ukraine: Wechsel des Elitenregimes oder Triumph des Parlamentarismus?* Soviet and Post-Soviet Politics and Society 13 (Stuttgart: *ibidem*-Verlag 2005); Anders Aslund and Michael McFaul, eds., *Revolution in Orange: The Origins of Ukraine's Democratic Breakthrough* (Washington, DC: Carnegie Endowment 2006); Taras Kuzio, ed., "Democratic Revolution in Ukraine: From Kuchmagate to Orange Revolution," *The Journal of Communist Studies and Transition Politics*, 23, 1(Special Issue) (2007): 1-179; Iurii Shapoval, ed., *U kol'orakh 'pomaranchevoï revoliutsiï'* (Kyïv: EksOb 2007).
19   Apart from the other papers mentioned here and many non-English articles, one could mention, for instance: Lucan Way, "Kuchma's Failed Authoritarianism," *Journal of Democracy*, vol. 16, no. 2 (2005): 131-145; Taras Kuzio, "Ukraine's Orange Revolution: The Opposition's Road to Success," *Journal of Democracy*, vol. 16, no. 2

However, the two books deciphering best what the Orange Revolution was actually about and which therefore would seem to constitute the most suitable complementary reading to *Aspects of the Orange Revolution* are Schedler's *Electoral Authoritarianism: The Dynamics of Unfree Competition*,[20] and Wilson's *Virtual Politics: Faking Democracy in the Post-Soviet World*.[21] In mainstream Russian interpretations of the Orange Revolution, the issue at hand in this event is, at best, presented as an extraordinary continuation of the ongoing power struggle between Ukraine's two competing political-economic clans with their geographically and culturally defined constituencies in Eastern and Western Ukraine, or, at worst, as a clash between two antagonistic civilizations with heavy involvement by the *amerikantsy*.

Doubtlessly, in these elections two clearly distinguishable Ukrainian political groups were set against each other and, though both were officially in favor of EU membership, one of them was more pro-Western than the other. Admittedly, the Orange Revolution was not a proper revolution comparable to the French, Russian or other social revolutions. Perhaps, the event should be instead classified as a mass action of civil disobedience in defense of the country's political order as defined by the Constitution of Ukraine adopted in 1996 (and it is rather the Kremlin's systematic deflation of Russia's nascent democratic institutions and silent devaluation of her Constitution since 2000 that might qualify as a political revolution from above). Yet, the 2004 actions that became known as the Orange Revolution were also not merely about *who* would win the elections. Rather, what mobilized both hundreds of thousands of

---

(2005): 117-130; *idem*, "Kuchma to Yushchenko: Ukraine's 2004 Elections, and 'Orange Revolution'," *Problems of Post-Communism*, vol. 52, no. 2 (2005): 29-44; *idem*, "The Orange Revolution at the Crossroads," *Demokratizatsiya*, vol. 14, no. 4 (2006): 477-493; *idem*, "Ukrainian Foreign and Security Policy Since the Orange Revolution," *The International Spectator*, no. 4 (2006): 1-18; Ararat L. Osipian and Alexander L. Osipian, "Why Donbass Votes for Yanukovich: Confronting the Orange Revolution," *Demokratizatsiya*, vol. 14, no. 4 (2006): 495-518; Olena Yatsunska, "Mythmaking and Its Discontents in the 2004 Ukrainian Presidential Campaign," *Demokratizatsiya*, vol. 14, no. 4 (2006): 519-534; Bohdan Klid, "Rock, Pop and Politics in Ukraine's 2004 Presidential Campaign," *Journal of Communist Studies and Transition Politics*, vol. 23, no. 1 (2007): 139-158; Alexandra Hrycak, "Seeing Orange: Women's Activism and Ukraine's Orange Revolution," *Women's Studies Quarterly*, vol. 35, no. 3/4 (2007): 208-225.

20 Schedler, *Electoral Authoritarianism*. See also Steven Levitsky and Lucan A. Way, "The Rise of Competative Authoritarianism," *Journal of Democracy*, vol. 13, no. 2 (2002): 51-65.

Ukrainians and several prominent international organizations was the issue of *how* the elections were conducted. In other words, the primary question was whether this presidential poll constituted a democratic election, or not. What the Russian noise concerning the Orange Revolution has been trying to obfuscate ever since 2004 is that this upheaval was not so much about which politician would rule Ukraine, but about what kind of rule the country should have. At stake was, only in the second instance, the composition of Ukraine's highest offices. The immediate and more fundamental issue was what the nature of Ukraine's post-Kuchma political regime would be.

To clarify this distinction Schedler's *Electoral Authoritarianism* and Wilson's *Virtual Politics* are helpful. Their books – Schedler's from a theoretical and cross-cultural, and Wilson's from a post-Soviet and intra-regional comparative perspective – are useful in drawing a clear line between Ukraine's pseudo-democratic regime before the Orange Revolution, and its more or less democratic political system after it. Schedler defines the generic regime-type, of which Kuchma's Ukraine was but one permutation, as "electoral authoritarianism." While seemingly pluralistic voting procedures defined as "elections" take place in such countries regularly, these states constitute, nevertheless, dictatorships – if, mostly, of a relatively soft type. At the heart of such systems lies a formal acceptance of multi-party and -candidate elections as a procedure to legitimize power. However, in electoral authoritarian regimes, such "elections'" overall socio-political context as well as their conduct on voting day are manipulated and/or their results falsified to an extent that they cannot be classified as democratic any more. From this viewpoint, it seems an open question whether these political systems should be understood as hybrid regimes between demo- and autocracy, or whether the attribute "electoral" in their title represents, in fact, a euphemism that distracts from the controlled – or, in Wilson's words, "virtual" – character of public politics in countries with electoral authoritarian regimes.

For those of us acquainted with the various "political technologies" to deprive formally democratic processes of their meaning in the post-Soviet context, Schedler's collection can be fascinating reading. Its papers show that

---

21 Wilson, *Virtual Politics*.

these phenomena are not as much region-specific as we might have thought.[22] While there is thus an argument to be made that we are dealing here with a larger phenomenon that invites cross-cultural comparison, Wilson's *Virtual Politics* shows us what is still specific about the post-Soviet context, and in which particular ways "political technology" works. Wilson demonstrates in admirable detail how hidden control of information flows, party-building, and electoral processes by the powers-that-be have been subverting democracy in the post-Soviet world to such a degree as to create a relatively novel system of state-society relations in which fundamental electoral procedures are formally observed, but made largely senseless through their more or less sophisticated manipulation.

Wilson makes here in so far a terminological innovation as he lifts the, until then, largely colloquial, peculiarly post-Soviet construct of "political technology" to a proper political science concept, i.e. to a term specifically designed to distinguish certain essentially anti-democratic political practices from those political PR campaigns that are also well-known in the West. Wilson's argument is that "political technology" should only partly be understood as a radicalization of some dubious Western political practices, such as the massive negative advertising that has been typical of recent US presidential election campaigns. Instead, Wilson shows that "political technology" is, above all, rooted in Russia's and the other republics' Soviet past, namely in the peculiar subversion strategies that the KGB and other Soviet bloc security services had developed in their fight against anti-Soviet dissent.

On the one hand, Wilson has thus strengthened the *Soviet* element within "post-Soviet transitions" lending support to those researchers emphasizing the continued relevance of the ideographic element in – as opposed to nomothetic approaches to – the study of contemporary Russia, Ukraine, etc. On the other hand, we might be dealing here with a case were post-communist studies can make a contribution to general political science: "political tech-

---

22 At least, that was my experience when reviewing the book for the Austrian Journal of Political Science. For a Ukrainian and Russian version of this review reprinted as an essay on Schedler and Wilson, see Andreas Umland, "Elektoral'nyi avtorytaryzm postsovets'koï demokratiï [– a clearly self-contradictory title formulated not by me, but by the editors of the journal]," *Krytyka*, no. 9 (2007), http://www.krytyka.kiev.ua/articles/s.1_9_2007.html; idem, "Elektoral'nyi avtoritarizm na postsovetskom prostran-

nology" or "virtual politics," as introduced by Wilson, are concepts that can travel to other regions of the world and could help us understand better various distortions of democratic procedures by spin-doctors who might not have had the benefit of serving in Soviet security services, but who may still be equally cynical and similarly original in their choice of instruments for stage-managing allegedly democratic processes.[23]

Ukraine's leaving behind of electoral authoritarianism and re-entry on a democratic transition path seems to be the major reason why the immediate reaction and continuing attention of Russia's currently ruling circles to the Orange Revolution has been so nervous: It was not only the more pro-Western approach of Yushchenko and supposedly pro-Russian sentiment of Yanukovych that was at stake for the Kremlin in Kyiv in 2004. The Orange Revolution appeared threatening as it concerned an issue that was then related to, and still touches upon, the core of Putin's "sovereign democracy." It provided a model for how a post-Soviet society can get out of the deadlock of electoral authoritarianism and use, with foreign support, remnants of democratic procedurality to topple a *de facto* dictatorship. It might have been the experience of the Orange Revolution that motivated the Kremlin to abandon, three years later, its earlier dramaturgy of staged political competition by controlled parties, and go, in December 2007, for an almost complete, largely

---

stve," *Sravnitel'noe konstitutsionnoe obozrenie*, no. 1(62) (2008), http://www1.kueichstaett.de/ZIMOS/forum/docs/a12Buchbespr2.pdf.

23 Wilson's *Virtual Politics* is of additional value because of the astonishing amount of – partly, little-known – facts, dates and names that he has amassed here, and the variety of large events and small affairs that his narrative chronicles. Russian or Ukrainian political scientists may find Wilson's emphasis on the role of "political technology" not very original, and be, at best, intrigued by the relative novelty of these phenomena to the comparative study of democracy. Even they will, however, be impressed by, and able to learn from, Wilson's book because it is such a dense and well-researched description. Sometimes, to be sure, certain small facts are wrong, a Russian or Ukrainian word is misspelled, or an interesting event is missing in the story. For instance, Wilson, in his description of Zhirinovskii's activities in 1990-1991, does not mention the LDP-leader's meeting with Vice-President Gennadii Yanayev shortly before the August Coup of 1991. See Andreas Umland, "Zhirinovsky Enters Politics: A Chronology of the Emergence of the Liberal-Democratic Party of Russia 1990-1991," *The Journal of Slavic Military Studies*, vol. 18, no. 1 (2005): 15-30. But such minor errors or omissions seem unavoidable in as wide-ranging a narrative as Wilson's clearly is. Rather, one is left overwhelmed by the amount of empirical data provided here.

undisguised restoration of an, in essence, singly-party system.[24] What has changed in Russia since the publication of Wilson's *Virtual Politics* is that, by late 2007, the Kremlin did not any longer bother to efficaciously fake political pluralism. Instead Russia has returned to its "special path" more or less openly denouncing the principle of checks and balances, and even re-discovering ancient Byzantine traditions to legitimize the country's now manifestly monistic political order.[25] This development is even more stunning in view of the fact that Ukraine – a country the history of which is closely intertwined with, and which had experienced an even deeper post-Soviet crisis than, Russia – was, by late 2007, still on the bumpy road to a consolidated democracy, and making slow, but steady advances in its rapprochement with such institutions as the WTO, NATO and EU.

The papers and documents assembled in the following six volumes can be seen as a concerted attempt to answer the question why Ukraine is – at least, as of late 2007 – developing differently than virtually all other states that grew out of the Soviet Union founded in 1922.[26]

---

24 Andreas Umland, "Kremlin Overkill: Why Putin's entry into party politics is the beginning of the end of Russian façade democracy," *Zerkalo nedeli*, 13-19 October 2007, http://www.mw.ua/1000/1550/60798/.

25 On the idea of Russia's special path, see Leonid Luks, *Der russische "Sonderweg"? Aufsätze zur neuesten Geschichte Russlands im europäischen Kontext*. Soviet and Post-Soviet Politics and Society 16 (Stuttgart: *ibidem*-Verlag 2005).

26 The other partial exception is, of course, Georgia that was playing the role of a model for Ukraine in 2004. As this book goes to print, it appears, however, that the Georgian democratization is encountering difficulties. See, on Georgia's difference from Ukraine, Taras Kuzio, "Georgia and Ukraine: Similar Revolutions, Different Trajectories," *Eurasia Daily Monitor*, vol. 4, no. 211 (2007), http://www.taraskuzio.net/media/pdf/Georgia_Ukraine.pdf. Moldova and the Baltic republics were annexed to the Soviet Union only later.

Democratization and Elections in Post-Communist Ukraine

Ukraine's 1994 Elections as an Economic Event

Robert S. Kravchuk, Indiana University
Victor Chudowsky, Meridian International Center

Abstract
This article explores the political, economic, and social forces underlying the east/west cleavage in the 1994 Ukrainian presidential and parliamentary elections. We demonstrate that economic factors – notably, variations in regional economic strength and changes in employment in the period preceding the elections – are stronger predictors of country-wide voting behavior and candidate support than ethnic and linguistic factors. The exceptions are the extreme eastern and western oblasts, where the analysis suggests the existence of significant differences in political culture.

Introduction: prospects for democratic consolidation
The literature on the political transformations in Eastern Europe and the former Soviet Union maintains that consolidation of democracy will be a lengthy process, marked by a prolonged stage of political instability which has been termed "postcommunism" (Bunce, 1995; Daedalus, 1994; Fish, 1993, 1995; McFaul, 1993a,b; Schöpflin, 1994; Tong, 1995). Schöpflin, for instance, asserts that the communist experience has atomized post-socialist populations, plunging them into a "semi-permanent" state of confusion and disappointment. Much of the literature holds that the legacies of communism (that is, mass alienation, ethnic nationalism, lack of democratic traditions, distrust of political parties, a fledgling civil society) pose serious difficulties for consolidating democracy. In this view, a highly chaotic political atmosphere will render it difficult for the masses to identify their interests. This will lead to "state-centered," or as we call them, "statist" political systems, in which there are ideological divisions, widespread distrust of government, and rampant corruption. The state fills the void that civil society cannot fill. In the nascent post-communist political culture, elections will turn on personalities, rather than on social or material interests. Inordinate faith will therefore be placed in strong leaders, essentially benevo-

lent dictators (Kubicek, 1994; Rose and Haerpfer, 1994; White et al. 1994). In interviews the authors conducted in 1993-1995, some prominent Ukrainian politicians described the people as "waiting for Pinochet." The vestiges of communism thus include both cultural and institutional pathologies that tend to produce a highly volatile brand of politics, which militates against development of democratic traditions.

To the casual observer, Ukraine exhibits symptoms of suffering from the "postcommunist condition." It is commonplace to focus on the floundering party system, fledgling civic organizations, occasional rhetoric of ethnic intolerance, and nascent nationalism. Commentators especially dwell on the political divergencies between Ukraine's eastern and western regions. In the 1994 presidential and parliamentary elections, the east voted predominantly communist or socialist, while the west was a bastion of nationalist and democratic support. The common interpretation of the election result is that differences in language, ethnic heritage, and political culture constitute the major fault lines in Ukraine; the east having been more thoroughly "russified" than the west, and therefore less enthused with market reforms and links with Western Europe (Arel, 1994, 1995; Arel and Wilson, 1994; Bilous and Wilson, 1993).

Much of the recent literature focuses on linguistic and ethno-regional factors as the key to understanding Ukraine's future path of economic and political development. Andrew Wilson is, perhaps, the most vocal proponent of this view, writing that, "it needs to be restated that ethnolinguistic and geopolitical factors and not economic issues decided the 1994 presidential contest" (Wilson, 2000). Wilson bases his conclusions on a study of maps. But the study of Ukrainian political culture is in its infancy, and many potential explanatory factors have yet to be thoroughly explored. Consequently, this article explores the political, economic, and social forces underlying the east/west cleavage in Ukrainian politics through an examination of the 1994 presidential and parliamentary elections.

Our main finding is that, contrary to the common view of Ukrainian politics, economic factors – notably, variations in regional economic strength and increases in state sector unemployment – are stronger predictors of political activity and voting behavior than ethnic or linguistic factors. The data support the conclusion that the strength of leftist forces in eastern Ukraine in 1994 was based on the relative economic decline there. Ethnicity appears to overlay Ukraine's 1994 electoral outcome, but does not constitute the sole foundation for Ukraine's 1994 political cleavage. Ethnicity was all but completely overshadowed by economic factors, except on a region-by-region basis, where ethnicity is a significant factor (albeit weaker than economic factors). These results will be seen to contradict the main contention of the "postcommunism" literature, that the voters are an amorphous mass, unable to identify their interests, and ultimately malleable by the demagoguery of the strong leaders that are certain to emerge.

Events leading to the 1994 elections

It has become commonplace to note the political divergencies between the eastern and western regions of Ukraine. Observers point out that the East votes predominantly communist or socialist, while the West is the traditional base of nationalism and democratic support. The common interpretation is that the main cleavage in Ukrainian politics results from differences in language, ethnicity, and political culture; the East having been more thoroughly "russified," and therefore less enthusiastic about market reforms and independent statehood, and more interested in reestablishing economic links and political ties with Russia, promoting Russian language and culture (Arel, 1994, 1995; Arel and Wilson, 1994; Bilous and Wilson, 1993; Sochor, 1995). The ethno-cultural cleavage has even been mentioned as a potential cause of Ukraine's possible future disintegration and collapse, but not recently (Solchanyk, 1994a; Larrabee, 1994; Weiner, 1994).

Ukraine's recent history reinforces perceptions of a regional ethno-cultural divide. The Ukrainian state was born in an atmosphere of defiance and internal political agitation. As the USSR collapsed "from within," nationalists led by Rukh, the Popular Front for Perestroika in Ukraine, spearheaded the drive for independence. Ukraine proceeded cautiously, however, until the bungled August 1991 Moscow coup attempt revealed the full extent of the Soviet system's decay. Ukraine declared its independence three days after the coup failed, on August 24, 1991. A mood of national euphoria set in, which was to be short-lived. At that time, eastern and western regions alike supported Ukrainian statehood. Indeed, there was overwhelming nationwide support for Ukraine's independence, which was approved by over 90% of Ukraine's citizens – including no less than 76% in any eastern oblast (54% in Crimea)din a referendum held on December 1, 1991 (Kuzio and Wilson, 1994).

Kravchuk's weakening electoral coalition, 1993-1994

Leonid M. Kravchuk, former ideology chief of the Ukrainian Communist Party, was elected president on the same date as the referendum in December 1991, garnering 61.6% of the popular vote (Kuzio and Wilson, 1994). Elected on a pro-nationhood platform, Kravchuk succeeded in identifying himself personally with Ukrainian independence in the eyes of voters, making possible an alignment of pro-independence forces (primarily Rukh and the nationalists), and the old apparatchiks and directors of state enterprises, who expected to enjoy unfettered economic freedom and prosperity in an independent Ukraine (Kuzio and Wilson, 1994). Lacking right-wing opposition, conservative elements in Ukraine also saw Kravchuk as the best bet to preserve their privileges, and other critical vestiges of the Soviet era.

The paradoxical consequence of Kravchuk's broad political appeal was that he sharply constrained his latitude to exercise leadership. Having appropriated Rukh's political program, the president appealed to pro-independence, pro-reform forces throughout Ukraine. At the same time, however, he needed to maintain his conservative base, especially in the rural districts. Kravchuk, therefore, combined numbers of both reformers and conservatives in his government, which served to infuse his administration with contradictory ideological orientations. Kravchuk himself appeared to be a true pragmatist, almost wholly lacking in ideological commitment. This proved to be a liability, as he was unwilling and unable to implement genuine market reforms without alienating his conservative political base. Yet, it is precisely a lack of progress to improve the material well-being of the populus that eroded support for Kravchuk's regime.

The hardships imposed by the dissolution of the economic space of the former USSR eroded the previous robust support for independence, especially in the east. Sharp contractions in economic output combined with high inflation to effectively pauperize large segments of the population (International Monetary Fund, 1992-1995). Popular dissatisfaction arose; confidence in governmental institutions declined steadily throughout 1993 (Tismaneanu, 1995). Kravchuk struggled to deal with the economic crisis while maintaining a grip on power. In order to relieve the growing political pressures from both sides, Kravchuk "semi-reformed" the economy, liberalizing in some sectors while retaining important, and intrusive, elements of state administration and planning in others (Kaufmann, 1995). The apparent strategy was to publicly embrace economic reforms, but to quietly undercut them, in a rather transparent effort to placate everyone.

Problems with parliament

Elected in March 1990, before Ukraine declared its independence, parliament was sharply divided. The dominant bloc was the so-called "Group of 239," socialists who had been raised under the old Soviet regime. A significant, but smaller, group was the "Democratic Bloc," which constituted the main body of opposition forces within parliament. The democratic forces were weak, however, themselves having been divided into three factions by year-end 1992, including the rival groups, "Rukh" (or, the Popular Front for Perestroika in Ukraine, led by the late Vyacheslav Chornovil), "Congress of National Democratic Forces" (created in mid-1992 when three prominent nationalists, Mykhailo Horyn, Ivan Drach and Larysa Skoryk, split with Rukh), and "New Ukraine" (formed by Volodymyr Lanoviy, former Deputy Prime Minister, and others). Kravchuk was able to build a stable coalition with neither conservatives nor the splintered reform factions. Further, as he was anxious to strengthen the institution of the presidency, throughout 1993 Kravchuk made repeated attempts to assume complete control of the government, including regional (oblast) administrations (Kravchuk, 2002). As the 1994 elections approached, relations with parliament remained quite unsettled.

The resurgence of the Left

Leftist parties emerged early, gaining strength throughout Kravchuk's tenure (Holdar, 1995). Three major leftist parties took root: the Socialist Party of Ukraine (formally the CPU, but really a reconstituted party of "old communists") was organized in October 1991; an Agrarian Party (CelPU), representing collective farms and agricultural workers, was formed in January 1992; and a new Communist Party of Ukraine (KPU) was founded in June 1993 in Donetsk, in the heart of eastern Ukraine. All three parties would figure prominently in the 1994 parliamentary elections. They tended to be hostile to market reforms, calling for a reinstatement of state economic controls, establishment of Russian as an official state language, and closer economic and/or political ties with Russia or the CIS. The communist party platform specifically called for the reestablishment of the former USSR (Dymytrychenko, 1994).

Regional political agitation

By early 1994, the challenge to Kyiv's dominance over regional affairs had been building in the Don River Basin (known as "Donbas") in eastern Ukraine for some time (Wilson, 1993; Solchanyk, 1994b). Political agitation for greater autonomy in the east was becoming commonplace, and was rumored to have received financial and other support from Russia. A debilitating strike by Donbas coal miners in June 1993, joined by sympathy strikes from metallurgical and other industrial workers, forced the government to accede to strikers' demands for new elections. Despite Kravchuk's political maneuverings, parliamentary elections were ultimately scheduled for March 27, 1994; presidential elections for June 26, 1994.[1] Regional and local elections would coincide with the presidential race.

Regional divisions on the question of Ukrainian independence and reunification with Russia appeared to reach the acute stage by year-end 1993. In a poll conducted in November 1993 by Kyiv's Democratic Initiatives Center (Democratic Initiatives Center, 1994b), 44% of Ukraine's citizens revealed that they were unwilling to suffer economic difficulties in order to maintain Ukraine's independence; 31% were willing to suffer for 1-2 years, and but 19% were willing to suffer as long as necessary (Kolomayets, 1994a). Of the 44% who were not willing to suffer for the sake of Ukrainian independence, 53% were from the Donetsk region of eastern Ukraine, and 19% were from oblasts in western Ukraine. A poll released on the very eve of the elections in March 1994 indicated overwhelming support for reunification with Russia in eastern Ukraine, where 62% favored reunion. This contrasted with western oblasts, where only 17% favored reunification (Pope, 1994).

---

1   Kravchuk originally promised elections for September 1993, but postponed them until 1994, arguing that a new election law and related administration issues would require more time to resolve. While undoubtedly true, this afforded Kravchuk an opportunity to time the election to coincide with a rise in his popularity. The postponement also permitted leftists in parliament to craft a new elections law which was inhospitable to development of nationalist and reformist parties (Kyriyenko, 1994).

Political demands emanating from Donbas coincided closely with the aims of the leftist parties, which included: recognition of Russian as a state language on an equal footing with Ukrainian; dual Russian and Ukrainian citizenship; open borders between Russia and Ukraine; regional autonomy within a Ukrainian federal government; and economic union with Russia within the framework of the CIS (Jung, 1994). On February 22, the Donetsk Oblast Council voted to hold a "consultative referendum" on the same day as the parliamentary elections, seeking public support for Russian as a state language, adoption of a federal system for Ukraine, and full membership in the CIS. On March 17, the Luhansk Oblast Council approved a proposal similar to Donetsk's. Further, on March 10, newly elected Crimean President Yuri Meshkov decreed that a referendum would be held on March 27 to decide Crimea's place within Ukraine. These referenda were nonbinding, but they would have potentially significant political effects beyond the elections.[2] For many observers then Ukraine's parliamentary and presidential elections of 1994 placed in rather sharp relief a growing polarization between Eastern and Western Ukraine (Birch, 1994; Marples, 1994; Holdar, 1995).

The remainder of this paper is divided into three sections: an analysis of the July 10, 1994 presidential runoff election; a discussion of factors which account for the results of several rounds of parliamentary elections held in 1994; and a concluding section that provides a summary of general findings, with recommendations for further research.

The 1994 presidential election

Ukraine's 1994 presidential and parliamentary elections were the result of a many months' long political struggle between president and parliament, and between political forces that appeared to support the notion of a territorial split in Ukraine (Kuzio, 1996). Held on June 26, challenger Leonid Kuchma garnered sufficient support in the first round of the presidential elections to force a runoff. Kuchma polled 31.3% to Kravchuk's 37.7%, in a hefty voter turnout of more than 68%. The runoff was scheduled for July 10, 1994.

---

2 President Kravchuk formally anulled these plebiscites on the basis that they violated the Ukrainian Constitution and other applicable laws. However, the referenda were held (albeit illegally).

The two candidates distinguished themselves sharply during the campaign. The former head of the huge Yuzhmaz missile factory in Dnipropretovsk, and founder of the Ukrainian Union of Industrialists and Entreprenuers (UUIE), a businessman's group, Kuchma ran on a platform of economic reform, federalism, Russian as a second official language, and closer economic ties with Russia and the CIS (Sverdlov, 1994).[3] The former prime minister thus appealed to the concerns of the heavily industrialized east, and much of southern Ukraine. Kravchuk, on the other hand, ran as the sole guarantor of Ukraine's statehood and territorial integrity. Having managed to avert civil strife and violence, Kravchuk portrayed himself as the source of stability and hope for a better future, despite his inability to press forward with reforms (Kolomayets, 1994c).

At a superficial level, results of the runoff elections appear to confirm the conventional interpretation of Ukrainian politics, providing rather graphic evidence of an East-West cleavage (see Table 1, like all further tables, at the end of this paper). Kuchma carried the whole of eastern Ukraine, with between 68 and 88% of the vote. Kravchuk dominated his native western Ukraine, where he captured an average of over 91% of the vote. By contrast, Kuchma, perceived as a serious threat to Ukrainian statehood, failed to gain even 4% in western Galicia, averaging but 8.2% throughout the whole of the west. It is tempting to conclude that these results reflect a deep ethno-cultural divide.

Regression analysis
The existing literature on the election suggests that language, ethnicity, economic strength, and political culture would account for the observed presidential election results (Birch, 1994, 1995). Multivariate regression analysis of the popular vote for Kuchma provides ample confirmation of this hypothesis. Oblast-level data have been employed throughout, extracted from the literature, appropriate sources in Ukraine, and over the world wide web. Crucial socio-economic data published by the Ukrainian Ministry of Statistics were checked for general consistency with other published sources. Data on ethnic heritage corresponds to the "nationality" stamped in a citizen's former

---

3 To clarify Kuchma's views on the language issue somewhat, during the campaign he advocated Ukrainian as the sole state language, "the language of diplomacy and

Soviet internal passport. (See Appendix 1 for the oblast-level detail, and data sources.)

We initially confine ourselves to the oblast level, ignoring for now the possible presence of regional influences that might transcend oblasts. Table 2 (see the end of this paper) provides the results of a "base model" which tests the influence of ethnicity, and an oblast's relative economic strength on Kuchma's percentage of the popular vote in the July 10, 1994 runoff. State sector job loss in 1993, the year preceding the election, and the proportion of Ukraine's 1989 agricultural output produced in each oblast were used as measures of relative economic strength.[4] It turns out that the most significant predictor of an oblast's vote for Kuchma is the proportion of that oblast's state sector employment base that was eroded in 1993. Also presented in Table 2 are models which include Hesli's indices as controls for degree of russification, levels of industrialization, social and agricultural development, and population growth. In each instance, the base model economic variables are positive and significant predictors of Kuchma's popular vote, particularly job loss.

Examination of the effects of state sector job loss by oblast reveals that the largest, most industrialized, and most russified oblasts – precisely those which voted overwhelmingly for Kuchma – are also those which suffered the most unemployment from the economic collapse over which Leonid Kravchuk presided. Relating unemployment in 1993 to the 1994 popular vote for Kuchma in Table 1 reveals that the eastern oblasts were precisely those that were most impacted by unemployment; those western oblasts that voted overwhelmingly for Kravchuk were precisely those which were least impacted.

There is a positive relationship between Kuchma's 1994 popular vote against 1993 state sector job loss for all oblasts (including the city of Kyiv). The economic conditions facing the voters appear to be an important factor in

---

law." However, he supported Russian as a second official language, "to apply in every other sphere" (Sverdlov, 1994, p. 47).

4 Other variables proved to be poor surrogates, including: percent of 1991 GDP by oblast; percent of 1989 industrial output by oblast; proportion of Ukraine's productive assets by oblast; and the level of urbanization. None of these variables produced significant effects, individually or in combination. (Interestingly, the urban/rural divide, perhaps the most significant vestige of the Soviet period's drive for industrialization, did not prove to be a factor in this analysis.) Further, the strength of the regional economic, dummy, and ethnic variables remained robust and significant in the presence of these other variables.

choosing to vote for Kuchma over Kravchuk. Sochor (1995, p. 209) has observed, "the elections were first and foremost about economic reforms." This observation finds confirmation here. Further, a measurable degree of economic rationality marks the Ukrainian voter. There is unambiguous evidence of retrospective voting behavior in the 1994 election.

Table 3 (see the end of this paper) presents results of the base model, controlled for Hesli's indices (see Appendix 2), as well as two other models which include selected predictors of Kuchma's popular vote, in order to permit the reader to evaluate the interaction effects between several of the more significant variables. In this case, the unemployment measure is significant across the entire array of models. In the service of thoroughness, Table 4 (see the end of this paper) regresses Hesli's control variables against Kuchma's popular vote, and evaluates the effect of the unemployment measure in the presence of the control variables. It turns out that the unemployment variable is positively correlated with population growth, and so its influence is dampened in models where the population strength index is included. The results are otherwise consistent with those in Table 2.

Impact of regional influences

It is reasonable to expect that the aggregate results would mask over any regional variation which might be present. Regional dummy variables are therefore introduced, based on Solchanyk's (1995) analysis of the regional presidential voting pattern. Table 5 (see the end of this paper) summarizes the regional groupings employed in the models. Introduction of regional variables has a dramatic effect on the country-wide analysis. Table 6 (see the end of this paper) provides models which include regional variables, with Hesli's indices as controls. In each case, the regional variables are very significant. Further, the ethnic variable is both positive and moderately to very significant. By contrast, agricultural output and state sector job loss, are no longer significant. Note that Russian ethnicity is also dominated by the regional variables, which have proportionately much larger beta coefficients.

These models demonstrate the explanatory power of region itself. The eastern region is especially significant, and positive, which reflects the extremely one-sided vote for Kuchma in these oblasts. The central regional variable also is positive and significant. The pattern is clear: in the aggregate, economic factors exerted a significant influence on the average voter's choice. However, regional variations also are present. Regional differences eclipsed the economic factors, but were independent of ethnic influences that usually are associated with Ukrainian regional politics.[5] These results support the notion that there are important historical differences in regional political culture, beyond language and ethnicity, and which also are independent of the existing differences in relative industrial, social, or agricultural development, and population growth.

Interpretation of the presidential election

The strong effects of oblast-level macroeconomic performance on presidential voting appears to contradict the arguments of Arel, Wilson, and Bilous and Wilson that language and ethnicity are the most crucial factors in Ukrainian politics (Arel, 1994, 1995; Wilson, 1995; Bilous and Wilson, 1993). Analysis of the nationwide result indicates the primacy of economic concerns for the average Ukrainian voter. However, when regional variables are introduced, ethnicity emerges as significant, lending credence to the more conventional view that there is an ethnic cleavage in post-independence Ukraine. Both views find support here, with their degree of credibility depending upon the level of analysis (regional or country-wide).

The second, and perhaps, most important finding is that region itself exerted a profound influence on the outcome. This suggests that the effects of regional political culture should be assessed apart from the more direct influence of ethnic heritage. This is not to say that eastern Ukraine's Russian ethnicity and language are unrelated to the political culture of, say, the Donbas. They are, in fact, crucial cultural artifacts, and fair game for study. Rather, it means that differences in regional political subculture in Ukraine appear to have manifested themselves in quite a different form than is generally presumed. It is not such a simple matter as "Ukrainian versus Russian." Regional political culture in Ukraine is a more subtle quantity. Its study must therefore contain an element of nuance.

Several observers of contemporary Ukrainian politics provide support for this viewpoint. Solchanyk notes that:

---

5   Russian ethnicity and language combined accounted for no more than 62% of the

in addition to the existing ethnic and linguistic differences, these two regions [east and west Ukraine] also had different views on Ukraine's political and economic future, with the eastern region inclined toward Russia and 'communism' and the western part supporting democracy and 'capitalism' (Solchanyk, 1995, p. 47).

Marples surmises that, "if Ukraine is split today, the division lies not between Ukrainians and Russians in themselves ... but in how different parts of the country view both the past and the future" (Marples, 1994, pp. 9-10). Finally, Kuzio argues for greater analytical rigor, insofar as

much western journalism on Ukraine ... include[s] the suggestion that Ukraine is under threat of disintegration with a 'nationalistic' west pitted against a Russian east. Any serious analysis of the Ukrainian regional inheritance has to discard such simplistic assumptions (Kuzio, 1995a, p. 21).

Consistent with these views, the present study finds evidence of decisive differences in political culture between eastern and western Ukraine, but which are separate and distinct from other measurable socio-economic characteristics, including the degree of russification.

The 1994 parliamentary elections

Ukraine's 1994 parliamentary elections pose more serious analytical challenges than the presidential race. The relative immaturity of the party system, together with Ukraine's rather arcane 1993 election law, resulted in an extremely large number of parties' candidates and non-party, independent candidates running in the first round. Consequently, it is difficult to systematize the results of voting. Further, the turnout requirements of the law resulted in parliamentary repeat elections being held in some six rounds held throughout

---

variation in the presidential vote, in the absence of other variables.

ASPECTS OF THE ORANGE REVOLUTION I   31

1994-1996, which makes it difficult to specify with precision the "final result"[6] (see Table 7 at the end of this paper).

In the first round, March 27, 1994, some 5833 candidates representing 29 political parties stood for 450 seats, an average of 13 candidates per district (Central Election Commission of Ukraine, 1994).

Due to the law's onerous registration requirements for party-nominated candidates, an inordinately high proportion of individuals ran as "independents" (officially "non-party"), amounting to 4271, or 73.2% of the total.[7] The law required that the Central Election Commission certify the convention endorsements of party nominees at both the okruh and oblast levels, in order to secure a place on the ballot. By contrast, to be nominated, independents needed a mere 10 voter signatures, either from residents, or from members of a "labor collective," as defined in the law. This feature of the law placed a decidedly conservative spin on the process, tending to reinforce regionalism. Consequently, the law has been criticized for weakening the fledgling multiparty system, encouraging "clientele politics," and preserving the status quo (Birch, 1994; Arel and Wilson, 1994; Commission on Security and Cooperation in Europe, 1994).

In the interest of practicality, we will examine only the results of the election and repeat voting held in 1994. Political conditions changed rather dramatically throughout 1995-1996, so that subsequent repeat votes are somewhat less related to the political and economic conditions that pertained in 1993-1994. The heavy voter turnout in the initial round (74.8%) indicates widespread voter disaffection with the performance of parliament (Kolomayets, 1994b). A March 1994 poll revealed that 63% of Ukrainians would not vote for the same candidate as in the 1990 parliamentary election (Democratic Initiatives Center, 1994a). There are also indications of the incumbents' self-perceived vulnerability, insofar as only 188 deputies stood for reelection.

---

6   Consequently, at year-end 1994, some 45 seats remained unfilled. For the text of the 1993 elections law, see "Law of Ukraine on the Election of Peoples' Deputies of Ukraine," November 18, 1993 (translated from the Ukrainian by Ukrainian Legal Foundation, 1993). While a decided improvement over the Soviet-era law, Shishkin provides an incisive analysis of the lack of protection which the law still does not afford to voters. See Shishkin (1994).

7   See Section VI, Article 23 of the 1994 Election Law, "Nomination of Candidates for Deputy" (Ukrainian Legal Foundation, 1993).

Ultimately, 56 of the 188 were successful. With an 88% turnover in membership, the new parliament was very different from its predecessor.

The critical campaign issues
Throughout 1994, three issues dominated the political scene: the state of the economy, relations with the CIS and Russia, and the status of the Russian language (Kuzio, 1995b).[8] The economy clearly was of primary concern. Wasylyk observes that public opinion polls at this time indicated that the state of the economy was the most important issue for most voters (Wasylyk, 1994). Indeed, in a poll released in March 1994, 68% of all adult Ukrainians cited "the condition of the economy" as their most important worry (Elections94 Press Center, 1994a). Thirty-nine percent cited "relations with Russia" as a significant concern. Just 6% mentioned the "Ukrainian language issue" as important (see Table 8 at the end of this paper).

Discontent with the economy coincides with negative attitudes towards the collapse of the former Soviet Union. According to a Democratic Initiatives Center poll conducted in November 1993, 52% of the population attributed Ukraine's economic problems to the disintegration of the USSR (Golovakha, 1994). Further, in a Socis-Kyiv poll conducted in January 1994, public approval of the former Soviet system was far higher than that of the present or hoped-for future system, with 55% approving the communist regime in general; 86% totally disapproving of the present economic system; and 76% approving the former non-market economy.[9]

Strong support for strengthening relations with member countries of the CIS was also evident in January 1994, with 70% of those polled calling for Ukraine to become a "full and equal member" in the CIS.[10] However, fully 82% favored "more cooperation and integration" with CIS member countries; only 10% opposed such cooperation (Kolomayets, 1994a). At approximately the same time, in November 1993, 38% supported joining the countries of the CIS into a unitary state (Golovakha, 1994). We may interpret positive attitudes

---

8 Other issues also were present, but as we will see below, these three issues received considerable attention in the winning candidates' official campaign issue position statements.
9 Rose and Haerpfer (1994). Interestingly, in the same poll, only 24% agreed that Ukraine should return to communist rule.
10 Elections 94 Press Center (1994b).

towards closer relations with CIS countries in terms of citizens' strong desire to rejuvenate Ukraine's economy, especially in light of the broad public perception that the Russian economy had reformed more successfully. In the same November 1993 poll, 64% of respondents thought that reforms in Russia were "more efficient" than in Ukraine.

The issue of Russian as a second official language for Ukraine appears to have been a regional issue, confined mainly to Russian-speaking areas. According to Table 8 the "Ukrainian language issue" (the obverse of the "Russian language issue") does not appear to have been particularly important on a country-wide basis.[11] In the unauthorized "consultative referenda" in the Donetsk and Luhansk oblasts, to coincide with the first-round parliamentary elections, nearly 90% of voters supported: making Russian an official state language, dual citizenship with Russia, and closer ties with the CIS. In the Crimean referendum, 75% wanted greater autonomy for the peninsula within Ukraine, and dual citizenship. In eastern Ukraine, support for closer links with the CIS coincides with support for an elevated status for the Russian language.

Parliamentary candidates' issue platforms

The campaign platforms of winning parliamentary candidates were reviewed for their positions on the three issues of: (1) privatization;[12] (2) relations with the CIS and/or Russia; and (3) Russian as a second official language.[13] Table 9 (see the end of this paper) summarizes the positions of the 405 deputies elected in 1994.

In so classifying the candidate's positions, a conservative approach has been employed. For instance, a candidate classified as "favors privatization"

---

11 This is consistent with an earlier poll, reported by Martyniuk, where 85% of all respondents were found to know Ukrainian, and 78% knew Russian (all nationalities included). But respondents in central and western Ukraine tended to be more in favor of Ukrainian language use than their counterparts in the southern and eastern regions (Martyniuk, 1992).
12 Privatization is the sine qua non of market reforms; in many respects, it is its defining principle. In the absence of broad privatization in all sectors, the sacrifices necessary to transform the economy which will accompany price liberalization, currency stabilization and market competition would be all for naught. Therefore, we have taken a candidate's support for privatization as an indication of his/her commitment to genuine market-oriented economic reforms.

means that the deputy unequivocally supports privatization of property in all sectors (which means no exceptions for land, leaseholding for small businesses, or state ownership of large, "strategically significant" enterprises). If the deputy supported, for example, "mixed forms of property" coexisting in the Ukrainian economy, they have been classified as being "against privatization." The deputies' positions on the other issues were treated in a similar fashion. (See the Notes section in Table 9 for specifics.)

Most successful candidates expressed no opinion on the elevation of Russian to be a second official language. If candidate statements are to be taken as an indication of their efforts to generate voter appeal, then Russian language appears third (195 deputies mentioned it), after privatization (318 mentions), and relations with the CIS and/or Russia (297 mentions) as salient campaign issues. Among these issues, the clearest expression of support is for closer relations with the CIS and/or Russia, followed by the Russian language. Concerning privatization, positions are fairly evenly split between supporters and opponents, reflecting the contentious nature of this issue, as well as the voters' own unsettled views concerning the virtues of a market economy.

Classification approach and threats to validity

The remainder of this chapter investigates the causal factors behind the proportion of each oblast's vote for successful candidates classified as "in favor" on each of the three issues. The winners' votes were summed across all okruhs within each oblast. The aggregate oblast vote serves as the denominator. Table 10 (see the end of this paper) provides the oblast-level vote for winning candidates, arranged according to their support for privatization, the Russian language, and closer ties with Russia and/ or the CIS.

Several potential threats to validity of this approach must be addressed prior to reviewing the results of regression analysis. First, due to the stringent turnout requirements of the election law, not every okruh successfully seated a deputy in calendar year 1994. Some 45 out of 450 seats, or 10% of the total, remained unfilled at year's end. Further, these empty seats were not uniformly, or even randomly distributed across the country. For instance, only some 7 of

---

13 The platforms of winning parliamentary candidates were found in English translation on the world wide web from the International Foundation for Electoral Systems Kyiv Office home page URL at: http://www.freenet.kiev.ua/ifes/ifes.htm.

ASPECTS OF THE ORANGE REVOLUTION I 35

23 seats in Kyiv City were filled, leaving over 70% of Kyiv's population unrepresented. This difficulty is not easily dealt with. However, with 90% of the seats filled, we feel reasonably safe to presume that the election results are broadly reflective of the popular will.[14]

A second threat lies in the problem that, unlike the presidential contest, not every okruh faced the same choices; neither in candidates, nor parties, nor issue positions (nor in their combination). A mitigating factor is the large number of candidates who stood for election in the first round, which provides some assurance – however limited – that a diverse array of issue perspectives was presented to the voters. To the extent that the choice provided to voters might have been constrained, however, by the candidates' (and potential candidates) choices to run (or not), their self-selection itself arguably represents an indication of voter preferences. Also, the election of some reformist deputies from Eastern oblasts provides a degree of comfort that the territorial configuration of okruhs was not necessarily unduly biased against reform-minded "centrists" or "national democrats."

Third, tabulations took a very conservative form. If anything, this method tends to understate somewhat the full extent of support for, for instance, Russian as a second official language. At least one anomalous oblast can be discerned in the case of the Russian language issue, Dnipropetrovsk. There, only some 13.34% of the vote went to winning candidates who supported Russian. The reason is simply that only some 4 out of 33 deputies from Dnipropetrovsk even mentioned the issue in their campaign platform statements. It is hard, indeed, to believe that the Russian language was not such an important issue in this oblast. The unspoken presumption in this case may have been that all candidates would naturally be presumed to support Russian; therefore, there may have been no need even to mention it.[15] Despite the potential for understatement, in the absence of more specific information regarding each

---

14   That is, elections were free and fair to the extent possible under Ukrainian law. This opinion was shared by foreign election observers (Commission on Security and Cooperation in Europe, 1994).
15   An important factor may be Ukraine's Declaration on the Rights of Nationalities in Ukraine, adopted by parliament on November 1, 1991, which specifically affirms the right of all Ukrainian citizens to use the Russian language. For the text of the law, see Demokratychna Ukrayina, November 5, 1991.

garding each deputy, we judged that a conservative approach would be the more conceptually defensible approach.

Fourth, and finally, the aggregated okruh-level vote was regressed across the same oblast-level economic and social data employed in the foregoing analysis of the presidential race. This approach is valid only to the extent that the oblast-level economic and social indicators are representative of okruh-level conditions. Some measure of aggregation bias may therefore be present. It can be demonstrated that aggregation bias can be avoided if the regression models are properly specified (Langbein and Lichtman, 1978). Specification is inevitably a problem in research on aggregate voting in parliamentary elections, however, to one degree or another. We are simply unable to incorporate the presumably strong influences of a candidate's personality, reputation, or name recognition. Institutional biases also would go undetected, for example, where members of a collective farm are instructed to vote for the kolhosp's director. In any event, even if detected and measured, these influences cannot be easily blended into an oblast-level composite. We will nevertheless take the regression results at face value. (Especially where the results appear to coincide with the results from analysis of the presidential election.)

Regression analysis

Compilation of the parliamentary vote by region again reveals an apparent EasteWest dichotomy. Models were developed which expressed the parliamentary vote as a function of the proportion of votes going to successful candidates, by oblast, for each issue area. Table 11 (see the end of this paper) presents several models which examine the relationship between the percentage oblast vote won by deputies who unequivocally supported privatization, and certain socio-economic factors. The base model measures the effects of the 1993 rise in unemployment and economic strength on the vote, as well as Russian ethnicity. In this case, both economic variables are significant. Table 11 also tests for the base model with controls for Hesli's indices. In each case, the increase in state sector unemployment exerts a significantly negative influence on the vote for candidates who supported privatization, as one might expect. Agricultural output is significant only in the case of models that control for the level of social development. The control variables for social develop-

ASPECTS OF THE ORANGE REVOLUTION I 37

ment and population growth also are significant, in their respective models. This is consistent with the analysis of the presidential election result.

Table 12 (see the end of this paper) introduces regional variables into the analysis, with controls for Hesli's indices. In this case, the regional variables are moderately to very significant in most cases. As in the analysis of the presidential race, the economic variables tend to be dominated by region, which indicates the strong influence of the "regional factor." Again, we observe that Russian ethnicity loses all significance in the presence of the regional variables. The influence of region is pronounced, even in the case of the parliamentary election, despite the myriad of other influences that may be present.

Table 13 (see the end of this paper) presents analysis of the vote for pro-privatization winners for the base model, plus regional controls, and controls for russification. With the exception of the model which controls for all of Hesli's indices in combination, region is significant and negative. Since region would only be expected to correlate closely with all of these regional attribute combined, its statistical effects are negligible here. However, consistent with the results in Table 12, its proportionately larger beta coefficients dominate all other potentially significant variables.

Analysis of the vote for winning deputies who supported closer ties with the CIS and/or Russia is presented in Table 14 (see the end of this paper). The base model variables are quite significant, as are the regional variables. Importantly, Russian ethnicity adds nothing to those models in which its effects are examined. In fact, region all but completely eclipses other variables, including Russian ethnicity. Ethnic heritage thus exerted little demonstrable effect on the vote for candidates who supported closer links with the CIS and/or Russia. Rather, region alone again accounts for the largest proportion of the variation, with overwhelmingly large beta coefficients.

Finally, we turn to analysis of the vote for deputies who supported Russian as a second official language for Ukraine. It should come as no surprise that support for the Russian language correlates closely with the proportion of an oblast's population that is of Russian origin (rZ0.763), as well as the proportion that considers Russian to be their native language (rZ0.705). Further, these relationships eclipse the influence of the economic variables in both the countrywide and regional analysis. Table 15 presents several models which seek to disentangle the effects of ethnicity, region, and other regional characteristics on the vote for deputies who supported Russian as a second official language (see the end of this paper). Table 15 indicates that the separate influence of the Russian ethnic variable can be discerned, even in the presence of the regional dummy variables. As can be seen, the level of russification is both positive and significant.

Interpreting the parliamentary elections

Consistent with the presidential race, on a countrywide basis economic factors dominated the parliamentary election, especially as regards the two key issues of privatization and links with the CIS/Russia. This is also consistent with public opinion polls taken immediately preceding and during the "election season," and reflects a hearty dose of retrospective voting behavior on the part of the electorate. It directly contradicts arguments that language and ethnicity are the most crucial factors in Ukrainian politics. Second, and also consistent with the presidential contest, the persistent influence of region is observed across all three issues which were used to dimensionalize and measure the parliamentary vote. The regional factor dominates the economic variables, having a robust, statistically significant influence on the outcome. In the case of the parliamentary vote, the regional factor eclipses, but is not separable from the influence of the ethnic factor. In the preceding analysis of the presidential vote, region was more clearly separable from the direct effects of ethnicity, however. These findings do not contradict those for the presidential contest, but point to a need for further research on the subtle features of political culture in the regions of Ukraine.

Several studies concerning Ukrainian regional electoral behavior and public opinion provide additional support for these findings. Indeed, a remarkable degree of convergence is discernible in the recent literature. For instance, Birch studied the geographical dynamics of party system formation and voting behavior in the 1994 parliamentary elections (Birch, 1994). In one of the few systematic studies of the parliamentary race to appear, she found that region and ethnicity are both important determinants of voting behavior in Ukraine, but that they have clear and distinctive effects. The most important factors that propel voter turnout, and sources of party support vary from region to region. She concludes that Ukraine's is a "proto-party system" which is disjointed at this early stage of development, but it is not fractured. Importantly,

Birch's results also identified "the region factor" as a separate and distinct influence from other explanatory factors.

Even more pertinent have been Hesli's findings concerning regional public opinion in Ukraine (Hesli, 1995). Particularly important for the present study are her analysis of regional variations in support for closer ties with the CIS, and public preferences for the use of the Ukrainian language only in official positions in government.[16] Hesli found that the greatest support for CIS control of Ukraine's nuclear weapons (which issue is now passé) – a surrogate for ceding of a degree of sovereignty to Russia – came mostly from Eastern Ukraine, where support was three times as strong as in the West. Further, support was twice as strong in the most russified oblasti as in the rest of Ukraine, and strongest among the most industrialized oblasts. Hesli's result is entirely consistent with those of the present study, insofar as she found huge differences between regions of Ukraine on the critical issue of CIS integration.

Hesli's examination of the Ukrainian language issue also demonstrates a degree of alignment between her study and ours, in that she found that there was not much support overall for limiting official employment to those who speak Ukrainian. However, significant regional variation was found to exist, with survey respondents from the West ten times more willing to reserve official jobs for Ukrainian speakers than respondents from the East. Indeed, consistent with our findings, the least russified areas were more willing to support this practice. Hesli thus unequivocally demonstrates the "extreme importance of regional context in determining political attitudes," and in so doing, establishes an opinion baseline for the present study. It is not too much to say that her results, in combination with ours, provide compelling evidence of convergence

---

16 Hesli (1995) examined public opinion on the use of Ukrainian language (which we take to be the obverse of the Russian language issue) using responses to a question on the 1992 Iowa survey which concerned "limiting the right to work in official establishments to those who Speak Ukrainian." The present analysis of electoral positions examined winning candidates' platforms on the issue of "Russian as a second official language" in Ukraine. Hesli's examination of the issue of Ukraine's relationship with the CIS was conducted using responses to a survey question about "support for CIS control of nuclear armaments" on the territory of the former USSR. Our study of winning candidates' issue platforms examined candidates' attitudes towards ceding any amount of economic and/or political sovereignty to Russia or the CIS. Arguably, these are different questions; however, we would maintain that they are directly analogous insofar as they deal with the very same subject matter. They seem to tap the same underlying sentiments in either case.

between Ukrainian public opinion and electoral behavior, which satisfies Fleron's recommendations that researchers strive for such convergence (Fleron, 1996).[17]

Conclusion: Ukrainians are rational voters

The foregoing analysis suggests that Ukrainian politics is not as volatile and unpredictable as the literature on "post-communist" states might suggest. First, Ukrainian voters seem to make fairly consistent choices of candidates based on their policy platforms, albeit with clear regional differences. Successful candidates who opposed privatization tended to come from the same regions as those who favored closer ties with the CIS/Russia, and use of the Russian language in official settings. As observed above, this is consistent with public opinion polling (Hesli, 1995; Miller et al. 1995).

Second, there are indications that Ukrainian voters engaged in retrospective voting behavior, insofar as those oblasts that suffered the most state sector employment erosion under Kravchuk tended to vote against him. Third, there are consistencies between the effects of significant explanatory factors in both the presidential runoff, and the parliamentary elections. Fourth, on a national basis, economic issues were more salient than ethnicity for the average voter. Ukrainians, like voters elsewhere, voted with their pocketbooks. Fifth, and finally, the national results mask over significant regional variations, but

---

17 In an exceedingly stimulating and useful article, Fleron (1996) surveys the recent literature on establishing connections between post-Soviet electoral behavior, public opinion, and political attitudes. He cautions against inferring any one from the other two, especially as regards the prospects for democratization in former Soviet states. He finds that much recent research raises serious questions about drawing causal connections between democratic practices and civic cultures. Its is simply not clear in which direction the "arrow of causation" operates (e.g., democracy can produce democrats, as surely as democrats can produce a democracy). In the case of studies such as the present one, he advises that care be taken in reaching inferences about voters' attitudes and values from voting behavior. There is a lower substratum of subcultures, many coinciding with geographic regions – such as is the case in Ukraine – and some within the same regions. Here we have taken care to ensure that meaningful contextual elements are contained within our models. Particularly, we have sought to avoid Fleron's caution that, "measures of political attitudes that fail to take account of changes in both subjective and objective economic factors can produce misleading results" (Fleron, 1996, p. 246). Some recent studies run afoul of this advice, and with predictable consequences, such as Wilson (2000). The present study strives for the sort of convergence among values, opinions and behaviors that

such divisions are separate and distinct from ethnicity and levels of oblast development along a number of critical dimensions. Indeed, region itself emerges as an important factor in understanding contemporary Ukrainian politics, apart from ethnic heritage.

We conclude that, despite expressions to the contrary in the literature on "postcommunism," Ukrainians are not an amorphous, depoliticized mass, ripe for ethnic or nationalist demagoguery. While vestiges of the communist region and mindset remain, Ukrainian politics contains within it elements which have great potential to attain a degree of stability, when compared to the politics of its neighbors in the former USSR. In this state of "perpetual disaster," opportunities for demagoguery and political violence were legion. Yet, there were also persistent democratic attitudes and behaviors, which served to dampen the potential for conflict. The basic characteristics of the Ukrainian political culture may well contain within them the seeds of compromise, consensus-building and accommodation which would mark the advance to political maturity that will be necessary to secure Ukraine's democratic future. The potential for democratic consolidation, it would seem, was high in Ukraine, despite the hardships of the 1990s.

Fleron recommends, explicitly by including considerations of economic well-being and regionalism as factors.

Tables and Appendices

Table 1: Presidential Runoff Election Results and 1993 State Sector Labor Departures - Eastern and Western Oblasts (Runoff Election of July 10, 1994)

Oblast (Region)	Kuchma (% of Popular Vote)	Kravchuk (% of Popular Vote)	1993 Sate Sector Job Loss (%)
Autonomous Republic of Crimea (Including Sevastopol)	*91.35*	*8.65*	*27.7*
Eastern Oblasts			
Luhanska Oblast	88.00	10.11	27.0
Donetska Oblast	79.00	18.49	25.5
Kharkivska Oblast	71.01	25.95	29.3
Zaporizhzhia Oblast	70.70	26.95	26.7
Dnipropetrovksa Oblast	67.81	29.72	25.3
Sumska Oblast	67.75	28.92	20.4
Average	*76.69*	*23.31*	*25.7*
Western Oblasts			
Ternopilska Oblast	3.75	94.80	14.7
Ivano-Frankivska Oblast	3.86	94.46	16.1
Lvivska Oblast	3.90	93.77	16.8
Rivnenska Oblast	11.04	87.25	16.5
Volynska Oblast	13.96	83.93	18.7
Zakarpattska Oblast	25.21	70.52	17.8
Average	*8.21*	*91.79*	*16.76*

Source: International Foundation for Electoral Systems, *Elections in Ukraine 1994* (Kiev-Washington: IFES, 1994): 133. (Weighted averages calculated by the authors.) For the data on state sector departures, see International Labour Office, Central and Eastern European Team, *The Ukrainian Challenge: Reforming Labour Market and Social Policy* (Budapest: Central European University Press, 1995): 71, Table 2.11.

Table 2: Predicting Percent of Popular Vote for President Kuchma Using Base Model with Controls for Regional Attributes (by Oblast, for July 10, 1994 Two-Way Runoff)

Independent Predictors	Base Model	Regression Coefficients with Controls for:									
		Russification		Industr. Develop.		Social Develop.		Agricult. Develop.		Populat. Growth	
		Unstandard Coefficient	Standard Coefficient	Unstandard Coefficient	Standard Coefficient	Unstandard Coefficient	Standard Coefficient	Unstandard Coefficient	Standard Coefficient	Unstandard Coefficient	Standard Coefficient
Base Model:											
1993 State Sector Employment Loss	.038** (.013)	.048** (.013)	.707	.041** (.013)	.616	.050** (.011)	.0740	.026γ (.015)	.382	.028* (.012)	.416
1989 Agricultural Output (% Ukr.)	.049 (0.20)	.039 (.025)	.178	.052γ (.028)	.238	.088** (.026)	.400	-.084 (.065)	-.384	.037 (.022)	.169
Ethnic Russian Population (%)	.033 (.003)	-.033γ (.018)	-2.043	.039 (.003)	.239	.025 (.003)	.151	.059γ (.003)	.364	.059* (.003)	.361
Hesli's Indices as Controls:											
Index of Russification		.087γ (.042)	2.160								
Index of Industrial Development				-.0064 (.005)	-.162						
Index of Social Development						-.016** (.005)	-.404				
Index of Agricultural Development								.024γ (.012)	.644		
Population Strength Index										-.012** (.004)	-.305
Constant	-.594	-.645		-.646		-.854		-.205		-.259	
R-square	.722	.813		.790		.854		.813		.855	

Notes: (1) Standards errors are given in parentheses beneath regression coefficients.
(2) Significance levels are: *p<.05; **p<.01; γmoderately significant (at .10 level).

Table 3: Predicting Percent of Popular Vote for President Kuchma Using Base Model and Selected Other Predictors from Among Hesli's Indices (by Oblast, for July 10, 1994 Two-Way Runoff)

Independent Predictors	Regression Coefficients					
	Selected Predictors - (A)		Selected Predictors - (B)		Base Model Plus Hesli's Indices	
	Unstandard Coefficient	Standard Coefficient	Unstandard Coefficient	Standard Coefficient	Unstandard Coefficient	Standard Coefficient
Base Model:						
1993 State Sector Employment Loss	.029* (.011)	.434	.038** (.013)	.561	.045* (.016)	.667
1989 Agricultural Output (% Ukraine)	.043^γ (.024)	.195	.006 (.064)	.027	.049 (.070)	.225
Ethnic Russian Population (%)					-.022 (.019)	-1.355
Hesli's Indices:						
Index of Russification	.015* (.006)	.377	.012^γ (.007)	.309	.064 (.044)	1.577
Index of Industrial Development	-.027 (.004)	-.068	-.003 (.005)	-.076	-.0038 (.005)	-.097
Index of Social Development			-.012* (.006)	-.304	-.0096 (.006)	-.241
Index of Agricultural Development			-.015 (.010)	.398	.0051 (.012)	.138
Population Strength Index	.011** (.004)	-.277			-.0031 (.006)	-.078
Constant	-.291		-.541		-.632	
R-square	.863		.873		.890	

Notes: (1) Standard errors are given in parentheses beneath regression coefficients.
(2) Significance levels are: * p<.05; ** p<.01; ^γ moderately significant (at .10 level).
(3) Selected predictors are as described in the text.

Table 4: Predicting Percent of Popular Vote for President Kuchma Using Hesli's Indices and 1993 State Sector Employment Loss (by Oblast, for July 10, 1994 Two-Way Runoff)

Independent Predictors	Regression Coefficients Hesli's Indices as Predictors		Impact of State Sector Job Loss	
	Including Population Growth	Excluding Population Growth	Including Population Growth	Excluding Population Growth
1993 State Sector Employment Loss			.0329* (.0121)	.0372 (.0112)
Index of Russification	.0279** (.0046)	.0285** (.0048)	.0143* (.0064)	.0127 (.0062)
Index of Industrial Development	-.0028 (.0052)	-.0050 (.0054)	-.0022 (.0046)	-.0030 (.0045)
Index of Social Development	-.0016 (.0063)	-.0082 (.0055)	-.0082 (.0060)	-.0018 (.0046)
Index of Agricultural Development	.0131* (.0059)	.0203** (.0047)	.0126* (.0052)	.0155 (.0041)
Population Strength Index	-.0099ʸ (.0054)		-.0047 (.0050)	
Constant	.2335	.0940	-.3841	-.5225
R-square	.830	.799	.879	.873

Notes: (1) Standard errors are given in parentheses beneath regression coefficients.
(2) Significance levels are: * p<.05; ** p<.01; ʸ moderately significant (at .10 level).

Table 5:   Geographic Classification of Ukrainian Oblasts

East	Central		West
Kharkiv	Chernhiv	Kirovohrad	L'viv
Donetsk	Odessa	Sumy	Ivano-Frankivsk
Luhansk	Mykolaiv	Poltava	Ternopil
Dnipropetrovsk	Kherson	Kyiv	Volyn
Zaporizhzhia	Chernivtsy	Cherkassy	Rivne
Crimea	Vinnytsya	Khmelnytskij	Zakarpattia
	Zhytomyr		

Note: Crimea is included among the eastern oblasts due to its demographic features as well as the voting patterns it shares with eastern Ukrainian oblasts (i.e., large ethnic Russian population; relatively low support for independence in the 1991 referendum; large margin for President Kuchma in the 1994 elections; regular and ongoing clamorings for autonomy).

Table 6: Predicting Percent of Popular Vote for President Kuchma Using Base Model with Controls for Region and Regional Attributes (By Oblast, for July 10, 1994 Two-Way Runoff)

Independent Predictors	Base Model with Regions		Regression Coefficients with Controls for Region and for:										Base Plus All Indices Controlled for Region	
			Russification		Industrial Development		Social Development		Agricultural Development		Population Growth			
	Unstandard Coefficient	Standard Coefficient	Unstandard Coefficient	Standard Coefficient	Unstandard Coefficient	Standard Coefficient	Unstandard Coefficient	Standard Coefficient	Unstandard Coefficient	Standard Coefficient	Unstandard Coefficient	Standard Coefficient	Unstandard Coefficient	Standard Coefficient
Base Model:														
1993 State Sector Employment Loss	-.00075 (.013)	-.011	.0031 (.011)	.046	.0037 (.012)	.055	.014 (.013)	.214	-.0040 (.012)	-.060	.0039 (.012)	.058	.0078 (.014)	.116
1989 Agricultural Output (% Ukraine)	-.019 (.016)	.104	-.0044 (.020)	-.020	.0081 (.024)	.037	.030 (.028)	.137	-.082 (.048)	-.373	.0025 (.021)	.012	-.0025 (.058)	-.114
Ethnic Russian Population (%)	.0056^ν (.003)	.341			.0059* (.003)	.361	.0049^ν (.003)	.301	.0081** (.003)	.499	.0070* (.003)	.430		
Regional Dummies:														
Central Region Control	.327** (.075)	.637	.352** (.071)	.676	.337** (.077)	.646	.283** (.081)	.543	.333** (.072)	.639	.287** (.083)	.550	.267** (.083)	.512
Eastern Region Control	.452** (.112)	.782	.441** (.104)	.760	.461** (.107)	.795	.373** (.109)	.644	.396** (.106)	.683	.355** (.116)	.612	.356** (.120)	.614
Hesli's Indices as Controls:														
Index of Russification			.016* (.006)	.385									.016* (.006)	.406
Index of Industrial Development					-.0043 (.004)	-.110							-.0034 (.004)	-.085
Index of Social Development							-.0083 (.004)	-.208					-.0049 (.005)	-.124
Index of Agricultural Development									.015^ν (.009)	.413			.010 (.010)	.282
Population Strength Index											-.0060 (.003)	-.149	-.00038 (.005)	-.009
Constant R-square	.039 .886		.051 .906		.0056 .906		-.205 .916		.250 .915		.087 .914		-.0085 .930	

Notes: (1) Standards errors are given in parentheses beneath regression coefficients.
(2) Significance levels are: *p<.05; **p<.01; ^ν moderately significant (at .10 level).

Table 7: Ukrainian 1994 Parliamentary Elections: Voter Turnout and Aggregate Results of Repeat Elections

Round	Dates	Deputies elected	Voter turnout	No. of seats remaining unfilled
1	27 March	49	74.8%	401
2	2-3 April	40		
	9-10 April	244	66.9%	117
3	24 July	20		
	31 July	12		
	7 August	27	51.2%	58
(Special Election[1])	25 September	1		57
4	20 November	10[2]	40.0%	47
	4 December	1		46
	Total	404		

Notes: (1) Former President Leonid M. Kravchuk won election to a seat from Ternopilska Oblast (Okruh 364) left vacant by the untimely death of Roman Kuper, who had been elected in the second round.

(2) Includes the election of Vasyl I. Yevtukhov, who replaces Leonid D. Kuchma, the latter having been elected President of Ukraine on July 10, 1994.

Source: International Foundation for Electoral Systems, *Elections in Ukraine 1994* (Kiev-Washington: IFES, 1994).

Table 8: Issues of Greatest Concern to Ukrainian Citizens In the Period Preceding the 1994 Elections (December 1993 - January 1994)

Citizen responses to the question: "Which of the problems Ukraine is facing today worries you most of all?"

Issue	(Percentage*)		
	Villages	Cities	All of Ukraine
(1) Condition of the Economy	56	73	68
(2) Relations with Russia	23	48	39
(3) Criminality	22	42	35
(4) Ukraine's Security	42	21	28
(5) The Nuclear Issue	11	7	8
(6) The Crimean Problem	16	3	8
(7) The Ukrainian Language Issue	2	8	6
(8) The Black Sea Fleet Problem	6	5	5
(9) Other Issues	3	1	2
(10) Hard to Tell	3	2	2

[* *Authors' Comment*: Obviously, respondents were permitted more than one choice.]

Source: Elections94 Press Center (1994). "Pre-Electoral Mood of Ukraine's Population." *Dateline: Ukraine* no. 4 (11 March):2-4. Results of a poll conducted by The KyivInternational Sociology Institute and the Sociology Department of the Kyiv Mohyla Academy among the adult population of Ukraine from mid-December 1993 through January 1994. There were 1737 respondents aged 18 and older in a random sample drawn from 183 villages, small towns, and cities of the 24 regions of Ukraine.

Table 9: Winning Candidate Positions on Three Critical Issues (Ukrainian Parliamentary Elections of 1994)

		Expressed no opinion	Against	In favor
(1)	Privatization[1]	86	156	162
		(21.24%)	(38.51%)	(40.25%)
(2)	Relations with the CIS and/or Russia[2]	108	53	244
		(26.67%)	(13.09%)	(60.24%)
(3)	Russian as a Second Official Language of Ukraine[3]	210	55	140
		(51.85%)	(13.58%)	(34.57%)

Notes: (1) *"Against"* means deputy opposes any aspect of private property, including land privatization; also includes those favoring "mixed" forms of property (i.e., workers' collectives, state enterprises in certain sectors, and/or collective farms). *"In favor"* means deputy unequivocally supports private property in all sectors.

(2) *"Against"* means deputy opposes any form of union with Russia or the CIS. *"In favor"* means deputy favors economic and/or full political participation in the CIS, *or* union with Russia and/or restoration of the Former Soviet Union.

(3) Refers to position on Russian as an officially-recognized state language of Ukraine.

Source: Data compiled by the authors from: International Foundation for Electoral Systems, *Platforms of Winning Parliamentary Candidates* (Kyiv: IFES, 1994). Available on the World Wide Web at IFES home page: <http://www.freenet.kiev.ua/ifes/ifes.htm>.

Table 10: Oblast-Level Vote for Winning Candidates Arranged According to Their Support for Three Critical Issues (Ukrainian Parliamentary Elections of 1994)

Oblast	Favor Privatization	Pro Russian Language	Favo Closer Ties with Russia and/or CIS
Kyiv City	84.36%	0.00%	0.00%
Crimean Republic*	27.85	50.13	84.85
Vinnytska Oblast	62.18	6.48	30.73
Volynska Oblast	43.72	0.00	17.53
Dnipropetrovska Oblast	38.06	13.34	74.25
Donetska Oblast	10.68	74.97	89.25
Zhytomyrska Oblast	16.10	22.06	74.94
Zakarpattska Oblast	100.00	0.00	0.00
Zaporizhzhia Oblast	28.69	55.31	80.58
Ivano-Frankivska Oblast	91.16	0.00	0.00
Kyivska Oblast**	57.09	7.76	41.20
Kirovohradska Oblast	16.59	38.04	54.10
Luhanska Oblast	16.79	82.24	87.42
Lvivska Oblast	75.26	8.43	0.00
Mykolaivska Oblast	7.57	48.31	64.17
Odesska Oblast	45.05	39.11	82.99
Poltavska Oblast	52.39	16.18	40.43
Rivnenska Oblast	93.58	0.00	14.07
Sumska Oblast	7.17	61.18	92.83
Ternopilska Oblast	80.44	0.00	0.00
Kharkivska Oblast	22.90	54.89	89.65
Khersonska Oblast	15.49	59.58	83.15
Khmelnytska Oblast	42.99	32.70	70.47
Cherkasska Oblast	19.48	19.66	75.64
Chernivitska Oblast	58.07	17.08	27.84
Chernihivska Oblast	13.32	28.76	74.70

Notes: * Including City of Sevastopol.
        ** Excluding Kyiv City.

Source: Compiled by the authors from campaign platforms of the candidates on file with the Central Election Commission of Ukraine, apportioned according to the proportion of each oblast's vote won by candidates expressing support on each issue.

Table 11: Predicting Percent of 1994-95 Popular Vote for Pro-Privatization Members of Parliament Using Base Model with Controls for Regional Attributes

Independent Predictors	Base Model	Regression Coefficients with Controls for:									
		Russification		Industrial Development		Social Development		Agricult. Development		Population Growth	
		Unstandard Coefficient	Standard Coefficient	Unstandard Coefficient	Standard Coefficient	Unstandard Coefficient	Standard Coefficient	Unstandard Coefficient	Standard Coefficient	Unstandard Coefficient	Standard Coefficient
Base Model:											
1993 State Sector Employment Loss	-5.065* (2.138)	-5.650* (2.140)	-.770	-6.319** (2.168)	-.861	-7.738** (1.826)	-1.054	-4.544^γ (2.515)	-.619	-4.295* (1.996)	-.585
1989 Agricultural Output (% Ukraine)	-7.522* (3.429)	-3.172 (4.405)	-.132	-5.485 (4.068)	-.229	-11.514* (4.224)	-.480	10.422 (11.182)	.436	-2.913 (3.724)	-.122
Ethnic Russian Population (%)	.434 (.522)			.379 (.509)	.213	.624 (.410)	.351	.202 (.553)	.114	.099 (.457)	.056
Hesli's Indices as Controls:											
Index of Russification		.867 (1.215)	.199								
Index of Industrial Development				1.103 (.825)	.257						
Index of Social Development						2.720** (.771)	.629				
Index of Agricultural Development								-2.623 (1.988)	-.654		
Population Strength Index										1.827** (.618)	.419
Constant	174.433	170.835		186.507		221.884		135.280		127.708	
R-square	.480	.480		.534		.687		.533		.646	

Notes: (1) Standards errors are given in parentheses beneath regression coefficients.
(2) Significance levels are: *p<.05; **p<.01; ^γ moderately significant (at .10 level).

Table 12: Predicting Percent of 1994-95 Popular Vote for Pro-Privatization Members of Parliament Using Base Model with Controls for Region and Regional Attributes

Independent Predictors	Base Model with Regions		Regression Coefficients with Controls for Region and for:								Base Plus All Indices Controlled for Region	
			Russification		Industrial Development		Social Development		Agricultural Development		Population Growth		
	Unstandard Coefficient	Standard Coefficient	Unstandar Coefficient	Standard Coefficient	Unstandard Coefficient	Standard Coefficient	Unstandard Coefficient	Standard Coefficient	Unstandard Coefficient	Standard Coefficient	Unstandard Coefficient	Standard Coefficient	Unstandard Coefficient	Standard Coefficient
Base Model:														
1993 State Sector Employment Loss	.889* (2.766)	-.117	-1.402 (2.417)	-.191	-1.989 (2.561)	-.271	-4.707ʸ (2.636)	-.641	-.995 (2.663)	-.136	-2.053 (2.419)	-.280	-3.667 (2.896)	-.499
1989 Agricultural Output (% Ukraine)	-4.355 (3.526)	-1.235	2.506 (4.324)	.105	-.113 (5.037)	-.005	-6.317 (5.427)	-.264	11.089 (10.434)	.463	.742 (4.224)	.031	-3.107 (12.383)	-.130
Ethnic Russian Population (%)	.220ʸ (.582)	.119			.109 (.537)	.062	.366 (.500)	.206	-.165 (.589)	-.093	-.119 (.517)	-.067		
Regional Dummies:														
Central Region Control	-34.747* (16.289)	-.589	-44.311** (15.025)	-.780	-39.353* (15.880)	-.692	-24.882 (15.965)	-.438	-40.499* (15.671)	-.713	-28.424 (16.822)	-.500	-23.017 (17.806)	-.405
Eastern Region Control	-49.701ʸ (24.167)	-.759	49.400* (22.027)	-.781	-51.347* (22.081)	-.812	-30.230 (21.542)	-.478	-43.256ʸ (23.119)	-.684	-29.272 (23.847)	-.463	-25.911 (25.646)	-.410
Hesli's Indices as Controls:														
Index of Russification			-1.05 (1.233)	-.024									.196 (1.378)	.045
Index of Industrial Development					.810 (.837)	.189							.177 (.896)	.041
Index of Social Development							2.034* (.881)	.470					1.494 (1.148)	.345
Index of Agricultural Development									-1.733ʸ (1.877)	-.432			-.383 (2.097)	-.096
Population Strength Index											1.247 (.708)	.286	.516 (.991)	.118
Constant	106.303		97.554		111.439		166.149		80.177		95.576		138.513	
R-square	.582		.643		.661		.725		.660		.696		.856	

Notes: (1) Standards errors are given in parentheses beneath regression coefficients.
(2) Significance levels are: *p<.05; **p<.01; ʸmoderately significant (at .10 level).

Table 13: Predicting Percent of Popular Vote for Pro-Privatization Winning Members of Parliament Using Base Model with Controls for Region and Regional Attributes

Independent Predictors	Regression Coefficients										
	Base Model		Base Model with Regions		Controlled for Russification		Hesli's Indices as Predictors		Hesli's Indices Controlled for Region		Base Plus All Indices Controlled for Region	
	Unstandard Coefficient	Standard Coefficient	Unstandard Coefficient	Standard Coefficient	Unstandard Coefficient	Standard Coefficient	Unstandard Coefficient	Standard Coefficient	Unstandard Coefficient	Standard Coefficient	Unstandard Coefficient	Standard Coefficient
Base Model:												
1993 State Sector Employment Loss	-5.065* (2.138)	-.669	-.889* (2.766)	-.117	-1.402 (2.417)	-.191					-3.667 (2.896)	-.499
1989 Agricultural Output (% Ukraine)	-7.522* (3.429)	-.361	-4.355 (3.526)	-1.235	2.506 (4.324)	.105					-3.107 (12.383)	-.130
Ethnic Russian Population (%)	.434 (.522)	.234	.220 (.582)	.119								
Regional Dummies:												
Central Region Control			-34.747* (16.289)	-.598	-44.311** (15.025)	-.780			-36.055* (14.190)	-.634	-23.017 (17.806)	-.405
Eastern Region Control			-49.701'^ (24.167)	-.759	-49.400* (22.027)	-.781			-44.252'^ (21.241)	-.700	-25.911 (25.646)	-.410
Hesli's Indices as Controls:												
Index of Russification					-.105 (1.233)	-.024	-1.856* (.776)	-.422	-.886 (1.003)	-.201	.196 (1.378)	.045
Index of Industrial Development							.344 (.894)	.080	.316 (.881)	.074	.177 (.896)	.041
Index of Social Development							.564 (1.079)	.130	.821 (.976)	.190	1.494 (1.148)	.345
Index of Agricultural Development							-1.568 (1.018)	-.391	-.625 (1.020)	-.156	-.383 (2.097)	-.096
Population Strength Index							1.539 (.916)	.353	.604 (.928)	.139	.516 (.991)	.118
Constant	174.433		106.303		97.554		56.662		72.429		138.513	
R-square	.480		.582		.643		.585		.701		.856	

Notes: (1) Standards errors are given in parentheses beneath regression coefficients.
(2) Significance levels are: *p<.05; **p<.01; '^'moderately significant (at .10 level).

Table 14: Predicting Percent of Popular Vote for Pro-CIS Winning Members of Parliament Using Base Model with Controls for Region and Regional Attributes

Independent Predictors	Base Model		Base Model with Regions		Regression Coefficients Controlled for Russification		Hesli's Indices as Predictors		Hesli's Indices Controlled for Region		Base Plus All Indices Controlled for Region	
	Unstandard Coefficient	Standard Coefficient	Unstandard Coefficient	Standard Coefficient	Unstandard Coefficient	Standard Coefficient	Unstandard Coefficient	Standard Coefficient	Unstandard Coefficient	Standard Coefficient	Unstandard Coefficient	Standard Coefficient
Base Model:												
1993 State Sector Employment Loss	4.972* (2.021)	.565	-.083 (2.355)	-.009	.466 (1.963)	.055					1.350 (2.441)	.160
1989 Agricultural Output (% Ukraine)	10.666*** (3.240)	.441	6.806* (3.002)	.281	.285 (3.511)	.010					1.260 (10.437)	.046
Ethnic Russian Population (%)	-.052 (.493)	-.024	.077 (.495)	.036								
Regional Dummies:												
Central Region Control			41.031** (13.867)	.608	49.833** (12.202)	.761			41.837** (11.455)	.639	37.027* (15.007)	.565
Eastern Region Control			65.705** (20.574)	.864	64.898** (17.890)	.890			61.149** (17.147)	.839	54.424* (21.615)	.747
Hesli's Indices as Controls:												
Index of Russification					.811 (1.001)	.160	2.778** (.731)	.548	1.213 (.810)	.239	.812 (1.161)	.160
Index of Industrial Development							-.561 (.843)	-.113	-.767 (.711)	-.155	-.715 (.755)	-.145
Index of Social Development							-.030 (1.017)	-.006	-.382 (.788)	-.077	-.631 (.968)	-.127
Index of Agricultural Development							1.872^γ (.959)	.405	.917 (.823)	.198	.810 (1.768)	.175
Population Strength Index							-1.480^γ (.864)	-.295	-.210 (.749)	-.042	-.181 (.835)	-.036
Constant	-95.727		-11.937		-3.968		25.427		5.007		-19.452	
R-square	.656		.776		.823		.722		.853		.856	

Notes: (1) Standards errors are given in parentheses beneath regression coefficients.
(2) Significance levels are: *p<.05; **p<.01; ^γ moderately significant (at .10 level).

Table 15: Predicting Percent of 1994-95 Popular Vote for Pro-Russian Language Members of Parliament Using Russification Level with Controls for Region and for Regional Attributes

Independent Predictors	Regression Coefficients with Controls for Region and for:												
	Ethnic Russians (%)		Russification		Industrial Development		Social Development		Agricultural Development		Population Growth		Russification Plus All Indices Controlled for Region	
	Unstandard Coefficient	Standard Coefficient	Unstandard Coefficient	Standard Coefficient	Unstandard Coefficient	Standard Coefficient	Unstandard Coefficient	Standard Coefficient	Unstandard Coefficient	Standard Coefficient	Unstandard Coefficient	Stand. Coeffic.	Unstandard Coefficient	Stand. Coeffic.
Russification Measure:														
Ethnic Russian Population (%)	.520 (.336)	.325												
Index of Russification			1.762* (.756)	.456	1.856* (.761)	.480	1.958* (.748)	.506	1.820* (.747)	.471	2.193** (.747)	.567	2.265** (.773)	.586
Regional Dummies:														
Central Region Control	20.334* (8.539)	.405	21.447* (7.777)	.429	21.801* (7.779)	.436	23.379** (7.684)	.468	29.366** (9.918)	.588	12.668 (8.648)	.254	20.536* (10.929)	.411
Eastern Region Control	37.716* (14.238)	.666	31.682* (12.867)	.570	35.584* (13.419)	.640	34.340* (12.655)	.618	40.404* (14.457)	.727	19.496 (13.698)	.351	26.387 (16.359)	.475
Hesli's Indices as Controls:														
Index of Industrial Development					-.563 (.554)	-.149							.188 (.678)	.050
Index of Social Development							-.720 (.490)	-.157					.188 (.752)	.049
Index of Agricultural Development									-.743 (.590)	-.211			-.949 (.785)	-.269
Population Strength Index											-.986ᵞ (.516)	-.258	-1.169 (.715)	-.305
Constant	-.893		-.025		1.576		2.930		4.998		13.921		21.615	
R-square	.637		.700		.714		.729		.722		.745		.770	

Notes: (1) Standards errors are given in parentheses beneath regression coefficients.
(2) Significance levels are: *p<.05; **p<.01; ᵞmoderately significant (at .10 level).

Appendix 1: 1994 Ukrainian Presidential Elections – Data Employed in the Models

OBLAST	(Col. 1) % Vote for President Kuchma [KUCHVOTE]	(Col. 2) Ethnic Russians (% 1989) [RUSSIAN]	(Col. 3) Native Russian Speakers (% 1989) [RUSLANG]	(Col. 4) Urban Dwellers (% 1989) [URBAN89]	(Col. 5) 1989 Industrial Output (% Ukraine) [INDOUT89]	(Col. 6) 1989 Agricultural Output (% Ukraine) [AGROUT89]	(Col. 7) Change in Industrial Output (1992-1993) [INDCH93]	(Col. 8) Job Loss in State Sector (1992-1993) [DEPLAB]	(Col. 9) Proportion of Industrial 1990 Assets (% Ukraine) [ASSETS]	(Col. 10) 1991 GDP (% Ukraine) [GDP1991]	(Col. 11) 1993 Fiscal Dependency [DEPEND93]
Crimea	,9135	67,00	81,67	70,00	2,60	5,60	-11,40	27,70	4,767	4,20	57,60
Vinnytsa	,4232	5,80	8,35	44,00	3,10	4,70	-13,90	18,90	2,953	3,64	72,80
Volynska	,1396	4,40	4,71	49,00	1,20	2,70	-30,90	18,70	1,309	1,94	70,10
Dnipropetrovska	,6781	24,20	36,49	83,00	11,20	5,30	-17,50	25,30	10.302	8,06	45,90
Donetska	,7900	43,60	66,74	90,00	13,70	4,90	-13,50	25,50	12.418	8,80	32,50
Zhytomyrska	,4156	7,90	11,53	53,00	2,10	4,00	-19,00	20,60	2,419	3,19	73,90
Zakarpattska	,2521	4,00	4,71	41,00	1,50	1,60	-26,20	17,80	1,169	1,84	67,90
Zaporizhzhia	,7070	32,00	48,03	76,00	5,90	4,30	-8,00	26,70	5,484	5,00	67,70
Ivano-Frankivska	,0386	4,00	4,23	42,00	2,20	2,10	-17,60	16,10	2,242	2,46	69,00
Kyivska Oblast	,3838	8,70	10,08	54,00	3,00	6,10	-11,60	20,90	3,833	3,93	80,30
Kirovohradska	,4972	11,70	14,53	60,00	1,90	3,90	-8,00	24,30	2,402	2,66	76,30
Luhanska	,8800	44,80	62,92	86,00	7,40	3,30	-20,80	27,00	6,163	4,66	60,40
Lviska	,0390	7,20	8,05	59,00	5,10	3,90	-27,80	16,80	4,072	5,74	67,40
Mykolaivska	,5280	19,40	32,88	66,00	2,20	3,50	43,80	22,70	2,803	2,82	70,30
Odesska	,6680	27,40	46,21	66,00	3,90	5,50	15,10	23,60	5,192	5,12	64,10
Poltavska	,5916	10,20	12,33	50,00	3,50	5,10	-17,10	21,50	3,997	3,96	63,80
Rivnenska	,1104	4,60	5,34	45,00	1,60	2,50	-27,30	16,50	1,911	2,19	67,70
Sumska	,6775	13,30	20,79	62,00	2,70	3,60	-13,80	20,40	2,469	3,20	79,80
Ternopilska	,0375	2,30	2,41	38,00	1,50	3,30	-26,70	14,70	1,668	2,18	73,10
Kharkivska	,7101	33,20	57,11	79,00	7,30	5,00	-8,30	29,30	6,120	6,58	57,00
Khersonska	,6464	20,20	29,84	61,00	2,20	3,80	-23,90	23,70	2,723	2,58	72,00
Khmelnytska	,3927	5,80	7,15	47,00	2,20	4,10	-,40	18,90	2,247	2,74	64,30
Cherkasska	,4572	8,00	9,53	53,00	2,60	4,70	n.a.	21,20	3,165	3,09	72,20
Chernivtska	,3527	6,70	10,16	42,00	1,20	1,80	-18,20	20,20	,921	1,38	80,30
Chernihvska	,7233	6,80	12,69	53,00	2,40	4,70	-22,00	18,90	2,033	2,91	54,90
M. Kyiv	,3558	20,90	40,32	100,00	5,80	,00	-,40	24,50	5,700	5,15	56,20

Sources:
(Col. 1): International Foundation for Electoral Systems, *Elections in Ukraine 1994* (Kyiv-Washington, 1994), p. 133. [Data supplied by Ukrainian Central Election Commission.]
(Cols. 2-3): Ministry of Statistics of Ukraine, *Narodnyeh Gospodarstvo Ukrayiny u 1992 Rotse* (Kyiv: Teknika, 1993), pp. 60-62.
(Cols. 4-6): Marian Dolishnii, "Regional Aspects of Ukraine's Economic Development," Ch. 14 in I.S. Koropeckyi (ed.), *The Ukrainian Economy: Achievements, Problems, Challenges* (Cambridge, Massachusetts: Harvard University Press, 1992), Figure 14-3, pp. 306-7. [Data originally from *Narkhoz Ukrayiny* (1988).]
(Col. 7): Ukrainian Center for Independent Political Research, *Table-Book About Ukraine*, No. 4 (November 1993), Table 2, pp. 7-8. [Data supplied by the Ministry of Statistics of Ukraine.]
(Col. 8): International Labour Office - Central and Eastern European Team, *The Ukrainian Challenge: Reforming Labour Market and Social Policy* (Budapest: Central European University Press, 1995), Table 2.11, p. 71. [Data originally from Ministry of Statistics of Ukraine, *Statistichniy Byuleten*, (2) Nov. 1993, Feb. 1994, and May 1994.]
(Col. 9): Ministry of Statistics of Ukraine, *Financi Ukrainy za 1993 rik* (Kyiv, 1994), pp. 114-115.
(Col. 10): Ministry of Statistics of Ukraine, *Narodnyeh Gospodarstvo Ukrayiny u 1992 Rotse* (Kyiv: Teknika, 1993).
(Col. 11): Calculated by the authors from oblast revenue data supplied by the Ministry of Finance of Ukraine.

Appendix 2: Hesli's Standardized Scores for Development Indices (Ukrainian Oblasts)

Oblast	Russification Score	Industrial Development Score	Social Development Score	Agricultural Development Score	Population Strength Score
Crimean Republic*	25.00	5.15	12.10	18.55	16.76
Vinnytska Oblast	1.37	3.60	5.13	23.79	1.72
Volynska Oblast	0.78	0.18	1.20	8.29	11.58
Dnipropetrovska Oblast	8.39	20.88	14.04	25.00	13.09
Donetska Oblast	18.29	25.00	8.24	20.35	4.09
Zhytomyrska Oblast	2.13	1.71	1.52	15.94	7.38
Zakarpattska Oblast	0.78	1.05	0.07	0.01	17.45
Zaporizhzhia Oblast	11.82	8.42	10.74	19.82	9.78
Ivano-Frankivska Oblast	0.69	1.44	3.62	3.05	14.41
Kyivska Oblast**	2.04	15.16	25.00	22.34	25.00
Kirovohradska Oblast	3.06	1.97	6.88	17.04	2.30
Luhanska Oblast	17.05	12.62	7.48	14.58	6.51
Lvivska Oblast	1.51	13.75	13.10	12.94	21.41
Mykolaivska Oblast	7.57	3.00	6.26	15.32	8.59
Odesska Oblast	11.43	8.37	18.94	24.56	9.21
Poltavska Oblast	2.57	6.74	7.41	22.49	1.07
Rivnenska Oblast	0.89	0.01	3.03	6.89	14.76
Sumska Oblast	4.65	2.51	3.66	15.48	0.82
Ternopilska Oblast	0.22	1.45	4.92	9.77	7.35
Kharkivska Oblast	11.56	10.07	24.60	23.33	3.73
Khersonska Oblast	6.86	2.01	6.24	16.69	10.37
Khmelnytska Oblast	1.33	2.48	2.84	16.00	4.59
Cherkasska Oblast	1.90	2.47	5.23	15.97	2.69
Chernivitska Oblast	1.73	1.63	4.68	1.21	9.46
Chernihivska Oblast	2.66	0.03	3.43	21.20	0.00

Notes: * Including City of Sevastopol.
** Including City of Kyiv.
Source: Vicki L. Hesli, "Public Support for the Devolution of Power in Ukraine: Regional Patterns." *Europe-Asia Studies*, vol. 47, no. 1 (1995): 100, Table 2.

References

Arel, D., Wilson, A. 1994. "The Ukrainian parliamentary elections." *RFE/RL Research Report*, 3 (26): 6-17.

Arel, D. 1994. "Voting behavior in the Ukrainian parliament: the language factor." In: Remington, T.F. (ed.), *Parliaments in transition: the new legislative politics in the former USSR and Eastern Europe*. Westview Press, Boulder, CO, pp. 125-158.

Arel, D. 1995. "Ukraine: the temptation of the nationalizing state." In: Tismaneanu, V. (ed.), *Political culture and civil society in Russia and the new states of Eurasia*. M.E. Sharpe, Armonk, NY, pp. 157-188.

Bilous, A., Wilson, A. 1993. "Political parties in Ukraine." *Europe-Asia Studies*, 45 (4): 693-703.

Birch, S. 1994. "The Ukrainian parliamentary and presidential elections of 1994." *Electoral Studies*, 14 (1): 93-99.

Birch, S. 1995. "Electoral behavior in western Ukraine in national elections and referendums, 1989-91." *Electoral Studies*, 47 (7): 1145-1176.

Birch, S. 1994. "The geographical dynamics of party system formation and voting behavior in the Ukrainian parliamentary elections of 1994." In: Kuzio, T. (ed.), *Soviet to independent Ukraine: a troubled transformation*. Macmillan, London.

Bunce, V. 1995. "Should transitologists be Grounded?" *Slavic Review*, 54: 112-127.

Central Election Commission of Ukraine, 1994. "Data concerning the candidates for people's deputy of Ukraine. Dani Pro Kandidativ u Narodni Deputati Ukrayini." Central Election Commission, Kyiv.

Commission on Security and Cooperation in Europe, 1994. "Ukraine's parliamentary election, March 27, 1994, April 10, 1994." United States Congress, Commission on Security and Cooperation in Europe, Washington, DC.

Daedalus, 1994. "After communism - what?" *Daedalus*, 123 (3) (special issue).

Democratic Initiatives Center, 1994a. "A political portrait of Ukraine: results of a public opinion poll conducted by democratic initiatives with the Institute of Sociology and Socis-Gallup, February-March 1994." Democratic Initiatives Center, Kyiv.

Democratic Initiatives Center, 1994b. "Public opinion in Ukraine: attitudes towards economic problems, based on sociological studies in 1992-1994." Reported at the International Scientific-Technical Conference, Societies in Transformation: Experience of Market Reforms for Ukraine, May 19-21, Institute of Public Administration and Local Government, Kyiv.

Dymytrychenko, S. 1994. "Ukraine from left to right: a brief tour of the political spectrum. " *IntelNews*, 22: 3-4.

Elections94 Press Center, 1994a. "Pre-electoral moods of Ukraine's population." *Dateline: Ukraine*, An Informational and Analytical Bulletin, 4 (11 March): 2-4.

Fish, S.M. 1993. "Who shall speak for whom? Democracy and interest representation in post-Soviet Russia." In: Dallin, A. (ed.), *Political parties in Russia*. University of California Press, Berkeley, CA.

Fish, S.M. 1995. *Democracy from scratch: opposition and regime in the new Russian revolution*. Princeton University Press, Princeton, NJ.

Fleron Jr., F.J. 1996. "Post-Soviet culture in Russia: an assessment of recent empirical investigations." *Europe-Asia Studies*, 48 (2): 225-260.

Golovakha, E. 1994. "The current political situation and the future of the political and economic development of Ukraine." *A political portrait of Ukraine*, 2. Democratic Initiatives Center, Kyiv.

Hesli, V.L. 1995. "Public support for the devolution of power in Ukraine: regional patterns." *Europe-Asia Studies*, 47 (1): 91-121.

Holdar, S. 1995. "Torn between east and west: the regional factor in Ukrainian politics." *Post-Soviet Geography*, 36 (2): 112-132.

International Labour Office, 1995. *The Ukrainian challenge: reforming labour market and social policy*. Central European University Press, Budapest.

International Monetary Fund, 1992-1995. *Ukraine: economic review* (annual). International Monetary Fund, Washington, DC.

Jung, M. 1994. "The Donbas factor in the Ukrainian parliamentary elections." *RFE/RL Research Report*, 3 (12).

Kaufmann, D. 1995. "Market liberalization by stealth: curse or blessing in disguise?" *The Ukrainian Legal and Economic Bulletin*, III (1-2): 13-30.

Kolomayets, M. 1994a. "Poll results depict a half-open society." *The Ukrainian Weekly*, 23 (3).

Kolomayets, M. 1994b. "Over 75% of electorate turns out to vote for parliament." *The Ukrainian Weekly*, 3 (1).

Kolomayets, M. 1994c. "Kravchuk, Kuchma to face off in presidential race on July 10." *The Ukrainian Weekly*, 3 (1).

Kravchuk, R.S. 2002. *Ukrainian political economy: the first ten years*. Palgrave Macmillan, New York and London.

Kubicek, P. 1994. "Delegative democracy in Russia and Ukraine." *Communist and Post-Communist Studies*, 27 (4): 423-441.

Kuzio, T. 1997. *Soviet to independent Ukraine: a troubled transformation*. London, Macmillan.

Kuzio, T. 1995a. *Ukraine: back from the brink*. The Institute for European Defense and Strategic Studies, London.

Kuzio, T. 1995b. "The 1994 parliamentary elections in Ukraine." *Journal of Communist Studies and Transition Politics*, 11 (4): 335-361.

Kuzio, T. 1996. "Kravchuk to Kuchma: the Ukrainian presidential elections of 1994." *Journal of Communist Studies and Transition Politics*, 12 (2): 117-144.

Kuzio, T., Wilson, A. 1994. *Ukraine: perestroika to independence*. Canadian Institute of Ukrainian Studies, Edmonton, Alberta.

Kyriyenko, M. 1994. "The three I's of Leonid Kravchuk: inconsistency, indecision, indterminateness." *Ukrayina Moloda*, 3, (7 June), Kyiv. (Translated from the Ukrainian in FBIS-USR-94-066, 21 June 1994, pp. 47-48).

Langbein, L.I., Lichtman, A.J. 1978. *Ecological inference*. Sage, Newbury Park, CA.

Larrabee, F.S. 1994. "Ukraine: Europe's next crisis?" *Arms Control Today*, 14-19 (July/August).

Marples, D.R. 1994. "Ukraine after the presidential election." *RFE/RL Research Report*, 3 (37): 7-10.

Martyniuk, J. 1992. "Attitudes toward language in Ukraine." *RFE/RL Research Report*, 1 (37): 69-70.

McFaul, M. 1993a. *Post-communist politics: democratic prospects in Russia and Eastern Europe*. Center for Strategic and International Studies, Washington, DC.

McFaul, M. 1993b. "Party formations after revolutionary transitions: the Russian case." In: Dallin, A. (ed.), *Political parties in Russia*. University of California Press, Berkeley, CA.

Miller, A.H., Reisinger, W.M., Hesli, V.L. 1995. „Comparing citizen and elite belief systems in post-Soviet Russia and Ukraine." *Public Opinion Quarterly*, 59 (1): 120-140.

Ministry of Statistics of Ukraine, 1993. *National economy of Ukraine for 1992*. (Narodne Hospodarstvo Ukrayiny, 1992.) Tekhnika, Kyiv.

Pope, V. 1994. "A struggle to remain independent." *US News and World Report*, 28 (20).

Rose, R., Haerpfer, C. 1994. *New democracies barometer III: learning from what is happening*. University of Strathclyde, Glasgow, UK.

Schöpflin, G. 1994. "Postcommunism: the problems of democratic construction." *Daedalus*, 123 (3): 127-143.

Shishkin, V. 1994. "The role of the courts in the electoral process of Ukraine." *Demokratizatsiya*, II (4): 651-661.

Sochor, Z. 1995. "Political culture and foreign policy: elections in Ukraine 1994." In: Tismaneanu, V. (ed.), *Political culture and civil society in Russia and the new states of Eurasia*. M.E. Sharpe, Armonk, NY, pp. 208-226.

Solchanyk, R. 1994a. "Ukraine: a year of crisis." *RFE/RL Research Report*, 3 (1): 38-41.

Solchanyk, R. 1994b. "The politics of state-building: centre-periphery relations in post-Soviet Ukraine." *Europe-Asia Studies*, 46 (1): 47-68.

Solchanyk, R. 1995. "Ukraine: the politics of reform." *Problems of Post-Communism*, 46-51 (November/December).

Sverdlov, B. 1994. "Leonid Kuchma: Ukraine cannot manage without economic alliance with Russia." *Rossiyskaya Gazeta*, 2 (Moscow, 31 May). (Translated from the Russian in FBIS-SOV-94-107, 3 June 1994, pp. 47-48).

Tismaneanu, V. (Ed.), 1995. *Political culture and civil society in Russia and the new states of Eurasia*. M.E. Sharpe, Armonk, NY.

Tong, Y. 1995. "Mass alienation under state socialism and after." *Communist and Post-Communist Studies*, 28 (2): 215-237.

Ukrainian Legal Foundation, 1993. *Zakon Ukrayini Pro Vibori Narodnix Deputativ Ukrayini*. (Law of Ukraine on election of people's deputies of Ukraine.) Kyiv: Ukrainska Pravnicha Fundatsia (enacted 18 November 1993).

Wasylyk, M. 1994. "Ukraine prepares for parliamentary elections." *RFE/RL Research Report*, 3 (5): 15-19.

Weiner, T. 1994. "CIA head surveys world's hot spots." *The New York Times* (Late New York Edition), A5 (26 January).

White, S., McAllister, I., Kryshtanovskaya, I. 1994. "El'tsin and his voters: popular support in the 1991 Russian presidential elections and after." *Europe-Asia Studies*, 46 (2): 285-303.

Wilson, A. 1993. "The growing challenge to Kiev from the Donbas." *RFE/RL Research Report*, 2 (33): 8-13.

Wilson, A. 1995. "The Donbas between Ukraine and Russia: the use of history in political disputes." *Journal of Contemporary History*, 30: 265-289.

Wilson, A. 2000. *The Ukrainians: unexpected nation*. New Haven and London, Yale University Press.

Regime Type and Politics in Ukraine under Kuchma

Taras Kuzio, George Washington University

Abstract
The article surveys and discusses different definitions of regime type in Ukraine and whether they provide a sound understanding of the regime emerging in Ukraine and other CIS states since the late 1990s. Ukraine and the CIS witnessed democratic regression and therefore could not be assumed that they were on a 'transition' path to a consolidated democracy. The majority of CIS states have either already moved to fully authoritarian regimes, such as Russia. Or, like Ukraine, they remained as unstable competitive authoritarian regimes which exhibited a 'hybrid' fusion of the former Soviet system and the emerging reformed economy and polity. Ukraine's oligarchs during Kuchma's second term preferred a fully authoritarian regime but they were also divided among themselves and faced a formidable opposition. These factors blocked the creation of a fully authoritarian regime under Kuchma and led to the victory of the opposition through Ukraine's Orange Revolution.

By the October-December 2004 presidential elections Ukraine will have experienced 13 years of rule under two presidents, Leonid Krawchuk and Leonid Kuchma. During this period Ukraine's two presidents and ten governments have continually claimed that Ukraine was in 'transition' to a liberal democracy and a market economy.

This article argues that transition towards these goals was sporadic at best, and more often than not faulting or regressing. By the end of two Kuchma's terms in office, Ukraine had regressed further from these declared goals and best defined as a 'hybrid' state with a 'competitive authoritarian' regime.

The article is divided into two sections. Section 1 discusses different political science models to define Ukraine's state and regime. Section 2 applies the terms 'hybrid' state and 'competitive authoritarianism' to Ukraine through the use of comparative analysis with other post-communist states.

Defining Ukraine's regime

Political scientists have been very adept in developing new terminology to describe CIS states. Many of these classifications are not necessarily different and therefore at times overlap.

One of the earliest attempts to classify Ukraine was made by Kubicek (1994) who himself drew on other democratization and transitology scholars (O'Donnell, 1994). Russia and Ukraine were defined as delegative democracies where a ruling elite faced an inactive population between elections. Elections remain one of the few facets found in the state that gave it some semblance of being a 'democracy'. The executive attempts to organize and control society so that the population remains passive between elections. The population defers to them on important matters of governance, making the system remarkably neo-Soviet in the manner in which it operates (Kuzio, 2002).

Kubicek (2000) also later developed this model to show how Ukraine had many of the features of a corporatist state of the type that was highly common in Latin America. Kubicek focused on an area of transition in Ukraine that had been largely ignored by other scholars, namely: why was civil society in Ukraine tired, defeated, alienated and stagnant at a time of mass corruption, enormous economic collapse, unemployment and unfulfilled expectations? Kubicek sought to explain why there was low trust and political efficacy, and citizens (or 'subjects') felt powerless to change anything.

Kubicek (2000) set out to add to the 'transitology' literature by examining how the institutions of the *ancien regime* influence political and economic reform through 'path dependence'. Kubicek therefore criticised the commonplace view in the 'transitology' literature that movement towards a democracy and a market economy is preordained. This view has since become more common among scholars (Carothers, 2002).

Kubicek believes that reform can be stopped, halted, it can stagnate or be reversed because, 'The goal of the system ... is actually to fragment civil society and prevent the emergence of true autonomous centers of power' (Kubicek, 2000, p. 5). Corporatism attempts to control change by preventing mobilization from below. It permits some elements of pluralism but also promotes social unity at the expense of conflict and competition.

Focusing upon 'path dependence' is important, Kubicek believes, because the ruling elite's of the *ancien regime* can reproduce themselves and thereby subvert reform or turn it to their own personal advantage. In the post-Soviet era old institutions survive and work against a radical restructuring of political life.

Much of the corporatist aspects of the Ukrainian state drew upon an inherited and deeply entrenched Soviet 'patrimonial' political culture found within centrist elites (Montgomery and Remington, 1994; Prizel, 1999; Van Zon, 2001). As Ukraine became mired in political crisis after the Kuchmagate[1] crisis in November 2000, and during the difficult 2003-2004 transition to the post-Kuchma era, Ukraine's centrist elites fell increasingly back on their neo-Soviet political culture.

Kubicek (2000) fails to provide us with the full picture of transition in Ukraine and the former Soviet Union. This is because he, like many other scholars, ignores a crucial influence upon the transition process – the national question – that is vital for understanding Ukraine's 'path dependence' (Kuzio, 2001). A more vibrant national identity in eastern Ukraine would have not required any negotiated transition in 1990-1992 between 'soft liners' in the *ancien regime* (that is, national communists) and moderates in the national-democratic opposition as the latter would have taken power themselves and instituted the radical changes that Kubicek laments did not take place.

This is what happened in the three Baltic states. In Ukraine the national democrats broke with this alliance only in 2000-2001 after Viktor Yushchenko's government was removed. Four years later he came to power through election victory and the Orange Revolution. His former centrist allies disintegrated.[2]

The author points out that eastern Ukraine is more alienated and less trustful of ruling elite. But he fails to ask why eastern Ukrainians should feel this

---

1   The Kuchmagate began on November 28, 2000 when tapes illicitly made in President Kuchma's office by presidential guard Mykola Melnychenko were publicly revealed in parliament. One of the tapes included an order by Kuchma to "deal" with opposition journalist, Heorhiy Gongadze, who was kidnapped on September 16, 2000. His decapitated body was found near Kyiv 2 months later. Melnychenko fled abroad and sought asylum in the USA where he has lived since 2001.

to a greater degree than western Ukrainians. The economic crisis in western Ukraine was more severe, and yet protests were not translated into votes for the Communist Party (unlike in eastern Ukraine). Kubicek (2000) admits that societies that are as polarised as Ukraine are prone to calls for consensus (zlahoda) politics over conflict. But his comparisons of Ukraine with Poland, the Czech Republic or Hungary as not being polarised are a poor choice as these three states are mono-ethnic. In addition, their transitions did not include Russian and Soviet imperial and totalitarian baggage.

Ukraine is best understood as only a partial delegative democracy as it is mainly Russophone eastern Ukrainians who are inactive between elections. Centrist political parties, often backed by Russophones, are top heavy and only mobilise citizens through pressure or financial inducements. This goes some way in explaining why eastern Ukrainians are so passive. Eastern Ukraine is the main base of support for oligarchs and centrist parties.

A passive population between elections is not the case in western and central Ukraine where civil society is continuously active, both during and between elections. Therefore, the delegative democracy label cannot be applied to western and central Ukraine. As numerous scholars have argued, Ukraine is very far from being a homogenous entity (Shulman, 1999). Shulman (2005) has pointed to a strong link between national identity and reformist sentiment. He divides Ukrainians into two political cultures: 'ethnic Ukrainian' and 'eastern Slavic' with only the former strongly supportive of reform. This link was clear when western and central Ukrainians played a decisive role in the Orange Revolution.

Western and central Ukraine remain strongholds of the democratic opposition. In the 2002 parliamentary elections these two regions voted primarily for three opposition forces: Viktor Yushchenko's Our Ukraine (NU), the Yulia Tymoshenko bloc (BYuT), and the Socialist Party of Ukraine (SPU). The only exception to this rule was the SPU's victory in the central-eastern Poltava oblast.

In the 1994 presidential elections the 'nationalist' candidate, incumbent President Leonid Krawchuk, won only west of the Dnipro river in central Ukraine while his opponent, Leonid Kuchma, won most votes east of the Dni-

---

2   See "Ukraine: weak opposition gives Yushchenko a free hand." *Oxford Analytica*, 25

pro river. The SPU's victory in Poltava in 2002, coupled with Viktor Yushchenko's strong support throughout central Ukraine in the 2004 presidential elections, showed that the opposition and national democrats had expanded their support throughout central Ukraine to a greater extent than that which Krawchuk had obtained in 1994. Central Ukrainian votes for Yushchenko, and Kyiv's hostility to his main opponent, Viktor Yanukovych, was a crucial element in Yushchenko's victory in 2004.

In the city of Kyiv the pro-presidential For a United Ukraine (ZYU) failed to even cross the 4% threshold while the Kyiv clan's Social Democratic united Party (SDPUo) just made it over. These results repeated those of the second round of the 1994 presidential elections when Kuchma lost in Kyiv to the 'nationalist' Leonid Krawchuk.

These election results show how an active civil society and anti-oligarchic views have prevented the Kyiv oligarchic clan's SDPUo from taking control of its home base of Kyiv. Another factor blocking this is the presence of the 'mini oligarch', popular Kyiv Mayor Oleksandr Omelchenko, who is aligned with Viktor Yushchenko. Omelchenko strongly backed Yushchenko in round two of the 2004 elections, providing crucial infra-structure support to sustain the Orange Revolution.

In contrast, the Labour Ukraine and Regions of Ukraine oligarchic clans monopolise Dnipropetrovsk and Donetsk, respectively.[3] In these two regions, especially Donetsk oblast and the Donbas in general, the classification of Ukraine as a 'delegative' democracy fits perfectly. ZYU's best electoral result in the 2002 elections was in Donetsk oblast where it won 37%, a result ensured by then Donetsk governor Yanukovych. The only opposition party with a strong base in eastern Ukraine is the Communist Party (KPU).

In states where there has been no 'economic reform', such as in Belarus, oligarchs have not appeared as the 'winners'. The Belarusian state has instead

---

3   January 2005.
    In Ukraine there are three main clans that bring together regional, political and oligarch interests. These are the same power bases that dominated Ukraine in the Soviet era. They include the Kyiv clan based on the Social Democratic united Party led by Viktor Medvedchuk, also head of the presidential administration in 2002-2004, the Dnipropetrovsk clan based on the Labor (Trudova) Party and led by Serhiy Tyhipko, and the largest and wealthiest in the Donbas based on the Regions of Ukraine Party. Prime Minister, Viktor Yanukovych, the presidential candidate in the 2004 elections supported by President Kuchma, is the leader of Regions of Ukraine.

been 'captured' by Lukashenka through a Sultanistic regime (Eke and Kuzio, 2000). In Russia, on the other hand, the oligarchs were removed from power after Putin was elected first to office in March 2000. An agreement was struck whereby the oligarchs could keep their ill gotten wealth on condition they stayed out of politics. Those that have refused to abide by this agreement have either been exiled (Boris Berezovskii) or imprisoned (Mikhail Khodorokovskii).

The oligarch's 'capture' of the Russian state has been replaced by that of Putin's allies in the security forces in what is now described as either a 'managed democracy' (Balzer, 2003) or, by Russian political scientists, as a 'militocracy' (Kryshtanovskaya and White, 2003). The prevalence of 'siloviki' (commonly referred to as representatives of the 'power ministries' in the Interior Ministry, Security Service and Defence Ministry) in the Russian state administration has grown under Putin, taking over power from the oligarchs who dominated state politics under Borys Yeltsin. Russia also has a confident party of power (Unified Russia) allied to nationalists (Rodina and the Liberal Democrtic Party) who together control two-thirds of the State Duma.

All of this makes Russia quite different from Ukraine. Whether oligarchs would distance themselves from politics would depend on who is to be elected Ukrainian president in 2004. A victory by the pro-presidential candidate (Yanukovych) would not have led to the separation of politics and business but rather the victory of Ukraine's largest and wealthiest oligarch clan. Yushchenko's victory ensures that there will not be a further consolidation of the oligarchic regime in Ukraine that was allowed to emerge under Kuchma. Yanukovych is associated with Ukraine's wealthiest Donetsk oligarchic clan. Russia's support for Yanukovych in the elections was also understood by Ukraine's ruling elites as an attempt to export Russia's 'managed democracy' model.

In Ukraine the first attempts to define Ukraine's regime type were undertaken during Kuchma's first term in office. An analysis of 'nomenklatura democratization' leading to 'electoral clientalism' in Ukraine was developed by Birch (1997). Birch's main arguments are that 'electoral clientalism' is favoured when elections are contested by candidates in single mandate (majoritarian) districts. This was the case completely in the 1994 elections and for half of the deputies elected in the 1998 and 2002 elections (the threshold in the 1998 and

2002 elections was 4%). The 2006 elections will be the first to be held using a fully proportional election law to a lower threshold of 3%.

Members of the pro-presidential parliamentary majority join together not through ideological unity, but to resolve certain economic or financial issues in their favour. These can include privatising factories, transferring land titles, obtaining credits and resolving difficulties with the State Tax Administration.

Although ZYU and the SDPUo together only elected 54 deputies in the proportional half of the 2002 elections this number was joined by another 140 deputies from majoritarian districts. Together with 30 defectors from the opposition this initially gave a 230-strong pro-presidential majority. With no ideological unity the majority disintegrated in Spring 2004.[4]

The 2006 elections will be the first to be held using a fully proportional election law. This is forcing centrist parties, such as Labor Ukraine, to begin to "deoligarchise" themselves in anticipation of the 2006 elections in order to portray a more acceptable public face. This may be important to accomplish as the centrist camp disintegrated after Yanukovych's defeat in the 2004 elections.

In Ukraine, due to economic reform being delayed until 1994, the oligarchs only rose to prominence during the 1998 parliamentary and 1999 presidential elections, 3-5 years later than in Russia. The oligarchs briefly developed an alliance with the national democrats in 1999-2001 which collapsed after the onset of Kuchmagate and the removal of the Yushchenko government in April 2001. Since then, and especially after the 2002 elections, centrists (who are dominated by three large clans who controlled 150 of the 230 deputies in the pro-presidential majority) attempted to rule Ukraine single handed.

A number of scholars have moved away from the transitology tautology underlining the assumptions that post-communist states are moving in a linear line from communism to democracy. D'Anieri (2001, 2003) has defined Ukraine's regime as 'electoral authoritarianism' (in contrast to Kubicek's 'delegative democracy' [1994] or 'electoral democracy' [2001]). This makes

---

4   See T. Kuzio, "Ukraine's pro-presidential parliamentary majority disintegrates." *Eurasian Daily Monitor* 1(83) (September 13, 2004) and "Ukraine: Parliamentary shift bodes ill for Yanukovych." *Oxford Analytica*, 15 September 2004.

greater sense as it avoids using the term 'democracy' in any definition of Ukraine's political regime under Kuchma.

The politics of "partial reform" (Hellman, 1998; Hellman et al. 2000) has been developed more recently by scholars who question whether 'transition' is a process that has a start (communism) and a finish (liberal market democracy). 'Partial reform' can lead to a halt in the transition creating a hybrid state. Such hybrid states are usually stable over time (for example, Mexico under the Institutionalised Revolutionary Party).

At the same time, during elections the survival of regime is threatened by unexpected developments, such as the strength of the opposition and civil society or outside pressure to hold free elections as a pre-requisite to obtaining international assistance. Serbia under Slobodan Milosevich in October 2000, Georgia under Eduard Shevardnadze in November 2003 and Ukraine under Kuchma in October-December 2004 are examples of how miscalculations by the regime during elections led to regime change.

A state only 'partially reformed' is similar to what other scholars have discussed as a 'hybrid state' that combines elements of authoritarianism and democracy (Levitsky and Way, 2002b). Such hybrid states account for the majority of countries in the world (Diamond, 2002).

'Hybrid states' are a better way of describing 'electoral democracies' (Kubicek, 2001) and 'electoral authoritarian' states (D'Anieri, 2001). Freedom House's annual Nations in Transit survey of 27 post-communist states describes one category of countries as 'transitional governments' or 'hybrid regimes'.

Ukraine entered the post-Soviet era through a negotiated pact between the national communists (who later became centrists and oligarchs) and the national democrats (Kuzio, 2000). The April 1990 Soviet Ukrainian elections had shown that Ukraine, along with Russia, Belarus and Moldova, was in the 'partial success' group of Soviet republics (Montgomery and Remington, 1994). The 'high penetration' group where the opposition was more powerful included Armenia, Georgia and the three Baltic states. Georgia experienced a democratic revolution in 2003-2004 and remains, together with Ukraine and Moldova, still classified as 'transitional governments' or 'hybrid regimes'. Armenia meanwhile, has regressed to a 'semiconsolidated authoritarian regime' (Table 1).

Table 1: Freedom House designation of CIS regimes (2004)

Transitional governments or hybrid regimes	Semi-consolidated authoritarian regimes	Consolidated authoritarian regimes
Ukraine	Azerbaijan	Belarus
Moldova	Russia	Turkmenistan
Georgia	Armenia	Uzbekistan
	Tajikistan	Kazakhstan
	Kyrgyzia	

Source: Freedom House, Nations in Transit, 2004 (http://freedomhouse.org/research/nattransit.htm).

The classification of three CIS states as 'transitional' (Nations in transit, 2003) is misleading. If true, there would have to be evidence of 'transition' that shows some progress towards democratic consolidation. Of these three states (Ukraine, Georgia, Moldova) Georgia underwent a democratic breakthrough in 2003-2004, but it remains too early to say whether this will lead to a successful consolidation of democracy. Ukraine's democratic breakthrough occurred during the 2004 elections.

'Transition', in the manner in which Carothers (2002) criticised the use of the concept as assuming a direct linear path from authoritarianism to democratic consolidation, is difficult to apply to the CIS. All 12 CIS states have witnessed democratic regression (rather than progress as implied in the traditional understanding of 'transition') since the late 1990s.

The Georgian democratic revolution of November 2003 and subsequent election by a landslide of reformer Mikhail Saakashvili in January 2004 is the exception, rather than the rule in the CIS. The November 2003 Azerbaijani and December 2003 and March 2004 Russian elections confirm the trend towards 'consolidated autocracies' in the CIS. Ukraine's Orange Revolution in late 2004 has added another country to Georgia and helped to break these negative trends.

The difficulties of the 'transition paradigm' were dissected by Carothers (2002) who found its premise of a 'democratic teleology' as its main failure to depict reality. Like Levitsky and Way (2002a,b), Carothers (2002) points out that only approximately 20 out of 100 transitions in the 1990s have achieved success in democratic consolidation. The majority of the states which were in transition remain in the 'political grey zone' and often combine elements of authoritarianism and democratic systems that scholars have increasingly referred to as hybrid regimes (Carothers, 2002).

Carothers (2002) defines Ukraine, Russia, Bulgaria, Bosnia, Moldova and Albania as hybrid regimes. These hybrid regimes have the following six features, all of which could all be found in Ukraine during Kuchma's second term in office:

- Citizens interests are under-represented or ignored;
- Low levels of political participation beyond voting as in a 'delegative democracy';
- Frequent abuses of the rule of law;
- Election outcomes produce uncertain results and lack legitimacy;
- Exhibit low levels of trust in state institutions;
- Poor performance of the state.

Carothers (2002) prefers to move away from the earlier classifications frequently used in the 1990s because they assumed that these regimes were merely stuck in a forward transition. Hybrid states can have long staying power. "Worse, these factors have, over time, coalesced to form a logically coherent system prone to stagnation and resistant to change" (Motyl, 2003, p. 19). In Mexico the hybrid state ruled by the PRI stayed in power until the 1990s by managing elections where it regularly received 80% of the vote. Russia is also increasingly referred to as a 'managed democracy' that could be stable over time (Balzer, 2003).

The main threat to regime stability in hybrid states is the requirement to hold periodic elections. If elections are mishandled, as in Serbia by Slobodan Milosevic in October 2000, Edvard Shevardnadze in November 2003 or Kuchma in Ukraine in 2004, regime turnover can lead to 'democratic breakthrough'. Kuchma miscalculated by selecting a candidate (Yanukovych) with a prison record that made it easier to mobilise against.

Carothers (2002) characterisation of the ruling elites as corrupt, disinterested in the country and dishonest is consistent with opinion polls in Ukraine which show that 90-92% of Ukrainians believed they had no influence over central or local affairs. In 2003, between 63 and 85% of Ukrainians believed the elites were corrupt, unable to increase living standards, were disinterested in protecting their rights, unprofessional and undemocratic. Seventy-one percent believed that the newly elected president in 2004 should change Ukraine's course. Meanwhile, 72% of Ukrainians had no faith in free and fair elections in 2004 (People don't match reforms, 2003). Only 22% of Ukrainians believed that the 2002 elections were held in a free and fair manner. As to the 2004 elections, only 12% believed they would be free and fair, a public view that was consistent with Ukraine holding its dirtiest ever election.

The political process in hybrid states is, 'widely seen as a stale, corrupt, elite-dominated domain that delivers little good to the country and commands little respect' (Carothers, 2002, p. 10). Ruling elites are as cut off from citizens as they were in the Soviet era by living in their own virtual world where actual policies and official rhetoric contradict one another (Wilson, 2001; Kuzio, 2003b). Maleyev (2004) sees this relationship as one where elite rule over Ukraine 'acts like a (foreign) occupation force'. This wide gulf between elites and parties led to the authorities miscalculating the mood within the population.

Carothers (2002) sees hybrid regimes as blurring the distinction between the state and the ruling party. The state's assets (finances, jobs, public information via state media, security forces) are placed in the hands of the ruling party (Carothers, 2002, p. 12). This is especially seen during elections when the party of power abuses its access to state administrative resources.[5]

Carothers (2002) describes hybrid regimes as 'dysfunctional' because they exhibit 'feckless pluralism'. Levitsky and Way (2002a,b, 2003) prefer to call this 'pluralism by default'. Pluralism by default exists in states which do not have either a strong civil society or united elites. Instead, there is, 'a fragmented and polarised elite and weak state unable to monopolise political control' (Way, 2003, p. 463).

In Roeder's (2002, p. 49) view, pluralism by default is inherently unstable because it incorporates 'autocratic incumbents and democratic rules' (Levitsky and Way, 2002a, p. 5). Neither side (authoritarian incumbents or the opposition) are powerful enough to either impose a fully authoritarian regime or to undertake a democratic breakthrough through regime change. Although they are at heart inherently unstable regimes, parties of power (such as Mexico's PRI) may have the capability to stay in power for long periods of time. Elections remain the greatest threat to upsetting this unstable relationship between the authorities and opposition a 'manifestation of democracy'. But, it is also an obstacle to authoritarianism. Pluralism within the state, such as we witnessed in Ukraine's hybrid regime under Kuchma provides, 'the least hospitable circumstance for preserving authoritarianism or creating new authoritarianism' (Roeder, 2002, p. 50). The ruling elites of the regime are incapable (for a variety of reasons that we shall discuss later) of introducing a fully authoritarian regime. This was the case during Kuchma's second term where from the Kuchmagate crisis until he left office (2001-2004) the ruling elites faced one of their strongest challenges from the opposition, albeit a disunited one. In the end, the opposition prevailed and launched an Orange Revolution that halted election fraud intended to support Yanukovych's election.

Ukraine as a hybrid state and a competitive authoritarian regime

As seen from the previous section, political scientists have a variety of tools at their disposal to integrate their analyses of Ukraine's regime type within the literature on democratisation. The definition developed by political scientists defines Ukraine as a 'hybrid' state with a 'competitive authoritarian' regime. The next section applies this definition to Ukraine under Kuchma.

During Kuchma's first term in office, centrists were too weak to move Ukraine to a fully authoritarian regime. Centrists were still disunited, unstructured and in the early stages of accumulating capital to transform themselves into oligarchs (Puglisi, 2003). During Kuchma's term in the late 1990s the centrists had transformed into oligarchs, and attempted to establish an authoritarian state to defend their political power and new wealth.

Why do centrists prefer authoritarian regimes? One important reason is that they are reluctant to risk ceding power. Being no longer in power in CIS states means not only going into opposition, but also the possibility of facing

---

5   See T. Kuzio, "Rising abuse of state-administrative resources in Ukrainian elections."

charges of corruption and, worse still, revenge by former political opponents who now constitute the country's new leadership.

Due to the close connection between business and the executive branch, if the executive loses power business empires built up by the president, his family, and oligarchic allies could be quickly lost. One way to overcome this is by a pact whereby oligarchs are left alone provided they redirect their loyalties to the chosen 'successor'. The 2003 clampdown on the Russian Yukos oil magnate can be attributed to the company's chief executive, Khodorkovskii, violating this unwritten agreement and openly expressing support for the opposition.

In a bid to insure themselves against legal proceedings and to protect the capital accumulated by their families and close associates, the presidents of both Kazakhstan and Kyrgyzstan introduced legislation in their respective parliaments guaranteeing them and their immediate families lifelong immunity from prosecution. Putin granted the same immunity to Yeltsin.

Since 1994 Krawchuk has never requested immunity from prosecution. The same was true of Kuchma in his first term in office. When Georgian President Shevardnadze was removed from power in 2003 he, like Krawchuk, also did not feel sufficiently threatened to seek immunity. In 2004, on the other hand, Kuchma was afraid of leaving office because of the numerous accusations against him and his allies. These accusations against Kuchma ranged from murder and violence, election rigging, high level corruption and abuse of office.

At issue was not only Kuchma's fate as he protected the business interests of his oligarchic allies in a two way process. On the one hand, he allowed their businesses and corruption to proliferate and in return he demanded political loyalty in a symbiotic relationship that has been described as a 'blackmail state' (Darden, 2001).

Ruling elites

The unity of the ruling elites is crucial for the imposition of a fully authoritarian regime. For this to be successful a united party of power is required. As Table 2 shows, it is not coincidental that CIS states with pluralism by default

Eurasian Daily Monitor 1(65) (August 3, 2004).

are also those lacking united parties of power, such as Georgia, Ukraine and Moldova.

The only exception is Belarus where no party of power exists. In Belarus the regime is built around a sultanistic cult of loyalty to Lukashenka (Eke and Kuzio, 2001).

Table 2: Parties of power in the CIS

Turkmenistan	Democratic Party
Uzbekistan	People's Democratic Party
Kazakhstan	Fatherland Party
Tajikistan	People's Democratic Party
Kyrgyzia	My Country; Agrarian Labour Party
Azerbaijan	New Azebaijan
Georgia	Union of Citizens of Georgia; For a New Georgia; Democratic Revival Union (Ajaria)
Armenia	Republican Party
Moldova	Agrarian Democratic Party
Russia	Russia's Choice; Our Home is Russia; Unity; Unified Russia (2001-)
Ukraine	NDP (1997-99); For a United Ukraine (2001-2002); SDPUo (2002-04)

Note: Belarus has no party of power. Parties of power in Georgia refer to the Edward Shevardnadze era (1992-2003).

Where there have been divisions within the ruling elites, and no one group has been able to establish its hegemony over the state, 'projects to maintain authoritarianism or establish new authoritarian constitutions failed' (Roeder, 2002, p. 40). In Ukraine its regional divisions worsened the already existing elite cleavages and prevented the creation of a unified party of power (Roeder, 2002, p. 45).

Tension within the ruling elites in Ukraine and Moldova over 'cultural or ethnic issues' have been an additional factor inhibiting the creation of unified parties of power. Regional divisions in Ukraine have prevented the consolidation of both the ruling elites and the opposition. In the 2004 presidential elections the Communists were more hostile to Yushchenko's candidacy than to the Kuchma camp's candidate, Yanukovych, because Yushchenko is seen by Communists as a 'nationalist' and an American stooge.[6]

The challenge of the transition to the post-Kuchma era, coupled with a powerful opposition, also reinforced cleavages within the ruling elites. One group of oligarchs are striving to become gentrified (Dnipropetrivsk) as capitalist entrepreneurs. Another (SDPUo) sought to continue to play by the old rules as corrupt oligarchs.

The first group is not necessarily afraid of an opposition victory as Yushchenko had ruled out re-opening privatisation conducted in the 1990s. Some within the Ukrainian elite also understood that there was a need for change in the post-Kuchma era.

Oleksandr Zinchenko, former deputy head of the SDPUo, and Viktor Pinchuk, one of Ukraine's wealthiest oligarch-businessmen, understood that the transition from oligarch to gentrification requires a divorce of politics from business (*Zerkalo Nedeli*, August 16-22, 2003). Only those who hold such views in the ruling elites are not threatened by an opposition victory. In June 2004 Zinchenko agreed to head Yushchenko's election campaign.[7]

In contrast, high ranking SDPUo member Nestor Shufrych believes it is impossible to divide politics and economics (Ukrayinska Pravda, September 20 and 21, 2004). The SDPUo have been the most hostile to the opposition, working alongside the Communists in denouncing Our Ukraine as 'Nashists' (a play on 'Nasha Ukrayina' [Our Ukraine] which resembles 'Nazis'). If the SDPUo had been able to dominate Ukrainian politics in the post-Kuchma era, Ukraine would have evolved towards a fully authoritarian regime.

The 'Young Turks' within the pro-presidential camp were also restless at the end of the Kuchma era. The Ministries of Foreign Affairs, Justice and Economics and European Integration voiced their opposition to Ukraine's admission to the CIS United Economic Space (YES) (Bukkvoll, 2004). The YES was signed by Ukraine, Russia, Belarus and Kazakhstan in April 2004.

Minister of Economics and European Integration Valeriy Khoroshkovskyi and Inna Bohoslovska, head of the State Committee for Regulatory Policy and

---

6 Yushchenko's wife is an American-Ukrainian. Examples of the anti-Yushchenko and anti-American tirade in the 2004 elections can be found in http://www2.pravda.com.ua/archive/2004/october/6/4.shtml, and http://www.razom.org.ua/album/150/.

Enterprise, resigned from the government in January 2004. Khoroshkovskyi and Bohoslovska are Dnipropetrovsk oligarch Viktor Pinchuk's proteges who funded their failed 2002 election bloc, the Winter Crop Generation (Kuzio, 2003c). Khoroshkovskyi and Bohoslovska cited deep disagreements with First Deputy Prime Minister and Minister of Finance Mykola Azarov, deputy head of the Party of Regions and Ukraine's main lobbyist for the YES.

Another line of tension was over corruption and the damage this had done to Ukraine's international image. As secretary of the National Security and Defense Council (NRBO), Yevhen Marchuk, came into conflict with Andrei and Leonid Derkach over their high level involvement in illegal arms sales in the second half of the 1990s. As a supporter of NATO membership, Marchuk understood how this kind of illegal activity damaged Ukraine's prospects for Euro-Atlantic integration. Former oligarch and presidential adviser Oleksandr Volkov also complained about mud slinging by the Derkach oligarchs against himself and the former head of Naftohaz Ukrayiny, Ihor Bakay (*Ukrayinska Pravda*, November 7, 2003).

In 2003, People's Democratic Party (NDP) leader Valerii Pustovoitenko complained that the presidential administration was pressing his party (Ukrayina moloda, November 19, 2003). Pustovoitenko believed that this was due to the signing by the NDP of an agreement of cooperation in 2003 with Our Ukraine, the same month the NDP protested at the removal of NDP member, Vasyl Shevchuk, as Minister for the Environment from the government. Although heading a pro-presidential party, Pustovoitenko was only a passive supporter of the centrist presidential candidate, Yanukovych, in the 2004 elections. The NDP was divided with a 'Democratic Platform' supporting Yushchenko.

With the power behind him of the SDPUo and the presidential administration, both of whom he led, Medvedchuk's tactics not only created tension with the opposition and within pro-presidential ranks, but also within his own SDPUo. In the 2004 election campaign regional branches of the SDPUo clamoured for their party to back Yushchenko in the 2004 elections. In Mukachevo, site of a severe battle between the SDPUo and Yushchenko's Our

---

7   See the hostile open letter from the SDPUo to Zinchenko that described him as a 'traitor' (http://www.sdpuo.org.ua, September 20, 2004).

Ukraine over who won the mayoral elections in 2003-2004, hundreds of SDPUo party members resigned.

The establishment of fully authoritarian regimes requires unified parties of power. This eluded Kuchma and some within Ukraine's elites remained united in the 2004 presidential elections only in opposition to Yushchenko as the 'Other'.

The attempt to launch the NDP as a party of power during the Pustovoitenko government (1997-1999) failed miserably. Despite the use of state-administrative resources to promote the NDP it only obtained 5.01% in the 1998 parliamentary elections. During Kuchma's second term another attempt was made with ZYU but it disintegrated into eight factions immediately after the 2002 elections.

Under Putin there has been a more successful attempt to institutionalise a party of power with Unified Russia, which combines Putin's Unity and Yevgenny Primakov and Yuriy Luzhkov's Fatherland-All Russia Party. Unified Russia is buttressed by nationalist and nationalist-Bolshevik allies in the State Duma.

Centrists in Ukraine who were grouped around Kuchma were also at a disadvantage to their Russian counter parts grouped around Putin as they could not link up with nationalists to give themselves a parliamentary majority. Centrists in Ukraine are anti-nationalist and the SDPUo denounce Our Ukraine as vehemently as do the Communists. The 2004 presidential election was filled with anti-nationalist (read anti-Yushchenko) campaigns.

'Nationalists' in Ukraine are also different from nationalists in Russia as they are reformist and pro-Western (that is, national democrats). This makes them very different from the anti-Western and anti-reform nationalists allied to Putin in Russia.

The lack of a party of power in Ukraine creates difficulties during transitions to new presidents, such as in 2003-2004. During his two terms in office Kuchma acted as a neutral umpire over three competing oligarchic clans who disliked each other as much as they disliked the opposition. Ideally, a presidential candidate from the Kuchma camp should have also been a new neutral umpire, rather than a representative of one of the three large clans, such as Yanukovych, who leads the Donbas clan's Party of Regions.

The December 2003 Constitutional Court's decision to allow President Kuchma to stand in the 2004 presidential elections was due to the fear by the executive of the splintering of pro-presidential elites during the election campaign (Mostova, 2003; Sobolev, 2003). SPU leader, Oleksandr Moroz, and russophone liberal, Vladimir Malynkowitch, believed that the threat of Kuchma becoming a candidate would thereby hang over the heads of the pro-presidential groups as a way of keeping them in line and not defecting to Yushchenko (Ukrayinska Pravda, January 2, 2004).

This policy has been shaped by past experience of defections within the ruling elites in Ukraine and elsewhere (Way, 2003, p. 455). Executives need to hold on to their allies and limit criticism.

In the 1990s some of the most serious challenges to incumbent's power came from Ukraine's prime ministers with Kuchma using this route himself to challenge Krawchuk in 1993-1994. Prime Ministers Yevhen Marchuk (1995-1996) and, more seriously, Pavlo Lazarenko (1996-1997) posed a direct challenge to Kuchma and threatened his 1999 election bid.

In 1997-1999 Lazarenko became the first oligarch to create a 'dissident party of power', the left-populist Hromada, which obtained 4.68% in the 1998 elections, only slightly less than the official party of power, NDP (5.01). Lazarenko's challenge was met by the executive instigating corruption charges against him, the stripping of his parliamentary immunity and Lazarenko being forced to flee abroad and seek asylum in the USA (Darden, 2001; Kuzio, 2003d, 2004a).

Yushchenko led the government in 1999-2001 and after he was removed by a centrist-KPU vote of no confidence he created his Our Ukraine bloc. Our Ukraine came first in that half of the 2002 elections which was based on proportional representation. In 2004 he was elected Ukraine's third president and made Tymoshenko his Prime Minister.

After Lazarenko fled abroad, Marchuk took up his anti-oligarch and anti-corruption populist rhetoric during the 1999 elections. Marchuk was then bought off in the second round of the elections when he was appointed secretary of the National Defense and Security Council (NROB) and in 2003-2004 occupied the position of Defense Minister.

As secretary of the NROB, Marchuk was never trusted by Kuchma because of his earlier opposition to himself from 1996 to 1999. This was made worse by strong rumours of his involvement with Mykola Melnychenko, the security service guard who illicitly taped Kuchma's office in 1999-2000 that led to the Kuchmagate crisis (Ukraine: an insider report, 2002). Melnychenko himself fled abroad in November 2000 just before the Kuchmagate crisis erupted, leading to another challenge to Kuchma's rule.

After Lazarenko fled abroad in early 1999, his business partner, Tymoshenko, split from Hromada to create her own right-populist Fatherland Party and an eponymous bloc for the 2002 elections. Marchuk's 1999 political allies on the populist right moved over to Tymoshenko. As with Lazarenko, similar executive-instigated corruption charges were launched against Tymoshenko, this time with the assistance of the region's 'counter hegemon', Russia (Levitsky and Way, 2003, pp. 13, 46, 47; Kuzio, 2004a).[8]

Incumbents in competitive-authoritarian regimes also need to dominate and manipulate parliaments. The left controlled the Ukrainian parliament from 1994 to 1999 but were then removed in a 'velvet revolution' in early 2000. In 2000-2001 during the Yushchenko government, the parliament was controlled by a centrist-national democratic alliance. The alliance had existed throughout most of the 1990s and was brought on by each side feeling threatened by the Communist Party domestically and Russia externally.

The national democratic-centrist alliance collapsed due to the Kuchmagate crisis and the removal of the Yushchenko government in April 2001 by a combined centrist and Communist vote of no confidence. The executive learnt these lessons well and attempted to ensure that their centrist allies took control of parliament after the 2002 elections.

Despite deep internal rivalries and disputes within the pro-presidential camp they were still able to forge a more coherent coalition of interests than the opposition. The reasons were the continued presence of Kuchma, the existence of a 'blackmail state' (Darden, 2001) and Medvedchuk's role as the 'crisis manager' of Ukrainian politics. Most members of the presidential camp were afraid of stepping out of line during the 2003-2004 transition to the post-Kuchma era.

Another factor, which has still to be fully researched, is the influence of Soviet era networks. These created common bonds that overcame internal

---

8   See Kuzio (2004a).

tensions – such as those outlined above – within pro-presidential oligarch clans.

In contrast to opposition left and right parties and blocs, pro-presidential groups are ideologically amorphous. At the same time, they do hold certain views, attitudes and – most importantly – a past common history forged within the top ranks of the Soviet Ukrainian nomenklatura, which provides them with a strong proprietary view of Ukraine. This, in turn, feeds into an added unwillingness to relinquish power.

In contrast, the opposition are divided between two groups: the KPU and the SPU/BYuT/Our Ukraine. The KPU regard the 'Nashists' (Our Ukraine) as a greater threat than pro-presidential oligarchs. Even within the two opposition camps there were divisions over whether to back constitutional reforms with the left (KPU, SPU) backing the changes while the right (BYuT, Our Ukraine) opposing them. Unlike Our Ukraine, BYuT continued to vote against them in the December 2004 compromise package that included constitutional changes going into effect in September 2005. The Kuchma camp had always wanted changes to go immediately into effect after the elections.

Twelve years after the demise of the Soviet Union, five of the 12 CIS states are still ruled by the same person who was already president at the time his country gained its independence. Entrenched elites throughout the CIS have rewritten constitutions and falsified elections in order to preserve their hold on power. The simplest way of extending the tenure of the incumbent president has been to amend the constitution and then argue that his second presidential term is actually his first because the country's post-Soviet constitution was adopted after the first term began. This argument was used by Russian President Boris Yeltsin (first elected in 1990, constitution adopted in 1993) and by Belarusian President Alyaksandr Lukashenka (first elected in 1994, revised constitution adopted in 1996). A referendum to change the constitution to allow Lukashenka to stand for a third term was successfully adopted in October 2004. The Constitutional Court ruled that Kuchma's 1999-2004 term was his 'first' and that he could therefore stand again in 2004, a ruling that he did not in the end act upon.

Former Azerbaijani President Heidar Aliev used the same line. He similarly argued that as he was first elected in 1993, but the current constitution was adopted 2 years after that, he was entitled to seek a third term in the ballot scheduled for October 2003. In the end, this proved impossible as he became incapacitated. Instead, his son was elected president in a transfer of power reminiscent of Syria or North Korea.

Referendums have extended the terms in office of the presidents of Turkmenistan (1994), Uzbekistan (1995), and Kazakhstan (1999). Turkmen President Saparmurat Niyazov subsequently secured for himself the option of remaining in power for life. In Tajikistan, voters were called on in June 2003 to endorse as a package some 50 constitutional amendments, the most important of which enabled incumbent President Imomali Rakhmonov to run for two further consecutive 7-year terms.

An alternative method of holding on to power has been electoral fraud. Since 1995, the OSCE has criticised violations and non-free parliamentary and presidential elections in Armenia, Azerbaijan, Belarus, Georgia, Kazakhstan, Kyrgyzstan, Russia, Tajikistan, Uzbekistan, and Ukraine. Ukraine was severely condemned by Western governments and international organizations for election fraud in round two of the 2004 elections. The US led the way in refusing to accept the official result of Yanukovych declared president.

In Ukraine attempts to change the constitution ahead of the 2004 election aimed to deny the most popular candidate (Yushchenko) the extensive levers of power accumulated by Kuchma. Initially, attempts were made to change the manner in which the president was elected from a popular vote to a parliamentary vote. This change was removed due to the unwillingness of the Socialists to back it.

Instead, the constitutional changes that were voted upon in April and June 2004 envisaged that elections would be held as normal in 2004 but that some of the presidential powers would be transferred to the prime minister and parliament. In return, the opposition would obtain what it had long sought; namely, a fully proportional election law.

The law on parliamentary elections was duly changed into a fully proportional system, albeit with a lower threshold of 3% than the 4% used in the 1998 and 2002 elections. But, when constitutional changes were put to the vote on April 8, 2004 they only obtained 289 votes, 11 short of a constitutional majority. The left (KPU, Socialists) voted in favour but some members of the pro-presidential camp who were elected in single mandate districts rebelled.

The December 2004 compromise package agreed to introduce constitutional changes in September 2005.

Finally, incumbents also need to maintain their 'monopoly over the use of violence'. In CIS states, such as Russia and Ukraine, the armed forces have been starved of funds.

This is not the case with the 'siloviky' (internal security forces from the Interior Ministry, the SBU, and the State Tax Administration) whose personnel, special force units and funding have grown. In the 2000 Serbian and 2003 Georgian revolutions the neutrality or defection of these internal security forces proved to be crucial for the success of the opposition. The same was true of these security forces in Ukraine, many of whom defected to the opposition during the Orange Revolution.[9]

These internal security forces have been implicated in corruption, human rights abuses in Chechnya, murders of journalists and political opponents, illegal arms sales and attacks on pro-opposition businesses. Opposition journalist Heorhiy Gongadze and Rukh leader Viacheslav Chornovil reputedly died at the hands of a Ukrainian Interior Ministry special forces unit 'Sokil' attached to the directorate to combat organised crime working together with an organised group.

Opposition

Ruling elites in hybrid states and competitive authoritarian regimes have little choice but to tolerate oppositions. This is one area that makes them different from fully authoritarian states. At the same time, this tolerance has its limits, especially when the elites are threatened with regime change during elections and at the end of the president's final term in office. Toleration is, of course, not the same as acceptance of the important role played by the opposition in democracies.[10]

In Central Asia, Azerbaijan and Belarus the opposition is not treated as a legitimate group from whom a new president could be elected. Opposition

---

9   T. Kuzio, Security forces begin to defect to Viktor Yushchenko. Jamestown Foundation, Eurasian Daily Monitor 1(137) (December 1, 2004) and Did Ukraine's secret service really prevent bloodshed during the Orange Revolution? Jamestown Foundation, Eurasian Daily Monitor 2(16) (January 24, 2005).

10 T. Kuzio, "Ukrainian officials increasingly denounce opposition as 'extremists' and 'terrorists'." *Eurasian Daily Monitor*, 1(96) (September 30, 2004).

parties are therefore stripped of legality by the passage of legislation setting impossible conditions they must meet in order to reregister (as was the case in 2003 in Kazakhstan). Or, they are de-legitimised through a political discourse that defines them as 'radicals,' 'extremists,' and bent on instigating 'instability,' as in Kyrgyzia, Belarus and Ukraine.

The opposition in Ukraine is denounced as 'nationalists' and 'Nazis', a view that is especially prevalent in SDPUo-controlled media. As in the Soviet era, 'Nashists' are labelled as 'anti-Russian', 'anti-semitic', rabid western Ukrainian nationalists who, if they come to power, would incite inter-ethnic conflict.

Ukrainians are disillusioned with politics as a whole, and not just with the authorities. All institutions – presidential and parliamentary – obtain low levels of public trust. A June 2003 Democratic Initiatives poll found that a striking 49-57% did not, or mainly did not, trust NGO's and political parties.

Most Ukrainians believed change was required but did not believe that they had the power to push these changes through. A poll cited by Ukrayinska Pravda (March 11, 2003) found that only 7% believed that changes were unnecessary in Ukraine.

Nevertheless, this did not necessarily translate into support for opposition activities. A poll by the 'Razumkov' Ukrainian Centre for Economic and Political Studies (Zerkalo Nedeli, September 27, 2003) found that half of Ukraine's population did not back the opposition protests. Another poll cited found even higher negative views of demonstrations with 69% unwilling to take part in them (*Interfax*, April 25, 2003).

Do the public desire to learn the views of the opposition? When asked if they knew the views of the opposition, 64% said 'no', according to a combined poll by four leading sociological organisations (Ukrayinska Pravda, May 28, 2003). When asked if they wished to learn more, only 37-46% said 'yes', whereas even more –43-54% – said 'no'.

How is this phenomenon explained? A Centre for Sociological and Political Research poll found that although 33% supported the opposition and only 15.9% the authorities, again a striking 31% supported neither side (Ukrayinska Pravda, April 25, 2003). Many Ukrainians seem to believe in the slogan 'A plague on all of your houses'.

A November 2003 poll by Democratic Initiatives found that if elections were held then, only 1% would vote for Kuchma. Three percent would have voted for then head of the presidential administration and leader of the SDPUo Medvedchuk.

The problem for the opposition was that large negative votes were to be found both for the authorities and for them as well. In a May 2003 Democratic Circle poll, Tymoshenko and KPU leader, Petro Symonenko, obtained two of the highest negative ratings of − 29 and − 27%, respectively. Both leaders suffered from different problems: Tymoshenko is a 'dissident oligarch' and Symonenko a hard line Communist. The promotion of Tymoshenko as Prime Minister under President Yushchenko is a bold move intended to win support from young activists in the Orange Revolution and to install somebody who is unafraid of undertaking radical reform measures.

Two of Ukraine's four opposition leaders (Tymoshenko and Symonenko) therefore have far higher negative than positive rankings. Symonenko is highly unpopular in western Ukraine and Tymoshenko is unpopular in eastern Ukraine. Symonenko is always fated to be a runner up in presidential elections but never to win them while Tymoshenko could never be elected Ukrainian president because of her oligarch past.

Even Yushchenko, who was the most popular politician during Kuchma's second term, did not escape some negative ratings. Our Ukraine leader Yushchenko was the only opposition leader who obtained higher positive than negative ratings and the lowest negative ratings. At the same time, 32% of Ukrainians would never vote for Yushchenko (*Ukrayinska Pravda*, August 18, 2003). These hard-line anti-Yushchenko voters undoubtedly backed Yanukovych in the 2004 elections.

Questions of 'trust' are also a factor in public attitudes to the opposition. A December 2002 Democratic Initiatives poll gave low levels of 'trust' (15%) and high levels of 'distrust' to Symonenko (47%), Tymoshenko (12:54), and Socialist leader Moroz (12:43). The September 2003 Democratic Circle poll found that Yushchenko was trusted fully or mainly by 48% of Ukrainians; even still, 37% still only distrusted him completely or partially. Higher levels of distrust than trust were found for all other leading Ukrainian officials and opposition leaders.

Large numbers of Ukrainians would never vote for the majority of leading politicians. According to the September 2003 Democratic Circle poll, this ranges from 34 to 36% for Medvedchuk, Tymoshenko and Symonenko. 20-25% would never vote for parliamentary speaker for Lytvyn, Prime Minister and Party of Regions leader Yanukovych and National Bank Chairman and Labour Ukraine leader Serhiy Tyhipko. Only opposition leaders Yushchenko and Moroz obtained the lowest number of Ukrainians who would never consider voting for them.

These different polls show general apathy and a widespread 'plague on all of your houses' for all politicians, whether from the opposition or the pro-presidential camp. Most Ukrainians felt they lacked efficacy and the power to change their lives. It is then remarkable how this radically changed in a short period of time in September-November 2004 during the elections. For many Ukrainians who joined the Orange Revolution the option of a 'plague on all of your houses' (moya khata z krayu!) was no longer a feasible option as they had to act now to block a Yanukovych fraudulent victory – or regret not having done so in the years ahead.

Elections

Elections are important for hybrid states and 'competitive authoritarian' regimes as the ruling elites seek legitimacy, domestically and internationally. Elections cannot be allowed to be free and fair as this could lead to regime turnover. This was clearly seen in the 2004 presidential elections which were the dirtiest in Ukraine's history.

Regime turnover, in turn, could lead to imprisonment, execution or exile of the ruling elites. At a minimum it could lead to a re-distribution of assets. This is the fate that befell oligarchs Berezovskiy and Khodorokovskii in Russia.

Elections need to be conducted in a not too blatantly un-free and unfair way in order to obtain approval by the OSCE and the Council of Europe. At the same time, elections should be successfully 'managed' to give an advantage to the authorities who: 'While quietly tilting the electoral playing field far enough in its own favour to ensure victory' (Carothers, 2001, p. 12).

The holding of even semi-free elections helps to provide a veneer of legitimacy for the ruling elites. This 'veneer of democratic legitimacy' (D'Anieri, 2003,p.14) maintains the regime in place with minimum coercion through control over economic goods made selectively available through the levers of the 'blackmail state' (Darden, 2001), patronage, selective application of the rule of law, and abuse of 'administrative resources'.

Kuchma's strategy in the 2004 elections attempted to tilt the playing field in favour of the authorities in four areas:

1. Constitutional changes: Their adoption would have meant that any potential election victory of Yushchenko would have been less of a threat to Kuchma and the oligarchs as constitutional changes envisaged the transfer of power from the executive to the prime minister and parliament where they possessed a tentative majority. The authorities could then 'allow' Yushchenko to be elected knowing he would possess few powers. Such a scenario would have allowed Kuchma to remain de facto leader of Ukraine until the 2006 parliamentary elections, working through Prime Minister Yanukovych, who would be the most powerful personality in Ukraine, and the pro-presidential parliamentary majority.
2. Dealing with the opposition: In December 2003 the pro-presidential camp and KPU voted to create a commission to investigate Western funding of NGO's in Ukraine. SBU surveillance and harassment of the opposition inside and outside Ukraine was stepped up. Serhiy Medvedchuk was transferred from Lviv to Kyiv to be deputy head of the State Taxation Administration. As head of Lviv oblast Tax Administration, Medvedchuk aggressively targeted pro-Yushchenko businesses and media outlets. After being transferred to Kyiv, Medvedchuk launched the Tax Administration against Yushchenko's political coordinator and main financial benefactor, Petro Poroshenko.
3. Curbing independent media: After Medvedchuk became head of the presidential administration it began to issue secret instructions ('temnyky') to television stations (Human Rights Watch, 2003; Kuzio, 2004c). Television stations controlled by Medvedchuk no longer allowed the opposition to have access. Information on key events were ignored and they provided a monolithic pro-Kuchma survey of events. The only large circulating newspaper sympathetic to the opposition, Silski Visti, was threatened with being closed down in January 2004 after being accused of publishing two anti-Semitic articles. Wide public access to Radio Lib-

erty's Ukrainian language service programs were reduced after its FM re-broadcaster, Dovira, was taken over by a business group belonging to the SDPUo. Other Western radio stations were also denied a FM re-broadcaster after their FM station, Kontynent, was closed.

4. Control over institutions: A new Central Election Commission (CVK) was formed with pro-Kuchma loyalist Serhiy Kivalov, close to the SDPUo, as its head. Of the 15 members of the CVK, three-quarters are from the pro-presidential camp. Kivalov worked closely with Medvedchuk and was implicated in election fraud. Medvedchuk placed new loyalists at the heads of the Interior Ministry, SBU and the Prosecutor's Office. These three institutions, coupled with the State Tax Administration, were seen as vital in attempting to prevent a repeat of the Serbian 2000 or Georgian 2003 revolutions in Ukraine that were sparked by protests at election fraud.[11] These attempts failed as Ukraine underwent its own Orange Revolution.

Avoiding international isolation

As Levitsky and Way (2003) have argued, many hybrid states and competitive authoritarian regimes have proved very successful in the post-Cold War era at manoeuvring to prevent sanctions or international isolation being implemented against them. Ukraine's multi-vector foreign policy under Kuchma could be understood as a response to short term changes in the international environment that require adjustments in foreign policy. These adjustments are in the interests of the ruling elite, not the state (Kuzio, 2004b).

Hybrid states and 'competitive authoritarian' regimes are compelled to hold elections and not abuse human rights on a massive scale (Levitsky and Way, 2003, p. 7). But, beyond that they can still maintain good relations with the West and avoid the kind of isolation that Belarusian President Lukashenka suffers from.

Ukraine utilised this very skilfully during Kuchma's first term in office when the NATO card was used to obtain concessions from Russia which recognised their common border. Ukraine's relations with the USA have also always been traditionally better when Washington's relations with Russia have

---

11   T. Kuzio, "Stratfor Report suggests democratic revolution possible in Ukraine." *Eurasian Daily Monitor*, 1(81) (September 9, 2004).

declined. When relations with Russia have improved, as after 9/11, US relations with Ukraine have worsened (Kuzio, 2003a).

After the Kuchmagate crisis Kuchma became isolated in the West. This worsened dramatically when the USA accused Kuchma of authorising in July 2000 (three months after President Bill Clinton visited Ukraine in a high profile visit) the sale of Kolchuga radars to Saddam Hussein's Iraq. Kuchma was advised not to attend the 2002 NATO summit in Prague and when he attended seating arrangements were made to ensure he did not sit next to the US President or British Prime Minister. Nevertheless, Kuchma was not prevented from attending the summit, unlike Lukashenka, who is fully isolated.

International isolation is not in the interests of the majority of the ruling elites and therefore domestic human rights abuses that are undertaken are relatively restrained. When international organisations have issued stark condemnations, such as the Parliamentary Assembly of the Council of Europe resolutions in 2004, the Ukrainian authorities have usually backed off and then re-assessed their strategy. A re-assessment of their strategy aims to reach the same end goals by not encouraging further, damaging international criticism.

Sanctions threatened by the US in the event of the holding of un-free and non fair elections in 2004 proved to be unsettling to the personal interests of Ukraine's oligarchs. This was because they targeted the ruling elites by threatening to deny them Western visas and to launch investigations of their bank accounts (*New York Times*, March 8, 2004). Such tactics in the field of the denial of visas were successfully used against Lukashenka and the Trans-Dniestr separatist leaders. In the 2004 elections Ukraine's leading oligarchs were placed on a US visa black list.

Conclusion

Within the many different political science classifications applied to CIS states the ones that are most applicable are a hybrid state and 'competitive authoritarian' regime. States, such as Ukraine under Kuchma, are failed authoritarian states, and democracies in transition that do not struggle to consolidated democracies.

Such a conclusion has important ramifications for our study of CIS states and confirms Carothers (2002) view that transitions can have more than one trajectory. From the late 1990s many CIS states could be more readily classified as failed authoritarian regimes, rather than on a transition path towards liberal democracies and market economies. Some of these CIS states are 'competitive authoritarian' (that is, semi-authoritarian) while others are already fully authoritarian states.

Ukraine under Kuchma was also a 'competitive authoritarian' state because of its stalemated domestic political configuration. The Ukrainian political spectrum is divided between three groups: centre-right national democrats, centrist oligarchs (who have their origins in the higher levels of the Soviet Ukrainian nomenklatura), and the KPU.

In the 1990s centrists were not powerful enough to rule Ukraine by themselves and relied upon national democrats to ward off internal threats from the KPU and external threats from Russia. During the 1990s Ukraine's oligarchic centrists were still in the early stages of capital accumulation and asset re-distribution (Puglisi, 2003).

Only during Kuchma's second term in office did centrists feel confident and powerful enough to rule Ukraine alone, and thereby move Ukraine from a competitive (semi) to a fully authoritarian state. Until then, Ukraine was stalemated by an opposition not strong enough to come to power (that is, launch a 'democratic breakthrough') or centrists able to fully impose their will (to install 'full authoritarianism'). This unstable regime in Ukraine could have moved to democratic consolidation (Yushchenko) or autocratic consolidation (Yanukovych).

Failed authoritarian regimes can remain relatively stable, as in Russia and Ukraine under Yeltsin and Kuchma, Peru under Alberto Fujimori or Serbia under Slobodan Milosevic (Levitsky and Way, 2001). But, regime stability is always threatened during elections and the end of an incumbent's term in office. The incumbent can attempt to rig elections, as in Serbia in 2000, Georgia in 2003 and Ukraine in 2004, but this could then tip the system leading to mass opposition protests and a democratic revolution (Kuzio, 2003-). In Ukraine Yushchenko's victory was only made possible by the democratic Orange Revolution (Kuzio, 2005a,b).

References

Balzer, H. 2003. "Managed pluralism: Vladimir Putin's emerging regime." *Post-Soviet Affairs*, 19 (3): 189-227.

Birch, S. 1997. "Nomenklatura democratisation, electoral clientalism and party formation in post-Soviet Ukraine." *Democratization*, 4 (4): 40-62.

Bukkvoll, T. 2004. "Private interests, public policy. Ukraine and the common economic space agreement." *Problems of Post-Communism*, 51 (5): 11-22.

Carothers, T. 2002. "The end of the transition paradigm." *Journal of Democracy*, 13 (1): 5-21. (See also the responses in *Journal of Democracy*, 13(3)).

D'Anieri, P. 2003. "Electoral authoritarianism in the former Soviet Union: a comparative analysis." Paper presented to the Association Study of Nationalities, Columbia University, April 4-6.

D'Anieri, P. 2001. "Democracy unfulfilled: the establishment of electoral authoritarianism in Ukraine. A decade of independence." *Journal of Ukraine Studies*, 26 (1-2): 13-36 (special issue).

Darden, K. 2001. "Blackmail as a tool of state domination: Ukraine under Kuchma." *East European Constitutional Review*, 10 (2/3): 67-71.

Diamond, L. 2002. "Thinking about hybrid regimes." *Journal of Democracy*, 13 (2): 21-35.

Eke, S., Kuzio, T. 2000. "Sultanism in Eastern Europe. The socio-political roots of authoritarian populism in Belarus." *Europe-Asia Studies*, 52 (3): 523-547.

Hellman, J.S., Jones, G., Kaufmann, D. 2000. "Seize the state, seize the day. state capture, corruption and influence in transition." *Policy Research Working Paper*, 2444, World Bank Institute and European Bank of Reconstruction and Development.

Hellman, J.S. 1998. "Winners take all: the politics of partial reform in postcommunist transitions." *World Politics*, 50 (2): 203-234.

Human Rights Watch, 2003. "Ukraine: informal political censorship." http://hrw.org/press/2003/03/ukraine031703.htm.

Kryshtanovskaya, O., White, S. 2003. "Putin's militocracy." *Post-Soviet Affairs*, 19 (4): 289-306.

Kubicek, P. 2001. "The limits of electoral democracy in Ukraine." *Democratization*, 8 (2): 117-139.

Kubicek, P. 2000. *Unbroken ties: the State, interest associations, and corporatism in post-Soviet Ukraine*. University of Michigan Press, Ann Arbor.

Kubicek, P. 1994. "Delegative democracy in Russia and Ukraine." *Communist and Post-Communist Studies*, 27 (4): 423-441.

Kuzio, T. 2005a. "Kuchma to Yushchenko: Ukraine's 2004 Elections and 'Orange Revolution'." *Problems of Post-Communism*, 52 (2): 29-44.

Kuzio, T. 2005b. "Ukraine's Orange Revolution. The opposition's road to success." *Journal of Democracy*, 16 (2): 117-130.

Kuzio, T. 2004a. "Dissident oligarchs under attack in U.S. and Ukraine." Jamestown Foundation, *Eurasia Daily Monitor*, 1 (30).

Kuzio, T. 2004b. "Ukraine's foreign policy: pro-Western, pro-Russian or simply pro-Kuchma?" *RFERL Belarus and Ukraine Report*, 6 (5): 10.

Kuzio, T. 2004c. "Russians run censorship in Ukraine." Jamestown Foundation, *Eurasia Daily Monitor*, 1 (35).

Kuzio, T. 2003a. "Ukraine's relations with the West: disinterest, partnership, disillusionment." *European Security*, 12 (2): 21-44.

Kuzio, T. 2003b. "National identities and virtual foreign policies among the Eastern Slavs." *Nationalities Papers*, 31 (4): 431-452.

Kuzio, T. 2003c. "The 2002 parliamentary elections in Ukraine: democratization or authoritarianism." *Journal of Communist Studies and Transition Politics*, 19 (2): 24-54.

Kuzio, T. 2003d. "When oligarchs go into opposition: the case of Pavel Pazarenko." *Russia and Eurasia Review*, 2 (11): 27.

Kuzio, T. 2003e. "The next revolution?" *Transitions-on-Line* (December 12).

Kuzio, T. 2002. "Clash of civilizations - why the postcommunist world is dividing." *RFERL (Un)Civil Societies*, 3 (46).

Kuzio, T. 2001. "Transition in post-communist states: triple or quadruple?" *Politics*, 21 (3): 169-178.

Kuzio, T. 2000. *Ukraine. Perestroika to independence*. Macmillan, London.

Levitsky, S., Way, L. 2003. "Ties that bind? International linkage and competitive authoritarian regime change in Africa, Latin America and post Communist Eurasia." Paper given to the American Political Science Association, Philadelphia, August 27-30.

Levitsky, S., Way, L. 2002a. "Autocracy by democratic rules: the dynamics of competitive authoritarianism in the Post-Cold War era." Paper given to the American Political Science Association, Boston, August 28-31.

Levitsky, S., Way, L. 2002b. "The rise of competitive authoritarianism." *Journal of Democracy*, 13 (2): 51-65.

Levitsky, S., Way, L.A. 2001. "Competitive authoritarianism: hybrid regime change in Peru and Ukraine in comparative perspective." Paper given to the American Political Science Association, San Francisco, August 30-September 2.

Maleyev, K. 2004. *Ukrayinska Pravda* (21 January).

Montgomery, K., Remington, T.F. 1994. "Regime transition and the 1990 Soviet republican elections." *Journal of Communist Studies and Transition Politics*, 10 (1): 55-79.

Mostova, Y. 2003. "Closed cycle of power generation." *Zerkalo Nedeli* (September, 13-19).

Motyl, A.J. 2003. "Ukraine, Europe, and Russia: exclusion or dependence?" In: Lieven, A., Trenin, D. (eds.), *Ambivalent neighbors: the EU, NATO and the price of membership* Carnegie Endowment, Washington DC, pp. 15-43.

Nations in Transit, 2003. "Democratization in East-Central Europe and Eurasia." http://www. freedomhou- se.org/research/nattransit.htm.

O'Donnell, G. 1994. "Delegative democracy." *Journal of Democracy*, 5 (1): 55-69.

Prizel I. 1999a. "People don't match reforms." *Zerkalo Nedeli* (April, 12-18).

Prizel, I. 1999b. "The first decade after the collapse of Communism: why did some nations succeed in their political and economic transformations while others failed?" *SAIS Review*, 19 (2): 1-15.

Puglisi, R. 2003. "The rise of the Ukrainian oligarchs." *Democratization*, 10 (3): 99-123.

Roeder, P.G. 2002. "Obstacles to authoritarianism." In: Anderson, R.D., Fish, S.M., Hanson, S.F., Roeder, P.G. (eds.), *Postcommunism and the theory of democracy*. Princeton University Press, Princeton, pp. 11-53.

Shulman, S. 2005. "National identity and public support for political and economic reform in Ukraine." *Slavic Review*, 64 (1): 59-87.

Shulman, S. 1999. "The cultural foundations of Ukrainian national identity." *Ethnic and Racial Studies*, 22 (6): 1011-1036.

Sobolev, Y. 2003. "Cornered." *Zerkalo Nedeli* (October, 11-17).

"Ukraine: an insider report", 2002. *Jane's Intelligence Digest* (September 13, 18, 27).

Van Zon, H. 2001. "Neo-patrimonialism as an impediment to economic development: the case of Ukraine." *Journal of Communist Studies and Transition Politics*, 17 (3): 71-95.

Way, L. 2003. "Weak states and pluralism: the case of Moldova." *East European Politics and Society*, 17 (3): 454-482.

Wilson, A. 2001. "Ukraine's new virtual politics." *East European Constitutional Review*, 10 (2-3): 60-68.

Rapacious Individualism and Political Competition in Ukraine, 1992-2004

Lucan A. Way, University of Toronto

Abstract
This article examines one reason for the failure of full-scale authoritarianism in Ukraine, 1992-2004. The monopolization of political control in Ukraine was partially thwarted by the disorganization of Ukraine's ex-nomenklatura elite that dominated the country after the Cold War. Elite Ukrainian politics in the 1990s can best be understood as an example of "rapacious individualism." This term was used by Martin Shefter to describe pre-machine New York city politics in the 19th century, dominated by a non-ideological and unstructured competition for power and rents. Rapacious individualism in Ukraine had a contradictory impact. It hindered full-scale democratization but also undermined efforts to consolidate authoritarianism. At one level, widespread corruption allowed the executive to concentrate political power because he controlled key patronage resources. At the same time, weak organization reduced the costs of open confrontation with the executive while corruption distributed resources to a broad range of future opposition leaders. The result was competitive authoritarian rule.

The Communist party monster has disappeared. What has filled the vacuum? Well nothing has filled it! (Grinev, 1992)[1]

They asked me to convene this whole bunch of [expletive] – they are all Hetmen! I can barely keep them together. (Melnychenko, 2002, p.22)[2]

---
1   Vladimir Grinev was a deputy representative of the Ukrainian Parliament during 1990-1993.
2   Mykola Azarov was a tax chief. This was how he described his efforts to create a government sponsored party.

This means, Leonid Daniilovich [Kuchma] ... we are giving money to the enemy ... Understand? We are strengthening them! (Melnychenko, 2002, p. 116)[3]

Between 1992 and 2004, Ukraine can best be described as a competitive authoritarian regime, in which elections were meaningful and created uncertainty but in which incumbent abuses were so regular and severe that the country could not be called democratic (Levitsky and Way, 2002). Elections were often highly competitive, leading to turnovers of power in 1994 and 2004. Yet, these same elections were also extremely undemocratic. Under pressure from the government, media coverage strongly favored the incumbent. Simultaneously, the government regularly bullied opposition leaders through periodic arrests and harassed them using the tax authorities, police and other government agencies. Finally, incumbents also heavily manipulated the election process itself, leading to outright stealing of roughly 3-10% of votes in elections.

Most studies have focused on the failure of democracy in this period. Yet, given the wide range of obstacles to democratic rule in Ukraine – including the absence of democratic history, the dominance of an old Soviet elite, concentration of resources in state hands – it seems equally important to ask why Ukraine never descended into full scale authoritarian rule. This article argues that full-scale authoritarianism in post-Soviet Ukraine was partially thwarted by the formal and informal disorganization of Ukraine's ex-nomenklatura elite that dominated the country since 1992-2004. Elite Ukrainian politics in the 1990s can best be understood as an example of "rapacious individualism", a term used by Martin Shefter (1976) to describe pre-machine New York city politics in the 19th century dominated by a non-ideological, and unstructured competition for power and rents. Rapacious individualism in Ukraine had a contradictory impact. It hindered full-scale democratization but also undermined efforts to consolidate authoritarianism. At one level, widespread corruption allowed the executive to concentrate political power because he controlled key patronage resources. At the same time, weak organization reduced the costs of open

---

3 Donetsk governor Viktor Yanukovich complaining to President Kuchma that budgetary funds were being transferred to the Prime Minister Viktor Yushchenko. (Melnychenko, 2002, p. 116).

confrontation with the executive while corruption distributed resources to a broad range of future opposition leaders. The result was competitive authoritarian rule.

Obstacles to democracy in Ukraine

While the fate of pluralism in the former Soviet Union did not meet early optimistic predictions, the extent and persistence of political competition in the area was still remarkable given the range of factors arrayed against democratic development. The highly undemocratic character of the Soviet inheritance raises questions about why incumbents in Ukraine were so unsuccessful at concentrating political authority and preventing the emergence of serious political competition.

First, post-Soviet Ukraine in the 1990s and early 21st century was dominated by an ex-nomenklatura elite with relatively weak commitment to democratic norms. Both Presidents Leonid Kravchuk (1991-1994) and Leonid Kuchma (1994-2004) demonstrated a readiness to use extra-legal and anti-democratic means to stay in power and to limit criticism. The first President Kravchuk, who is often considered more democratic than his successor, tried both to limit anti-governmental media and to crack down on opposition. His government put pressure on newspapers and television stations that aired criticism of the administration (*Nezavisimost*, 6 March 1993, p. 8; September 3, 1993, p. 1; 22 December 1993, p. 1). During the 1994 Presidential election, the President successfully shut down the television station, Gravis that came out in favor of Leonid Kuchma. In addition, Kravchuk also was prepared to use physical force against his opponents when his power was threatened. Thus, in 1993, Kravchuk decided to shut down the legislature and only changed his mind when the Minister of Interior refused to cooperate (Kravchuk, 2002, pp. 227-228). The second President Kuchma also used extensive coercion against opposition journalists and opposition politicians, and engaged in outright censorship of the electronic media (Human Rights Watch, 2003; OSCE, 2000). In the late 1990s and early 21st century, Kuchma actively sought to manipulate elections through blackmail and systematic efforts at ballot stuffing (Darden, in press; Herron and Johnson, 2003). Finally, it seems likely that Kuchma was at least indirectly involved in the murder of independent journalist, Georgii Gongadze, in 2000, and the poisoning of opposition candidate, Viktor Yushchenko, in late 2004.

This willingness to use anti-democratic measures has not necessarily coincided with a strong desire for greater power and control. Thus, most agree that Kravchuk, in contrast to Kuchma (or Alyaksandr Lukashenka), was content to have a relatively limited role in the day-to-day management of the country.[4] However, he clearly was willing to use extra-legal and anti-democratic means to keep his position. In addition, antidemocratic efforts to stay in power may be driven by laudable long-term goals, such as the destruction of Communism, economic reform, or political independence.[5] Finally, an important motivating factor for virtually all executives and their staffs has been the desire to avoid prosecution for corruption after leaving power (*Nezavisimost*, 19 July 1993, p. 2). Staying in power may sometimes be considered the most effective means of avoiding prosecution. Thus a willingness to use extra legal means to stay in power has not necessarily been the outgrowth of a desire for power per se.

The weakly democratic character of the Ukrainian ruling elite was matched by the relative weakness of a rule of law that could prevent anti-democratic action. The absence of a strong legal tradition meant that leaders had a relatively free hand in manipulating laws and state agencies to harass political opponents (Darden, in press). Further, economic legacies of Soviet rule concentrated resources in state hands, providing executives with significant assets to buy off potential enemies and monopolize political control. Finally, organized civil society in Ukraine, as in other post-Communist countries, has been extremely weak (Howard, 2002). Thus, with a few important exceptions, Ukrainian leaders faced relatively little organized societal opposition to their rule in the post-Soviet era.

In sum, Ukrainian leaders demonstrated a readiness to use anti-democratic measures to stay in power, had significant state economic and administrative resources at their disposal, and confronted a mostly disorgan-

---

4　Observers at the time suggested that Kravchuk was primarily interested in being a kind of contemporary English monarch – secure in his position but uninvolved in the day to day operations of the government (Nezavisimost 7 April 1993, p. 2).

5　In the Russian context, one can believe Boris Yeltsin that at least one motivation behind his initial decision to cancel elections in 1996 was a genuine desire to prevent the return of Communist rule.

ized societal opposition. Yet, these same leaders also continued to meet serious political competition throughout the post-Soviet era. In this period, Ukraine witnessed two democratic transfers of power, a relatively dynamic media, and a surprisingly powerful legislature. To understand this puzzle, we need to examine both the organization of the ruling elite and the interaction between economic and political power in post-Soviet Ukraine.

Rapacious individualism in Ukraine, 1992-2004

The relative openness of the political system in Ukraine in the 1990s in the face of important obstacles can be partially explained by the disorganization of the political and economic elite after the fall of the Soviet Union. According to Martin Shefter, rapacious individualism is characterized by "the weakness of political organizations ... and the fluidity of ... political alignments" (Shefter, 1976, p. 21). Shefter describes a situation in which corruption was extremely rampant but also extremely unstructured and unorganized. Non-ideological politicians constantly shifted alliances and acted as more or less free agents unconnected to any constituency.

Rapacious individualism helped to generate political competition for two central reasons. First, weak organization promoted opportunism and uncertain attachment to any particular leader or organization within the governing elite. The executive was relatively susceptible to defection by allies in the face of perceived vulnerability. Signs of government weakness have encouraged mass defections, or at least fence sitting that have made it all the more difficult for the government to withstand crisis. Second, the large scale corruption and insider privatizations ended up giving individuals the resources they needed to mount serious challenges to the government.

Two elements of rapacious individualism – high fragmentation and the rampant use of government for personal enrichment – have been dominant features of Ukrainian elite politics since the fall of the Soviet Union. First, the ex-nomenklatura elite has been extremely fragmented throughout the post-Soviet period. In the Soviet era, the Communist Party of the Soviet Union provided a key mechanism of elite control (Hill, 1991). However, Gorbachev's promotion of open discussion, his failure to seriously punish dissenters, and introduction of competitive elections fundamentally undermined this tradition and made it increasingly difficult for party leaders to reign in the party members seeking to destroy the system. The failed coup of August 1991 discredited the Party and led to its dissolution throughout most of the former Soviet Union, including Ukraine. In the wake of the failed coup in 1991, all high level officials abandoned the Communist Party as part of a strategy to hold onto power (Polokhalo et al. 1995, pp. 150-155).[6]

Virtually no effort was made to replace the Party with any formal political organization to coordinate support for the executive. Instead, the "party of power" that emerged after the Party's fall in Ukraine as well as in other post-Soviet countries in the 1990s was characterized by a total absence of organization or coordination (Kuzio, 1997, pp. 21-22; Wasylyk, 1994). Rapacious individualism was first reflected in an extraordinarily fragmented executive in the 1990s. Under Kravchuk, the executive was split between a "state Duma" created by Kravchuk in early 1992, the Cabinet of Ministers, and the Presidential administration itself. Reformers in the early 1990s complained that nothing was getting done because of constant fighting between these three bodies (*Nezavisimost*, 23 May 1992, p. 2). Observers in the mid and late 1990s also noted that conflicts over property distribution created severe and often open battles among functionaries within the Presidential hierarchy or vertikal (*Zerkalo nedeli*, 16-22 November 1996). Thus, while many of the people remained the same from the Soviet era, the hierarchical organization of the elite had totally disappeared.

Within the parliament, the role and importance of governing parties evolved after 1991. In the early 1990s, Kravchuk made virtually no effort to create a formal base of political support. Instead, he sought alliances with existing national democratic parties and numerous individual political leaders and parliamentary deputies. In the late 1990s, certain government leaders around Prime Minister Valerii Pustovoitenko attempted to create a single governing party – the National Democratic Party – encompassing the entire government elite. However, by late 1999 the party had mostly disintegrated. By the beginning of the 21st century, a series of relatively well-organized parties developed around specific government officials and regional elite groupings, such as Batkyvshyna or Fatherland headed by Yulia Tymoshenko, Social Democratic Party (United) headed by Viktor Medvedchuk, and Party of Regions headed by

---

6 Communist party organization was left to third and fourth tier elites with a genuine

Mykola Azarov and Viktor Yanukovich, who all gave their support to the President. In addition, for a brief period of time during the 2002 parliamentary election, Kuchma sought to create the party "For a United Ukraine." However, this fell apart shortly after the election.

The failure of any single and dominant pro-executive political organization to emerge in post-Soviet Ukraine (or 1990s Russia, Moldova, or Belarus) can partially be explained by a lack of interest on the part of the executive. The absence of any strong ruling party organization was self-reinforcing. Existing parties either lacked popularity or were unknown to most people. Thus, Kravchuk and Kuchma in Ukraine seem to have felt that attaching their names to such organizations offered them few immediate political benefits. In turn, the relative lack of executive attention to party building meant that parties could not benefit from the resources or the individual popularity that these leaders enjoyed at different points in the 1990s. Further, Kuchma apparently feared concentrating too much power in any single organization. By keeping his allies mutually antagonistic and competitive, the President would remain "the uniting, cementing force that keeps all of his allies together" (*Zerkalo nedeli*, 23-29 March 2002).

In the absence of strong pro-executive political parties, many observers stressed the importance of informal networks or "clans." In particular, some argued that Kuchma's power was rooted in networks based on his home region of Dnipropetrovsk (Pikhovshek, 1997). Yet, informal elite networks in Ukraine have in fact been relatively weak. Cooperation has been almost entirely restricted to short term instrumental exchange involving relatively low levels of loyalty and group identity.[7] As a result, regionally based allies frequently abandoned their former patrons. Indeed, some of the most important opposition to Kuchma's rule emerged from within the President's own "Dnipropetrovsk clan." Following his ouster as Prime Minister, Pavlo Lazarenko, a former governor of the region, openly opposed Kuchma and transformed the oblast into a center of anti-Kuchma activity in 1998. Subsequently, Yulia Tymoshenko, also a product of the "Dnipropetrovsk clan," became a major leader of the

---

commitment to Communist ideology.

7 Simultaneously, Kuchma's informal networks simply do not seem to have been large enough to secure control over the state. Thus, when Kuchma came to power in 1994,

opposition in the early 2000s and was appointed Ukraine's first post-Kuchma Prime Minister in 2005.

The second component of rapacious individualism in addition to organizational fragmentation has been the rampant use of government connections and resources for private gain. Ukraine is widely regarded as one of the world's most corrupt countries. In 2004, Transparency International ranked Ukraine as one of the 25 most corrupt countries in the world (http://www.transparency.org/cpi/2004/cpi2004.en.html#cpi2004). Such corruption has manifested itself in the strong and direct connection between government actors and business. Government connections have been a key source of cheap privatization, underpayment of taxes, and access to government-controlled monopolies. As in Russia, such corruption led to the emergence of a relatively powerful group of businesspeople or "oligarchs" who relied extensively on government connections for their wealth. In 2000, it was estimated that 386 deputies in parliament controlled 3954 businesses, accounting for 25% of Ukraine's imports and 10% of its exports (Melnychenko, 2002, p. 15).

Under Prime Minister Pavlo Lazarenko 1996-1997, the connection between government and business was perhaps the most striking. Thus the start of his tenure in the summer of 1996 was marked by an attempt on his life that was widely viewed as a response to his business dealings in the energy sector (*Zerkalo Nedeli*, 20-26 July 1996). Economic conflicts have often provided a key source of political battles among pro-presidential forces. Thus, conflicts between Mikhail Pozhivanov and Vladimir Shcherban in Donetsk in 1996 as well as between "energy oligarchs" Viktor Medvedchuk and Yulia Tymoshenko a few years later appear to have been rooted in economic conflicts of interest (*Zerkalo nedeli*, 22-28 June 1996).

Rapacious individualism and competitive authoritarianism in Ukraine

The relationship between weak elite organization and corruption that characterized rapacious individualism, and political competition is contradictory. At one level, rapacious individualism provided important opportunities for executives to concentrate political authority since the executive in power had

---

he was forced to rely almost entirely on regional representatives from the Kravchuk period (Nezavisimost 8 December 1995).

dominant access to rents and property to buy off support. As a result, businessmen and officials tended to flock to the executive, increasing presidential power. Further, as Keith Darden (in press) has shown, corruption combined with extensive surveillance was used by Kuchma to create a system of blackmail against potential regime opponents. Kuchma, in fact, seems to have actively encouraged corruption among officials and allies in order to increase the available blackmail material. Finally, while many initially thought that the distribution of property to "oligarchs" would lead to the growth of an independent business class, subsequent events throughout the former Soviet Union have shown that the government retained important levers of control even after privatization. In the absence of direct ownership, state actors still had numerous mechanisms of pressure and influence over businesses. In particular, tax audits and fines have provided extremely effective sticks the executive could use to punish any business leaders who challenged him. Thus, in Ukraine, as in Russia, businesses that funded opposition faced tremendous pressures from the government in the post-Soviet era. As Evhen Marchuk, former head of the SBU (Ukrainian KGB) reported, "If [your business is] loyal to the authorities, they will ignore or overlook anything. If you are disloyal, you or your business will be quashed immediately." (*National Security and Defense*, 4 2004). Because the legal system in Ukraine is so weak, the executive has been largely successful at severely reducing or even eliminating the sources of income business people who openly opposed the government.

At the same time, key economic and organizational aspects of rapacious individualism generated important sources of political competition in the system. First, the widespread lack of coordination among political actors sometimes made it possible for officials to oppose the President even while remaining within the government. In the early 1990s, for example, some cabinet ministers openly joined parties opposed to Kravchuk (*Nezavisimost*, 1 July 1992, p. 3). Under Kuchma, Roman Bessmertnyi headed the "Our Ukraine" campaign in late 2001 and early 2002 at the same time that he was also the President's representative in parliament.

Further, Kuchma's active encouragement of multiple pro-presidential parties allowed political leaders to gain the organizational and financial resources for future opposition activity. In the late 1990s and early 2000s, numerous future opposition leaders obtained resources by allowing themselves to be coopted into the government and then using those resources to challenge the President. Thus, after the government had frozen her bank accounts in the late 1990s, Yulia Tymoshenko distanced herself from the anti-Kuchma former Prime Minister, Pavlo Lazarenko, and created the pro-Presidential "Batkyvshyna" (Fatherland) party. As a result, her assets were released to her. However, by the end of 2000, Tymoshenko and her party had gone into opposition (*Zerkalo nedeli*, 23 February – 1 March, 2002). Viktor Yushchenko provided another striking example of what might be called "opposition through cooptation." When he started the "Our Ukraine" movement, he made strenuous efforts to portray the party as pro-Presidential. He referred to Kuchma as a "father" figure and actively distanced himself from openly oppositionist parties such as the Socialists and Tymoshenko's Batkyvshyna. Partly as a result, he was given significantly better access to media resources than these two parties in the 2002 parliamentary elections. Such coverage likely contributed to the overwhelming success of the bloc in the 2002 parliamentary elections that presaged the Presidential victory in 2004. (By contrast, politicians such as Oleksandr Moroz, one of the few who consistently opposed the government throughout the post-Soviet era, have been mostly marginalized and unsuccessful.) In this way, the President's choice to disperse power among competing organizations provided a key opening for opposition actors who would have otherwise been locked out of the political system.

Key elements of the oligarchic system generated important sources of business autonomy even in the face of government harassment. First, the widespread practice of transferring money abroad has allowed oligarchs to keep their funds from the reach of the government (Melnychenko, 2002, p, 86). Oligarchs such as Lazarenko (or Boris Berezovsky in Russia), who managed to accumulate enough resources in Cyprus or Switzerland, could create problems for the government even if their businesses were destroyed in Ukraine. In this way, capital flight created important possibilities for political entrepreneurship that would otherwise be much more difficult. In addition, many oligarchs have been protected by the robust institution of parliamentary immunity that protects them from criminal prosecution. The institution of immunity has been a key factor limiting the possible use of blackmail by the executive. Parliamentary immunity was particularly important in protecting the leadership of the Yushchenko movement that was dominated by parliamentary deputies. Finally, to a lesser extent, some oligarchs appear to be protected by connections to foreign investors, whose potential flight raises the cost of crackdown by the government.

Rapacious individualism among Presidential supporters has created important levels of political competition both at the executive and, to a lesser extent, parliamentary level. First, within the executive rapacious individualism has created powerful challengers to the presidency. Second, rapacious individualism among presidential supporters in parliament has weakened executive capacity to subordinate the legislature.

Defection within executive

Rapacious individualism has permitted the emergence of competitors to the executive from within the government. In line with their counterparts in other post-Soviet countries, Ukrainian leaders have mostly faced their most serious challenges from former subordinates and allies rather than civil society or regional elites. Thus, Kravchuk was defeated by his former Prime Minister Leonid Kuchma. Kuchma was in turn threatened by almost every one of his numerous Prime Ministers until 2001, including Evhen Marchuk, Pavlo Lazarenko and obviously Viktor Yushchenko.

Prime Ministers have been a particular threat because their access to media and government resources has facilitated the construction of powerful political bases. Thus, while Presidents could prevent outsiders from gaining access to political resources, they had a much harder time preventing government leaders from accumulating their own power base using governmental resources. For example, one commentator noted that after less than a year in office, Pavlo Lazarenko had at his disposal "about a hundred deputies indebted to him, a large number of appointees in both the regions... and power structures.media [and] a reliable business structure and money" (*Zerkalo nedeli*, 22-28 March 1997).

Kuchma was acutely aware of this danger created by Prime Ministers and other former allies, complaining at one point, "I do not think that any father likes it when his sons start dividing up the land even before he is dead" (*Zerkalo nedeli*, 28 Septembere4 October 1996). In 1996, he fired Prime Minister Marchuk for paying too much attention to the Prime Minister's personal reputation. Kuchma also successfully destroyed the political career of Lazarenko after the latter had become too powerful.

Yet, Kuchma was only been able to control events partially. His most stark failure was his inability to stop the rise of Viktor Yushchenko. As Prime Minister 2000-2001, Yushchenko made an extremely effective use of the media to build up his popularity (Melnychenko, 2002, p. 109). Like Vladimir Putin in Russia, he was also lucky enough to become Prime Minister at a moment when the economy began to significantly grow for the first time in the post-Soviet era. As a result, Yushchenko gained wide popularity during his tenure. Yushchenko was joined by a large number of former Presidential supporters. By the author's count, at least 20 of the 32 members of the National Salvation Committee that managed the pro-Yushchenko movement (as well as virtually all of the top leaders) in late 2004 had at one point been allied to the President (http://www.obozrevatel.com/index.php?rZthemes&idZ169000 accessed on February 1, 2005).[8]

Simultaneously, a key element to Yushchenko's rise was the defection from Kuchma's camp of a range of government-business figures who joined Yushchenko's bloc "Our Ukraine." In 2002, at least a quarter of the top 40 party list seats were set aside for businesspeople. Oligarchs (those who ran businesses when they were elected to parliament) accounted for roughly a third of the membership of the pro-Yushchenko National Salvation Committee in 2004. Petro Poroshenko, Yulia Tymoshenko, and Oleksandr Zinchenko were the most prominent oligarchic figures who abandoned Kuchma to join the opposition. Petro Poroshenko, who had been previously allied with Viktor Medvedchuk's SDPU(o) as well as Yanukovich's Party of Regions, played a particularly prominent role in the campaign as both principal financier and media owner. With a business empire ranging from chocolates to cars, he was thought by many observers to have provided the key source of financing to the campaign (Skachko, 2004). In addition, his cable Channel 5, while limited in its presence in many parts of Ukraine,[9] provided the only serious pro-Yushchenko

---

8 If we exclude the several sports stars and artists from this list – who probably did not have much decision-making power in the movement – then the share of ex-Kuchma allies is even higher.
9 As of November 2004, it was available in roughly 40% of the country. Its news had a market share of about 5% (Andriy Shevchenko, Editorial Director 5th Channel, NDI presentation, Kyiv, 18 November 2004).

source of TV coverage in the country during the campaign. By most accounts, he suffered significant harassment from the government for his support of the opposition. Nevertheless, his connections to business interests both in Russia and western countries such as Switzerland apparently saved him from an all-out assault from the government. Thus, despite his conflict with the government, he maintained prominent business interests in Ukraine (Skachko, 2004). Other prominent businessmen who supported Yushchenko included those in banking (Viktor Topolov), the beverage industry (Anatolyi Matvienko), and a large number in energy (Mykola Martynenko, David Zhvania, Aleksei Ivchenko, Andrei Derkach).

Funding by these and other figures that reached at least US $150 million facilitated the purchase of advertising, the holding of campaign rallies that often rivaled rock concerts for their high cost technical displays, and ubiquitous orange logo shirts, scarves, and flags that spread throughout Ukraine before the election. In the face of overwhelming administrative resources and Yushchenko's virtual total absence from the electronic media, such contributions to the campaign were key to the opposition leader's emergence as a serious threat in 2004.

Rapacious individualism and parliament

Rapacious individualism within the pro-presidential camp also helps to account for the surprising strength of Ukrainian parliament in the 1990s. Parliament was especially strong in the early 1990s. Between 1992 and 1995, the legislature thwarted numerous executive initiatives (*FBIS-SOV*, 29 November 1993, p. 61; 26 November 1993, p. 53; 10 November 1993, pp. 77-78; 15 November 1993, p. 68). It played the key role in choosing Prime Ministers and successfully sought early presidential elections in 1993. Between mid 1995 and late 1999, the power of parliament was reduced significantly. However, even then the parliament, particularly under Moroz, effectively blocked numerous reform measures. As in other competitive authoritarian regimes, the parliament in Ukraine provided a center of opposition to executive authority. In the early 2000s, the legislature successfully thwarted efforts by the President to strengthen executive rule.

Further, throughout the post-Soviet era, executive control over parliamentarians was never strong enough to infringe on their corporate interest as deputies. Thus, in 1996 even the otherwise pro-presidential national democratic deputies rejected presidential efforts to impose a two level parliament that would have considerably weakened it. Perhaps even more significantly, parliamentarians strongly defended immunity of legislatures, which as noted above, was an important source of defense for oppositionist oligarchs. In the post-Soviet era, only three deputies have reportedly been stripped of immunity (Skachko, 2004).

While much has been written about the battles between president and parliament that ensued in Ukraine – as well as Moldova and Russia – in the early 1990s, no scholar that I am aware of has sought to explain legislative strength. The influence of parliament is puzzling for at least four important reasons. First, the overwhelming majority of post-Soviet government and legislative officials had been socialized until 1989 in a Soviet institutional context characterized by façade legislatures and highly powerful executives. While advocates of presidentialism in the 1990s often argued that making the legislature stronger would strengthen "soviet" rule, it is obvious that the main Soviet legacy was not powerful "soviets" (literally translated as "assemblies") but dominant executives. It is not immediately obvious why the Soviet institutional legacy did not quickly reassert itself. Second, given the left's domination of Russian and Ukrainian legislatures in the 1990s, both the West as well as well as the democratic opposition tended to favor executive authority in both Russia and Ukraine (Talbott, 2002; Way, 2003). Thus, legislative influence probably cannot be understood as a product of international pro-democratic pressures. Third, the legislature was often strong even when controlled by purported presidential allies. Thus, the legislature effectively opposed President Kravchuk when it was controlled by Pliusch who was widely considered to be a presidential ally (Whitmore, 2004, chapter 3). Later in November-December 2004, parliament was the first governmental institution to back anti-government protestors, despite the fact that the head of parliament, Volodymyr Lytvyn, was Kuchma's former chief of administration.

Fourth, and perhaps most importantly, the legislature throughout the post-Soviet era included large numbers of non-ideological deputies who should have been open to patronage appeals by the executive. During Kravchuk's tenure, almost half of the legislature (including Kuchma) was unaligned to any party. Such deputies were often referred to as boloto or marsh. Many felt that even the supposedly ideological deputies were in fact quite fluid (*Nezavisimost*, 1993, p. 4).[10] Deputies were initially highly disorganized and frequently belonged to multiple factions simultaneously (until 1994) and switched factions extremely frequently. Some commentators complained that the legislature rarely achieved the necessary quorum to operate. "One deputy is in commercial structures, another person solves his personal problems, another never comes to Kyiv and another combines work with the executive structures" (*Nezavisimost*, 27 October 1993, p. 2).

While ideological stakes apparently increased under Kuchma, parliament continued to contain large numbers of non-ideological deputies. The left never accounted for a majority of the legislature, controlling between 30% and 43% of seats between 1994 and 2000 (Whitmore, 2004). Given that the right (which accounted for between 10 and 30% of the legislature in this period) consistently supported the President, the only true obstacle to presidential control of the legislature was the non-ideological and often highly rapacious "center." In principle, this should have made the legislature open to manipulation by the executive, with his control over jobs and government resources. So it is puzzling why the legislature nonetheless regularly opposed the executive so openly and often effectively.

Disunity and disorganization within the executive and among presidential supporters are key to understanding legislative power in the post-Soviet era. First, in the early 1990s, disorientation caused by the sudden collapse of the Communist Party hierarchy created widespread uncertainty about the location of central power that helped parliament to thwart executive initiatives. Thus, finance ministry officials in Donetsk, Ternopil, and Kharkiv provinces interviewed by the author, reported widespread uncertainty in the early 1990s about which Kyiv officials they should follow.[11] If the Communist Party had been quickly replaced in 1991-1992 by another well-disciplined elite party or coordinated informal elite alliance, it seems likely that this confusion would not have persisted given the Soviet legacy of centralization. However, the absence of

---

10 In mid 1992, for example, the deputy head of parliament, Vladimir Grinev, complained that the legislature lacked any structure and often was victim to constantly shifting emotions of deputies. "It is always impossible to predict when the legislature will vote "yes" or vote "no"" (*Nezavisimost*, 12 June 1992, p. 8).
11 Interviews by author with Department of Finance officials in Donetsk (June 1996), Ternopil (July 1997), and Kharkiv (June 1995).

such organization created room for the parliament radically to increase confusion about the location of central power. Even in the absence of a strong rule of law, well-organized structure, or robust legislative apparatus, the parliament was still in a position to undermine central initiatives. The mere formal existence of a legislature that wanted to increase its prerogatives and that had access to media was enough in the transitional context to increase uncertainty about the extent of executive authority.

Second, the lack of strong pro-presidential support among deputies hindered executive control over parliament. Both Kravchuk and Kuchma had an extraordinarily difficult time obtaining support from the legislature despite disproportionate access to state resources and patronage. In 1993, Kravchuk was repeatedly turned down in his efforts to centralize political control and was ultimately forced to submit to early presidential elections. Kuchma had greater success in securing de jure and de facto authority to fire and appoint Prime Ministers but still faced constant opposition from parliaments controlled by his opponents. At least part of such difficulty may be traced to the fact that Kuchma faced problems controlling non-ideological deputies. Data from Protsyk and Wilson (2003, p. 715) suggest that "centrist" parties and nonaffiliated deputies (representing about 40% of deputies) supported the President just under 60% of the time between 1994 and 1998.[12] This suggests that presidential patronage had a relatively mild effect on deputy decision-making even among the least ideological deputies presumably most open to such patronage appeals. Kuchma appears to have gotten better at attracting such support in the 1998-2002 Parliament. Thus, Kuchma loyalist Volodymyr Pustovoitenko created the National Democratic Party (consisting of roughly 20% of the legislature at its height) that voted 93% of the time with the President (Protsyk and Wilson, 2003, p. 715).[13] At the same time, the President failed to prevent the emergence of the highly oppositionist "centrist" Hromada faction (Whitmore, 2004, chapter 5). More importantly, Kuchma failed to get support on key efforts to strengthen presidential power and eliminate parliamentary immunity. In

---

12   Calculated from their data plus data on faction size from *The Ukrainian Weekly*, LXIV (3) (January 21, 1996).

13   Overall, "centrist" and non-alligned deputies voted with the President about 80% of the time. Calculated from Protsyk and Wilson data as well as data kindly provided by Paul D'Anieri.

2000-2002, parliament repeatedly failed to pass such changes in the constitution that would have greatly increased Kuchma's leverage over the legislature.

At least part of this failure to control deputies was the result of the different corporate interests of the presidency and parliament. Deputies in parliament wanted to strengthen and preserve parliamentary prerogatives, while the President was interested in undermining them. "The long-term goals" of the President and his parliamentary supporters, noted one commentator "are in opposition to one another, if not antagonistic" (*Zerkalo nedeli*, 22-28 February 1997). The lack of trust inherent in rapacious individualism appears to have made it more difficult to overcome these differences despite the President's overwhelming access to state resources to buy off recalcitrant deputies. The strength of corporate interests of deputies and lack of trust in the President was evidenced in the early 2000-2002, when parliamentarians refused to approve constitutional changes that would have considerably weakened legislative powers. Such lack of trust also was shown in the mid 1990s by the initial reluctance of the pro-governmental National Democratic Party to endorse Kuchma's reelection (although later the party did support Kuchma) as well as by Kuchma's open efforts to investigate party members (*Zerkalo nedeli*, 8-14 February 1997; 22-28 February 1997). Further, close observers felt that the combination of business and political interests undermined deputy discipline. Thus, Viktor Pinchuk, Kuchma's son-in-law, complained that [if a prime minister threatens a businessman's interests, the businessman may say], "my faction will vote against your law. [it is hard] to split your head [and decide that] this part will think about business, and this part about the interests of the country. If I am a businessman, first I will think about my shirt, because my shirt is closer to my body." (*The Economist*, 16 December 2004).

The President's failure to pass constitutional amendments strengthening his power combined with the emergence of the Yushchenko threat seems to have convinced Kuchma to focus energy on creating a strong pro-presidential parliamentary party, "For a United Ukraine." Partly as a result of increased efforts,[14] pro-presidential forces did much better in the East than in 1998 when the Communists still dominated (Wilson, 2002). Starting in 2002, parliament

---

14 For example, in the 2002 election, pro-presidential media gave the party twice the television coverage that it had given Pustovoitenko's pro-governmental NDP in the 1998 parliamentary elections (*EIM*, 2002, p. 34).

was controlled by pro-presidential deputies. Yet, this majority proved to be incredibly tenuous. "United Ukraine" quickly fragmented. Yulia Mostovaia noted that by this point there were few politicians remaining willing to fight hard for Kuchma (*Zerkalo nedeli*, 16-22 August 2003). In September 2004, just before the elections, head of parliament, Lytvyn, Kuchma's former chief of staff who was once considered the President's "closest ally" (*Zerkalo nedeli* 27 November – 3 December 1999) openly broke with the President.

In sum, rapacious individualism in Ukraine generated tremendous political competition in the face of overwhelming structural obstacles to democracy. While state leaders most of the time faced relatively few serious challenges from civil society, they confronted serious competition from former allies and subordinates.

Conclusion

Studies of post-Soviet regimes have often implicitly taken as their starting point that we should expect to find democracy. Thus, analyses have tended to focus on the extremely serious abuses of democratic procedure that have pervaded most post-Soviet countries since the end of the Cold War. Similarly observers have often drawn attention to the weak organization of democratic opposition and civil society and their failure to prevent such violations. Indeed, throughout the 1990s in most post-Soviet countries, opposition democrats were at best junior partners in governments dominated by Soviet era elites. Yet, given the extraordinarily anti-democratic legacies of Soviet rule, we can be equally surprised by the persistence of very real political competition in many post-Soviet regimes throughout the 1990s. Such a perspective is important because it reminds us that autocrats, just like democrats, can fail. Especially in the post-Cold War era, autocracy, just like democracy, requires organizational and state resources to succeed.

This article has focused on an important example of autocratic failure in post-Soviet Ukraine. While individual members of the ex-nomenklatura elite managed to retain control of the state in the 1990s and early 21st century, they lacked the organization and cohesion to monopolize political control. Rapacious individualism created a governing elite filled with opportunists unwilling to defend the regime when it looked weak. It also generated relatively wide distribution of organizational and financial resources that produced significant opportunities for opposition to emerge in the face of otherwise daunting structural obstacles to democratic rule. Without such resources, it seems unlikely that the orange revolution could have ever succeeded.

References

Darden, K. "The Integrity of Corrupt States: Graft as an Informal State Institution." *Politics & Society*, in press.

European Institute of the Media (EIM). "Monitoring the media coverage of the March 2002 parliamentary elections in Ukraine. Final Report." Düsseldorf, August 2002.

Grinev, V. 1992. *Nezavisimost*, (12 June):8.

Herron, E., Johnson, P.E. 2003. "It doesn't matter who votes, but who counts the votes: assessing election fraud in Ukraine's 2002 parliamentary elections." Ms. University of Kansas.

Hill, R.J. 1991. "The CPSU: From Monolith to Pluralist?" *Soviet Studies*, 43 (2): 217-235.

Howard, M.M. 2002. "The weakness of postcommunist civil society." *Journal of Democracy*, 13 (1): 157-169.

Human Rights Watch. 2003. "Ukraine: negotiating the news. Informal state censorship of Ukrainian television." New York. http://hrw.org/reports/2003/ukraine0303.

Kravchuk, L. 2002. "Maemo te, shcho maemo." Kyiv.

Kuzio, Taras, 1997. *Ukraine Under Kuchma*. Centre for Russian and East European Studies. The University of Birmingham.

Levitsky, S. Way, L.A. 2002. "The rise of competitive authoritarianism." *Journal of Democracy*, 13 (2): 51-65.

Melnychenko, N. 2002. "Kto est Kto na divane Prezidenta Kuchmy." Kyiv.

OSCE, 2000. "Ukraine presidential elections 31 October and 14 November 1999. Final report." http://www.osce.org/odihr/documents/reports/election_reports/ua/ukr 99-1-final.pdf.

Pikhovshek, V. 1997. *Dnipropetrovska Sim'ia*. Ukrainskyi nezalezhnyi tsentr politychnykh doslidzhen, Kyiv, Ukraina.

Polokhalo, V., et al. 1995. *The political analysis of post-communism*. Politychna Dumka, Kyiv.

Protsyk, O., Wilson, A. 2003. "Center party politics in Russia and Ukraine: power, patronage, and virtuality." *Party Politics*, 9 (6).

Shefter, M. 1976. "The emergence of the political machine: an alternate view." In: Hawley, W.D. et al. (eds.), *Theoretical perspectives on urban politics*. Prentice Hall, Englewood Cliffs, NJ.

Skachko, V. 2004. Interview. *Kievskii Telegraf* (17 November).

Talbott, S. 2002. *The Russia Hand*. Knopf, New York.

National Security and Defense, 4:21. 2004. "The system of democratic civilian control over law-enforcement bodies: its effectiveness and shortcomings." Razumkov Center, Kyiv.

Wasylyk, M. 1994. "Ukraine on the Eve of Elections." *RFE/RL Research Report* (25 March): pp. 44-50.

Way, L. 2003. "Pluralism by default: challenges of authoritarian state-building in Belarus, Moldova, and Ukraine." *Studies in Public Policy* (working paper #375).

Whitmore, S. 2004. *A State-Building in Ukraine: The Ukrainian Parliament, 1990-2003*. Routledge-Curzon.

Wilson, A. 2002. *Ukraine's 2002 elections: less fraud, more virtuality*. EECR, Summer.

Further reading

"Democratic elections in Ukraine." 1994. Report on the 1994 Presidential Elections. Kyiv.

Kubicek, P. 1994. "Delegative democracy in Russia and Ukraine." *Communist and Post-Communist Studies*, 27 (4): 423-441.

The Ukrainian Orange Revolution Brought More than a New President: What Kind of Democracy Will the Institutional Changes Bring?

Robert K. Christensen, Indiana University
Edward R. Rakhimkulov, Parliamentary Development Project
Charles R. Wise, Indiana University

Abstract
The authors discuss the institutional changes proposed in Ukraine's constitutional framework and election laws that could fundamentally alter the separation of powers and the responsiveness of Ukrainian government to the electorate. We analyze the proposed institutional changes from the perspective of what they portend for Ukraine's democratic transition. Building on the most recent vein of democratization studies examining institutional factors affecting democratic stability, we emphasize that it cannot be assumed that Ukraine is "in transition to democracy." We conclude that comprehending the likelihood of achieving democratic stability must be contextualized in an understanding of intervening factors-political, economic, and historical-that ultimately influence democratic stability. Our analysis reminds government reform advocates that it is necessary to go beyond the basic institutional framework of proposed governmental changes in order to obtain a more comprehensive picture of democratization.

Introduction
The victory of opposition candidate, Viktor Yushchenko, after three rounds of presidential balloting, unprecedented political demonstrations and outpouring of citizens into the streets, invalidation of the fraudulent second round by the Ukrainian Supreme Court, and action by the parliament to replace the election machinery is widely appreciated as the culmination of the Orange Revolution. While many look forward to sweeping democratic changes following the revolution and Yushchenko's electoral victory, the realization of

meaningful democratic change is likely to depend on more than Yushchenko's leadership. Sustained change in Ukraine's democracy will also be heavily affected by another, perhaps less noticed, aspect of the Orange Revolution: significant changes in Ukraine's governmental institutions brought about by fundamental changes in Ukraine's Constitution and election law that were made during the presidential contest. Indeed, one of D'Anieri et al.'s conclusions is that "the success of democracy is based both on societal and institutional factors" (D'Anieri et al. 1999, p. 272). As such, the dynamics of the presidential election that altered the system of governance may extend the effects of the Orange Revolution far beyond Victor Yushchenko's term as President.

The question remains, however, whether these institutional changes add to or detract from Ukraine's procession to a fuller democracy. While the results of the Orange Revolution suggest a "peak" in democratization, D'Anieri (2001) reminds us that we have seen such peaks before (for example, in 1994 when two national elections took place under competitive conditions), which were followed by democratic deterioration. Numerous observers have raised doubts about Ukraine's ability to consolidate its progress toward democracy. As has been pointed out (Åslund, 2003, p. 107), Ukraine is a "most delicately situated major country [where] everything appears to be up for grabs. Semi-democratic Ukraine could become a dictatorship or a fuller democracy." Protsyk (2003, p. 1077) emphasizes this point by noting that "while constitutional debates about the underlying institutional framework in most of the countries in the post-communist region have already settled down, allowing politicians to turn to everyday political issues, the debates about the basic issues of government organisation in Ukraine are as topical as ever." While many factors have a bearing on a country's path toward democratic development, Ukraine's direction will be heavily influenced by institutional changes enacted by political elites in 2004, the outcome and dynamics of the 2004 presidential, and the 2006 parliamentary elections.

This article discusses the institutional changes proposed in Ukraine's constitutional framework[1] and election laws[2] that could fundamentally alter the

---

1   The constitutional changes seek to move Ukraine from a presidential-parliamentary form of government to a parliamentary-presidential form.

separation of powers and the responsiveness of Ukrainian government to the electorate, and demonstrates how the dynamics of the 2004 presidential election interacted with long-developing institutional reform proposals to produce a significantly altered political structure. We then examine these changes from the perspective of what they portend for Ukraine's transition in terms of its democratic development.

We cannot assume that Ukraine is "in transition to democracy" and that only the question of institutional choice affects its path of democratization. Scholars have pointed out the dangers of presupposing that once a country embarks on the transition to democracy it will inevitably proceed, however circuitously, along the path to a consolidated democracy (Carothers, 2002; Diamond, 2002; O'Donnell, 2002). Carothers draws our attention towards the existence of a "gray zone" of democratization. He suggests that less than one-fifth of the "transitional" countries are visibly moving towards consolidated democracy. The vast majority of transitioning countries remain trapped in a gray zone characterized by dominant-power politics and/or feckless pluralism (where Carothers places Ukraine), "rendering political life an ultimately hollow, unproductive exercise" (Carothers, 2002, p. 10). O'Donnell (2002, p. 8) asserts that the gray zone is not virgin conceptual territory sandwiched between autocracy and consolidated democracy, but is home to a detailed, if incomplete and uneven, taxonomy of hybrid regimes including "competitive authoritarianism, electoral authoritarianism, and delegative democracy."

This analysis builds on the most recent vein of democratization studies examining institutional factors affecting democratic stability. We conclude that comprehending the likelihood of transcending the "gray zone" must be contextualized in an understanding of intervening factors-political, economic, and institutional-that ultimately influence democratic stability.

In part one we review relevant literature on democratic stability and specific institutional factors relative to that stability. In part two we turn to the laboratory of Ukraine, and introduce key components of its historical and recent political development. We focus on two interrelated institutional complexes that are crucial to understanding Ukraine's current and potential democratic composite: constitutional separation of powers and electoral systems.

---

2   The changes in election laws generally seek to move from district-based to propor-

We examine the institutional changes adopted by Ukraine's Parliament during the presidential election in light of the political dynamics of the country. We conclude with implications for the stability of Ukraine's democracy.

Institutions and factors affecting democratic transition

A vast scholarship exists enumerating institutions and factors that affect the transition to democracy (Mainwaring and Shugart, 1997; Power and Gasiorowski, 1997; Przeworski et al. 2000; Shin, 1994; Shugart and Carey, 1992; Stepan and Skach, 1994). For example, some analyses have demonstrated that the decisions that elites make in the composition of a country's fundamental governmental institutions profoundly affect the subsequent political dynamics and its transition path (Geddes, 1996; Luong, 2000; O'Donnell and Schmitter, 1986; Pigenko et al. 2002; Wise and Brown, 1999). Alternative streams of research have sought to conceptually and empirically clarify and synthesize thinking on regimes and democratic stability.

One of the most focused debates to emerge has been the examination of parliamentary and presidential systems, with a particular focus on which political regime best promotes democracy. The work of Linz (1990a,b, 1994) and Horowitz (1990) illustrate the founding conceptual limits of this debate, Horowitz championing the presidential system and Linz pointing out the follies of a presidential regime.

Subsequent empirical work testing Linz's and Horowitz's concepts have done little to settle the debate. For example, Stepan and Skach (1994) and Przeworski et al. (2000) recommend parliamentary regimes for democratic stability as strongly as Shugart and Carey (1992), Shin (1994), Mainwaring and Shugart (1997), and Power and Gasiorowski (1997) have pointed out the weaknesses in the research on the "perils of presidentialism."

Lijphart (1984, 1999) has demonstrated that from institutional standpoint the democracies tend to cluster into two main types: majoritarian and consensus democracies. The institutional elements of a consensus democracy are a proportional electoral system, multiparty coalition executives, executive-legislative balance, a multiparty system, and a corporatist form of interest intermediation. The institutional elements of a majoritarian system are characterized by a disproportional election system, a one-party majority executive,

---

tional voting.

an executive that dominates over the legislature, a two-party system, and a plurality interest groups system. The argument for the consensual model is that it tends to restrain majority rule, and shares, disperses, and limits political power.

The role of proportional representation (PR) is particularly emphasized. Voter turnout tends to be higher under proportional representation rules for a number of reasons (Blais and Carter, 1990; Jackman and Miller, 1995). Scholars argue that PR is fairer because people feel less alienated and thus are more inclined to vote. PR increases the number of parties and the variety of options among which people can choose, and so it makes elections more competitive in that most parties have a chance to win at least one seat, and so they attempt to mobilize their electors throughout the country. Lijphart argues that for divided societies, ensuring the election of a broadly representative legislature should be a crucial consideration, and PR is the optimal way of doing so (Jackman and Miller, 1995; Lijphart, 2004). The multiplication of parties, however, has a positive effect on representation only up to a point. As Bielasiak (2002, p. 204) has pointed out for Eastern European and former Soviet countries, the advent of PR systems has allowed for the entry of many parties along a wide political spectrum but has led to party systems with too many competitors for effective strategic behavior by voters, thus producing extreme indices of volatility.

Another institutional aspect, a governing coalition in the form of a multiparty cabinet, represents a more diverse group of voters than a governing party in exclusionary majoritarian systems (Birchfield and Crepaz, 1998; Powell, 2000). Systems that lean toward the majoritarian model tend to concentrate power in the hands of a bare majority, or even only a plurality, and tend to be more exclusive, competitive, and adversarial (Lijphart, 1999).

Application of Lijphart's majoritarian-consensus model is not a straightforward matter. This is especially true when analyzing hybrid regimes such as Ukraine's, which combines elements of both models. As Roberts (2003) demonstrates, the new democracies of Eastern Europe do not fall clearly into Lijphart's consensus and majoritarian camps. Instead they exhibit more hybrid forms. Thus, while the models cannot be used in their pure forms, they are nonetheless, suggestive for analyzing the dynamics of Ukraine's institutional and political condition.

Further evidence of the need to nuance Lijphart's model is found when considering the effects of political institutions on political party fragmentation. For example, Shugart and Carey (1992) and Mainwaring (1993) concluded that strong executive institutions, irrespective of the electoral institutions – whether proportional or single-member districts – discourage large party coalitions with the potential to control a legislative agenda. Clark and Wittrock (2005) find that strong presidents undermine the rationale for the formation of parties seeking control over the policy and governmental control functions of the legislature. They argue that if one assumes that the primary goal of a political party is to gain the largest number of seats possible to gain control of the legislative agenda, then there is less rationale for a political party to attempt to do so when the parliamentary control of the legislative agenda is undermined by the existence of a president with the powers to legislate by decree. It is further undermined when the legislature's control of the process of making and breaking governments is compromised. Moreover, weak legislative powers also serve to obscure the locus of responsibility in the eyes of the electorate, which in turn decreases the incentive for voters to cast their ballots for parties or candidates likely to win an election. (p. 176)

Accordingly, while Ukraine's institutional governing structure may be hybrid in form, it has exhibited several majoritarian elements including a partially disproportionate election system (one-half of seats in parliament elected on a district basis); a one-party executive (the president appoints the prime minister); and executive (the president) that has dominated the legislature; and a pluralist interest group system. The one consensual component has been a multiparty system.

Ukraine's experience since independence has, as Lijphart's characterization predicts, exhibited exclusive, competitive and adversarial relations between the president and parliament, and between the dominant block and minority block in parliament. Exclusive power of the president has allowed scant room for consensus building in parliament to be translated into government policy, and has led to repeated clashes over basic institutional prerogatives. Such clashes have periodically led to attempts by one branch to eliminate the other by attempting to alter the country's constitution. Issues of democratic representation and policy reform have often been subordinated to a fundamental struggle for power.

The scholarly debate has been mirrored in Ukraine by political debates over the best governmental institutional structure – president-centered or parliament-centered. Battles over Ukraine's separation of powers governmental system and electoral system have been venues for contestation of power by major political forces since Ukraine's independence. These continuing struggles have significant implications for Ukraine's potential transition to democracy. As Linz and Stepan (1996, p. 4) point out, "indeterminacy about core procedures necessary for producing democracy may not only leave the transition incomplete, but also postpone any consolidation of democracy." Several scholars have pointed to the necessity of examining research that focuses on intervening institutional factors for their impact on regime stability (Baylis, 1996; Frye, 1997; Mainwaring, 1993, 1997). Two core institutional elements examined in the Ukrainian context are the structure of the system of elections and the constitutional separation of powers.

The question for institutional changes made during the 2004 presidential election period is whether they will provide an institutional environment that permits more consensual policymaking that is representative of Ukrainian society. Our argument is that such an answer is predicated upon the contextual and intervening factors that lead to the institutional changes.

Frye's (1997) work is particularly useful in illustrating this point. In his study of 24 post-communist countries, Frye found that the structures of presidential powers were influenced by (1) the perceived political power of the favored candidate and (2) the uncertainty of the outcome of the election. We interpret these findings to suggest that there are significant relationships between intervening factors (such as electoral uncertainty) and subsequent institutional arrangements. This point is particularly critical for understanding of the convergence of political tensions and to the outcome of the Orange Revolution. Therefore, we dedicate to it a subsection below.

The Ukrainian laboratory

We examine below how the contested changes in Ukraine's core institutions of (1) electoral systems and (2) the constitutional separation of powers have been subject to historical and recent parliamentary action potentially shifting the allocation of power. In this section, we demonstrate that specific components of these institutional elements are associated with the distribution and contestation of economic and political powers and how this interaction of interests portends significant ramifications for Ukraine's transition. As an introductory note, while most of our discussion will focus on political powers, we agree with D'Anieri's (2003) observation that economic and political power are particularly concentrated in Ukraine and are inseparably connected.[3] Although the following subsections are chronologically arranged, we highlight the themes of diverging and converging political tensions that intervened in Ukraine's institutional arrangements.

Divergent tensions: 1991-2002

The themes underlying the context of institutional change highlight the processes of ideological power struggles and political self-preservation. In the initial period following independence, against the collective membership preferences of the Communist, or the Left, dominated parliamentary majority, the independent democrats successfully proposed a presidential-parliamentary form of government by amending the inherited from the Soviet period Republic Constitution. This was done largely on the basis that a president was needed to guarantee the national sovereignty of Ukraine. However, the Communists did not cede the creation of a presidency based on the support for the constitutional principle, but rather on the situational factor of conceived political power gain (Leonid Kravchuk, the Communist Party secretary, was likely to win the president's seat). Consequently, during both Kravchuck's presidency and that of his successor, Leonid Kuchma, inter-branch relations were characterized by repeated clashes not only over policy but over the unresolved question of fundamental constitutional allocation of power (Wise and Pigenko, 1999). The differences between Kuchma and the Left were much more than policy differences and represented cleavages based in fundamentally different visions of the future development of the Ukrainian economy and state. Such ideological differences first manifested themselves in epic political battles over the formation of the interim constitution and then over the formation of the permanent constitution. In these battles, Kuchma constantly pressed for most governmental powers to be placed in the office of the presidency. The Left

---

[3] In D'Anieri's (2003) words, "in Ukraine there are relatively few barriers to the use of money to gain political power, and there is an extraordinary capacity to use political power to make money."

pressed for elimination of the presidency altogether, having witnessed what a president opposed to their economic and social vision could do.

Adoption of Ukraine's Constitution in 1996 established a presidential-parliamentary form of government. The new constitution was a compromise, but one that still left the president in a powerful position, particularly since he controlled the administrative resources of the government. The powers allocated to Ukraine's presidency, following the 1996 Constitution, made Ukraine's president one of the strongest, on a par with those of Russia and Belarus (Frye, 1997, p. 547). As Protsyk has discussed, the dual nature of the executive has led to an off-again, on-again competition between the president and various prime ministers and a high rate of cabinet turnover in Ukraine, "undermining the efforts at creation of a stable political environment, which is an important ingredient of any recipe for successful democratic consolidation" (Protsyk, 2003, p. 1085).

The adoption of the interim constitution and then the permanent constitution reduced the level of ferocity of the battles over constitutional prerogatives between Kuchma and the Left in parliament. Wise and Brown explain that constitutional rules reduce institutional contention by providing parameters within which "neither the president nor parliament can eliminate the other from a role in determining future institutional or policy changes" (Wise and Brown, 1999, p. 42). Within these boundaries, however, both the parliamentary majority Left and the president continually sought to alter the constitutional framework to shift power to themselves (Pigenko et al. 2002; Protsyk, 2003).

Utilizing his control of the administrative apparatus of government, an expansive use of presidential decrees, and some hard-fought legislative victories, Kuchma began the dismantling of the state economic complex Ukraine inherited from the Soviet Union. However, these measures did not move Ukraine to a full, open-competitive-market system, but one in which various economic and regional elites or "clans"[4] assumed ownership of many large enterprises.

The economic changes Kuchma enacted largely through use of unilateral presidential powers, fundamentally influenced the political transition as it cre-

---

4 These regional elites are subdivided into Kyiv group (Medvedchuk, Surkis, and others), Donetsk group (Yanukovych, Akhmetov, and others), and Dnipropetrovsk group (Pinchuk, Tihipko, and others).

ated a new class of economic-political elites. They occupy one point of the political competition triangle that now dominates politics in Ukraine (the other two points are occupied by the Left and the democratic-market reformers). The new economic elites, popularly referred to as "oligarchs" developed into the President's primary political power base in parliament. The importance of core institutions is illustrated by the fact that the rise of the oligarchs as a major political force was facilitated by Ukraine's single member district first-past-the-post electoral system that allowed prominent wealthy enterprise owners to dominate district elections in which as many as twenty or more party or individual representatives were vying. Oligarchs' wealth and coercive power over enterprise employees brought many such enterprise directors or business-owners into parliament, and led to the Communists losing their majority and becoming minority Left.

While opposed by the minority Left, numerous economic changes were initially passed with support of a combination of parties representing the oligarchs and the democratic-market reformers. The pace of reform was particularly brisk when Victor Yushchenko served as a prime minister. However, the alliance fell apart when the oligarchs saw the extent to which Yushchenko was prepared to go in reforming the system by introducing much more open competition.

Ukraine's first parliamentary election followed a single-member district format,[5] where each of the Verkhovna Rada's 450 members was directly elected from 450 districts. Despite repeated attempts by parliamentary deputies to substitute proportional representation, Kravchuk, and later Kuchma, maintained the single-member district format through repeated vetoes, sensing (with good reason) the threat to their authority in the proposed proportional scheme. However, partial reform of the parliamentary election system was passed in 1997 and in 1998 and 2002 half of 450 deputy mandates were elected in single member districts with the other half elected according to proportional party voting.

---

5   The Law on Election of National Deputies of the USSR was passed in October 1989. Experts say the document was more democratic than its Soviet counterpart. In particular, the 1989 law provided for (1) direct declaration of citizen's will by secret vote, (2) division of the Republic's territory into single-member electoral districts, and (3) advanced model of nominating: the right to nominate candidates was given to meetings of voters, labor collectives, as well as public and political organizations.

In the 2002 parliamentary election, the oligarch parties that backed Kuchma combined into the electoral coalition United Ukraine. The democratic-competitive market parties combined their forces into the electoral coalition Our Ukraine headed by Victor Yushchenko. This was the first parliamentary election that produced significant party voting blocs by the electorate. While Our Ukraine finished first in the proportional voting, United Ukraine did better in the single member districts.

The oligarchic factions' candidate for parliamentary chairman was elected, as presidential pressure was put on some members of the Our Ukraine coalition (most of which were businessmen) to support the president's candidate. Parties of the Our Ukraine coalition charged that the oligarchs had hijacked the Parliament and defeated the democratic choice of the voters, in that the party coalition that had finished first on a national basis was denied the chairmanship by defections of members elected under the Our Ukraine banner enticed by bribes or governmental coercion.

Battles over the constitutional separation of powers continued to rage simultaneously with strife over forms of electoral systems. Since 2002, the oligarchic coalition parties have enjoyed a slight parliamentary majority but one that is not large enough (300 votes are required) to amend the Constitution. Since then, the parliamentary political dynamics has been dominated by the drive by the oligarchic factions to consolidate their hold on power either through arranging for re-election of Leonid Kuchma (or his hand-picked successor), or failing that, amending the constitution to shift power to the parliament where they expected to continue to dominate.

Converging tensions: 2002-2005
The impact of the presidential election of 2004 extends much further than the defeat of the oligarchic clan candidate and the installation of a reform president. The sweeping changes made to Ukraine's governmental institutional structure arising out of decisions made by the contending political blocs will have far-reaching consequences for the functioning of Ukrainian government. So too, the decisions made during the 2004 presidential contestation will impact politics far beyond the Yushchenko's administration (although they will also vitally impact Yushchenko's style of governing and his potential to put through his reform program). In essence, we observe that some long-standing

proposals for institutional change came together with tactical election priorities to produce a new Ukrainian political-institutional framework.

From 2002 through 2004, President Kuchma continually attempted to push changes in the Constitution and election system through parliament. His proposals appeared to be a function of a quest for continuity of power. As one observer stated in 2002, "the major issue (for Kuchma) is about establishing continuity of power and securing prosperity and a stable future for himself and his entourage" (cited in Polityuk, 2002). Kuchma was, no doubt, disturbed by repeated public opinion polls that showed that the leader of the right-wing opposition, Yushchenko, was the most popular presidential contender. Kuchma became fearful not only over the sustainability of his policies, but also over his personal future after leaving the presidency (Protsyk, 2003, p. 1087). Some have even suggested that Kuchma's concerns might be rooted in fear of liability for questionable actions taken while president. As previously mentioned, Kuchma forces followed a dual-strategy during 2004: either push for Kuchma's reelection (or one of their elite who would support the same policies), or change the Constitution to shift power to the parliament (making the presidential incumbent challenger's victory hollow).

We note, however, that proposals to change the allocation of power between branches have not been the preoccupation of any one group. Various parliamentary political groups on both sides of the ideological line have supported the idea of achieving a more equal balance of powers between the parliament and the presidency. Since 1999, several constitutional reform bills shifting more power to the parliament were introduced by the leader of the Socialist Party, Oleksandr Moroz. Members of the parties of the Right also generally supported reallocation but favored doing this primarily by passing constitutionally required laws such as the Law on the Cabinet of Ministers, and the Law on Central Executive Bodies. The oligarch parties voiced their support for constitutional change only recently, after this change was supported by President Kuchma in August 2002. By the fall 2003, two constitutional reform bills were supported by the pro-president majority in parliament.

In the aftermath of his declining popularity and accusations of criminal and political scandal, Kuchma, in a television broadcast on March 5, 2003, urged the Ukrainian public to support changes in Ukraine's constitution that would shift governmental powers from a presidential-parliamentary to parliamentary-presidential form of government. Kuchma also argued that Ukraine needed to change its election law and elect parliament on party lists for a five-year term. Frye's work offers some insight into these moves by suggesting that under uncertain conditions (Kuchma's declining popularity), "powerful actors tend to hedge their bets and create institutions that are less biased in their favor" (Frye, 1997, pp. 546-547). Notwithstanding, Kuchma then proposed to amend the constitution and introduced a respective bill in parliament that called for a bi-cameral legislature where the lower chamber would dominated by proportional representation, but in the upper more powerful chamber, single-member districts would be the rule (Ukrainian president agrees to step down in 2004, 2003). This latter system would have favored Kuchma and other oligarch candidates as it had done in previous elections.

Almost immediately, the parliamentary task force on constitutional amendments introduced its own bill while a group of deputies headed by leader of the Socialist Party, Oleksandr Moroz, fielded yet another alternative set of constitutional amendments (Bill 3207-1). This latter alternative had gone through numerous parliamentary deliberations since 1999 when it was first introduced by Moroz and other parliament members that represented opposition to Kuchma.

The group of parliament members headed by Moroz, as well as most other opposition members, favored a transition to a fully proportional parliamentary election system. It became evident that without enlisting support of the politicians that favored a strictly proportional electoral system, the constitutional amendments that required 300 votes to pass was doomed to fail. Thus, Kuchma and his allies in parliament had no choice but to agree to enact the proportional system, although many pro-president deputies elected in single member districts opposed the change.

To implement the shift to a more parliamentary form of government, the Verkhovna Rada needed to first pass the bill on amending the constitution by a simple majority of 226 votes and then send it for review and approval of Ukraine's Constitutional Court. To become law, the draft had to be approved by 300 of the 450 lawmakers in parliament, after it received endorsement of the Constitutional Court, in the next consecutive session after the one during which it was passed by 226 votes, and the president had to sign it.

In the debate over the political and constitutional changes that ensued, the political forces, roughly representing the democratic-competitive market forces, communists, and socialists, argued that the president's constitutional proposals failed to comply with needs of citizens of Ukraine, would destroy parliamentarianism and also judicial independence, and ruin local self-governance. To answer this criticism President Kuchma, in June 2003, filed a revised bill in which his previous proposal to provide for a bicameral legislature was eliminated.

Kuchma's revised proposal, however, still contained an ambiguous provision concerning Kuchma's ability to serve as president for an additional two years, ostensibly in order to make presidential and parliamentary elections simultaneous in 2007. In addition, the possibility of Kuchma running for the third term remained likely. Opposition leaders petitioned the Constitutional Court to decide whether Kuchma was allowed to run for a third term,[6] despite the apparent prohibition of a third term in Ukraine's Constitution which was passed three years before Kuchma's second term began (Vickery, 2003). The leader of the opposition to Kuchma's proposals was the former Prime Minister and 2004 presidential favorite, Viktor Yushchenko, who called for a moratorium on constitutional changes until after the presidential elections (Vickery, 2003). Fearing Yushchenko's popularity relative to his own, Kuchma chose to support the candidacy of his Prime Minister, Viktor Yanukovych. This choice reinforces Kuchma's strategy of maintaining political power by ensuring that the president's seat, in case constitutional reforms failed, would be occupied by one sympathetic to Kuchma's ideology. Pursuance of this strategy arguably added to the impetus for the mass fraud and corruption seeking to ensure Yanukovich's election.

---

6 On December 30, 2003, the Constitutional Court ruled on this petition stating that Kuchma can run for president. Answering in the affirmative, the Court explained that "the clause of part three of Article 103 of the Constitution of Ukraine (254k/96-VR), under which one and the same person cannot be the President of Ukraine for more than two consecutive terms, shall be interpreted as concerning only a person elected the President of Ukraine after the Constitution of Ukraine entered into force in 1996. The person elected the President of Ukraine for the first time in 1999 under the Constitution of Ukraine in force (254k/96-VR) has the right to run for the office at the regular elections of the President of Ukraine in 2004" Constitutional court of Ukraine, decision n 22-rp/2003, case n 1-46/2003, 2003. Kyiv.

By mid-October 2003, three prominent constitutional amendment proposals (3207-1, 4105 and 4180) and nine others, some of which proposed various proportional models, were on parliament's agenda. Bill 4105 was prepared over the summer by Kuchma' Chief of Staff, Viktor Medvedchuk, in cooperation with Communist Party leader, Petro Symonenko, to replace the presidential proposal. In this new bill, a provision was made for election of the president by the parliament. Enactment of such a provision would have eliminated the presidential election and negated the chances for Yushchenko to become a president in that the oligarchs had a majority in parliament. Bill 4180 was essentially similar to 4105 but for some procedural provisions.

Throughout the parliamentary maneuvering, the main objective of the pro-presidential forces appeared to be the passage of the constitutional amendments, while the main objective of the opposition was to change the electoral system to a fully proportional model. Some opposition deputies were willing to trade support for the constitutional reform in exchange for a fully proportional electoral system. On October 16, 2003, all nine of the proportional system bills were voted on and failed. The majority then wanted to move to consideration of the constitutional amendment. The Socialist Party and Yuliya Tymoshenko Bloc factions supported by deputies from the Our Ukraine (Yushchenko) faction started blocking the parliament's work to prevent passage of amendments to the Constitution. They demanded that the parliament pass the law on proportional representation first. Movement on the electoral system reforms was a prerequisite for the communists and socialists to acquiesce to majority constitutional reforms.

Meanwhile, the Constitutional Court declared that provisions of 3207-1 were repugnant to the Constitution's provisions ensuring separation of powers. Later in November and December 2003 the Constitutional Court ruled, respectively, that both 4105 and 4180 were compliant with constitutional requirements.[7]

---

7 Reacting to these events, the Venice Commission, on December 15, 2003, passed a resolution stating that "the precise solutions chosen in the various drafts do not yet seem to have attained that aim [of bringing Ukraine closer to European democratic standards] and introduce other amendments to the Constitution that would appear to be a step backwards." Venice commission opinion no. 230/2002: On three draft laws proposing amendments to the constitution of Ukraine, 2003. European (Venice) Commission for Democracy through Law: Council of Europe.

On December 24, 2003, following the long-term blocking of parliament's work by the opposition, Parliamentary Chairman Lytvyn announced that he was imposing a new voting procedure for consideration of the amendments to the Constitution. He called for parliament to vote on 4105, by a showing of hands. Although a highly irregular voting procedure, the chairman declared that 4105 was supported with 276 votes. However, the opposition charged that there was an insufficient number of deputies even present in the session hall to constitute a majority. This decision was followed by a very tense stand-off between the pro-presidential camp and the opposition. The pro-presidential camp even attempted to pass a resolution to discharge opposition deputies from their parliamentary committee leadership positions, but passage of the resolution violated parliamentary rules and, in the end, the committees' chairmanship remained unchanged.

The December 24 vote to approve bill 4105 received harsh criticism both from domestic observers and from the international community. In January 2004, the presidency of the European Union declared that "the EU believes that any debate on constitutional changes aimed at changing the procedures to elect the president should take place separately from the elections" [5614/1/04 (press 32), 2004] (EU presidency, 2004).

Notwithstanding international criticism of Ukraine's timing, Chairman Lytvyn again coupled the constitutional reform processes and election legislation changes by announcing his willingness to consider a draft law on proportional representation as long as the threshold to gain proportional representation were lowered from 4%. Thus, while many pro-presidential factions seemed to prefer single member districts, their tolerance of proportional elections increased as the required representation decreased. Ultimately, the pro-presidential forces were persuaded to compromise with the Socialists and Communists to insure their support for the vote on the constitutional changes. As one analyst observed, "the adoption of a law on fully proportional parliamentary election ... is the sine qua non for support of both the Communist Party and the Socialist Party to the constitutional-reform bill in the second reading" (Maksymiuk, 2004). The Socialists would not go along, however, with a provision for parliamentary selection of the president. In February, the Verkhovna Rada passed a resolution to remove the provision of electing the president by parliament from 4105.

ASPECTS OF THE ORANGE REVOLUTION I   133

On the same day, an extraordinary parliamentary session was convened to allow for voting on the revised 4105 bill and forwarding it for Constitutional Court's review. After this, the pro-presidential forces needed to pass the bill with 300 or more votes in support before the end of the plenary session on July 2, 2004, when coincidentally the presidential election campaign was scheduled to begin.

By mid-February 2004, the leaders of ten factions, including opposition factions of the Communist Party and the Socialist Party, had entered into an agreement to coordinate their constitutional reform efforts and the reform of the election system, seen by some to also detract from the campaign for presidential hopeful Viktor Yushchenko (Ten Ukrainian parliament factions reach agreement, 2004). Fourteen draft proposals were introduced concerning a shift to a fully proportional system of parliamentary elections. One point of difference in these bills concerned the threshold required to enter parliament with some proposals offering to lower the national minimum required to register a party in parliament from the current 4% to 1%.

In March 2004, the agreement making the proportional electoral system part and parcel of proposed amendments to the Constitution was formalized in the promulgation and passage of the bill granting power to the Parliament's Temporary Special Commission to expedite and consolidate pieces of draft legislation including bills on parliamentary election and constitutional amendments bill 4105. On March 25, 2004, parliament passed a new parliamentary elections bill introducing the fully proportional system of parliamentary elections as of October 1, 2005, and lowering the requirement from 4 to 3% of the national vote (Ukraine's parliament votes on proposed election law, 2004).

Now, with all requirements of the opposition Communists and Socialists concerning the proportional model fulfilled, the pro-president camp turned their attention to the passage of the constitutional amendments bill. Word went out from all pro-president faction members that the parliamentary session to consider the amendments was a "must attend" session. However, on April 8, 2004, bill 4105 received only 294 votes, six votes short of the constitutionally required 300. The problem was that some of the unaffiliated deputies and even a few members of the pro-president majority factions did not vote on the amendments motion. This defeat has important implications for post-presidential election developments on the implementation of or future consideration of the constitutional amendments.

According to the Constitution, the bill to amend the Constitution cannot be legally voted upon again for one year after it is defeated. However, the pro-president forces, eager to pass the constitutional reform bill, circumvented (whether without future contestation remains in question) this Constitutional requirement. They returned to consideration of bill 4180 that was essentially identical to bill 4105, which had been narrowly defeated. In June 2004, they passed 4180 in the initial reading and sent it for the Constitutional Court's review. The Constitutional Court approved 4180 in October. This action left open the possibility of still achieving constitutional change before the presidential election.

After the presidential election's first round on October 31, 2004, the discussion about the need to pass the constitutional reform bill was renewed in the parliament. However, opposition leader, Viktor Yushchenko, refused to discuss the passage of the constitutional reform. He said that he supported the changes, but stated that they should be discussed and adopted after the presidential election. He argued that bill 4180 was nearly identical to the substance of bill 4105, and therefore, under the Constitution, it could not be put to a vote less than a year after the date of the defeat of 4105 on April 8, 2004. In essence, Yushchenko argued that one should not change the rules of the game during the game by taking presidential powers away in the middle of the finale of the presidential campaign.

His opponent, Prime Minister Viktor, Yanukovych, and his parliamentary faction Regions of Ukraine, continued to voice their backing for the constitutional reform. However, they were not able to put the constitutional reform bill onto the parliament's agenda prior to the run-off round of the presidential election, because Socialist Party leader, Moroz, would not support them in that timeframe.

The runoff round of the presidential election on November 21, 2004, pushed the political situation in Ukraine in the direction where many political as well as individual interests of oligarchs and politicians converged to produce a final push for the constitutional reform.

Yushchenko gained the endorsement of Moroz for his presidential candidacy after signing an agreement unifying their political forces and agreeing that Yushchenko's 100-member parliamentary faction would discuss the constitutional reform in parliament at the beginning of December (2004) and would vote for it before the end of year (Moroz says political reform voting must take place November 16-17, 2004).

On November 23, the Central Election Commission (CEC) announced results of the runoff round of the presidential election. According to the CEC, Viktor Yanukovych received about 3% of the votes more than Viktor Yushchenko. This decision was announced in the middle of allegations of widespread fraud and rigging of election results in the east and south of Ukraine, the regions that supported Yanukovych. These allegations were also supported by parliament, which convened for several extraordinary sessions, and passed a resolution rejecting the decision of the Central Election Commission as fundamentally flawed. While this resolution did not have legal force to void the Commission's action, it lent support to the Supreme Court that ultimately acted in such a way. The parliament also passed a vote of no confidence in the government headed by Prime Minister Yanukovych.

Yushchenko filed a complaint in the Supreme Court and submitted documented evidence confirming the election fraud. On December 3, the Supreme Court sustained Yushchenko's complaint, cancelled the results of the runoff election and ordered a repeat runoff round for December 26, 2004. On December 26, Viktor Yushchenko won the presidential election gaining 51.99% of the votes, while Viktor Yanukovych received 44.2%.

Simultaneously with these developments, people supporting Yushchenko took to the streets to protest against election fraud. In the middle of this political crisis President Kuchma, parliament's Chairman Lytvyn, and two presidential contenders, Viktor Yushchenko and Viktor Yanukovych, started rounds of political negotiations to find a way out of the political crisis. Yushchenko, supported by people in the streets, demanded that election law be changed before the repeat runoff round of elections, the composition of CEC be changed, and Prime Minister Yanukovych be dismissed. For some time, Yushchenko held fast and would not concede to President Kuchma's demands to support passage of amendments to the Constitution. Nonetheless, Yushchenko had made a commitment to Moroz to support constitutional change, and after several rounds of tense negotiations was able to secure sufficient changes in the provisions of bill 4180. Yushchenko then agreed to compromise.

Among the changes secured were (1) the president would continue to appoint the heads of the local state administrations, (2) the president would continue to appoint the heads of the enforcement ministries – Ministry of Interior, National Security Agency, Prosecutor General, and (3) the proportion of nominees the president, parliament, and the judiciary for the Constitutional Court would remain at 6-6-6. This compromise illustrates both of Frye's (1997) arguments relative to the bargaining of the electoral favorites and the uncertainty of the electoral outcome. The fraud and corruption surrounding the election (particularly the campaign media) created a very uncertain electoral environment, which may have caused Yushchenko to agree to changes he otherwise would not have agree to, in order to gain Moroz's support. Notwithstanding, despite the uncertain electoral environment, Yuschenko was widely perceived, particularly by Moroz, as holding greater political bargaining power. Yushchenko was thus able to obtain changes to 4180 that preserved some presidential powers.

On December 8, 2004, after prolonged negotiations between political forces in parliament with the involvement of President Leonid Kuchma, parliament passed three decisions lumped together in one package: (1) two Constitutional amendment packages (bill 4180 and another bill involving local self-government provisions); (2) Law on Specifics of Conduct of the Repeat Vote of the Runoff Presidential Election drafted to eliminate possibilities for electoral violations; and (3) the decision to dismiss existing members of the Central Election Commission.

The passage of this "packaged" deal became possible due to the convergence of longer-term interests of major political actors (President Kuchma, opposition leaders, and oligarchs) in the Ukrainian political environment; 402 national deputies voted to support the package.

The timing for the constitutional changes reallocating power among the branches was made contingent on the passage of the local government bill in final reading. If the local self-government bill passes (spring 2005), the reallocation of powers provision will go into effect on September 1, 2005. If not, the provisions of 4180 will go into effect on January 1, 2006.

Throughout this two-and-half year period, the electoral prospects of the presidential candidates representing the contending political blocs have been highly influential. As just illustrated, parliamentary coalitions have shifted in their willingness to champion institutional reforms based on how they saw "their" candidate fairing in the presidential race. While once championed by the oligarchic pro-president forces to diminish the influence of Yushchenko should he be elected, the call to constitutional reform was then picked up by Moroz as part of a political bargain to ensure his ideology a place at the table, again, should Yushchenko be elected. In other words, the constitutional reforms in bills 4105 and now 4180 have been used as means for various political blocs to try to allocate power to the branch where they expect to have the most influence in the immediate future.

Institutional changes: whither Ukraine's transition to democracy?

In this section we draw implications for what this latest round of contestation over the core institutions may mean for Ukraine's transition to democracy. As discussed, the pressures and incentives embedded in presidential election politics came together with some long-standing political dynamics seeking changes in the political institutional structure of Ukraine to produce a new allocation of power between the political branches of government. Thus, the significance of the events of the political campaign will extend beyond the elevation of Yushchenko to the presidency or even his policy reform program, but also to the operation of the political system in the near term and in the future. In turn, the changed institutional framework will affect the ability of the new president to gain adoption and implementation of his reform program. Here we analyze the institutional changes that were enacted and their potential effects. Understanding the reforms is essential for grasping their potential impact on the future of Ukrainian democracy.

Election law reforms have primarily concerned (1) parliamentary election law, and (2) sub-national government election law. In both instances the reforms have led Ukraine from district-based elections to proportional representation.

The major changes in the election law that applies to the election of parliamentary deputies include:

1. Elimination of the mixed system with half of the members elected from single member districts to a proportional representation system with all members elected from party lists.

2. A lowering of the threshold for parties electoral blocs of parties being eligible to enter parliament from 4% to 3%.

3. Increasing the maximum amount that may be spent on party campaigns up to 500,000 Hryvnia (approximately 100,000 US dollars).

If election reforms can be summarized as a move from district to proportional representation, changes to the balance of powers between president and parliament can be summarized as a move from strong president-parliamentary system to a strong parliamentary-president system of government. The most recently approved constitutional reforms retain the president's power to appoint a prime minister, but the bulk of government appointments will now be parliament's domain. The constitutional changes include:

1. The parliamentary majority will be convened within one month of a new convocation of parliament, or within one month following the dissolution of parliamentary majority. If the parliamentary majority is not constituted within the time required, the president has the right to disband the parliament and call for new elections.

2. The majority will submit proposals to the president for candidates for prime minister and other ministers of the government.

3. The president shall propose the prime minister's candidacy to parliament for approval after consultations with a coalition of deputy factions that constitute the majority in the parliament.

4. The parliament, upon submission by the president, will appoint the prime minister, the minister of defense, the minister of foreign affairs, and the head of the security service. The parliament would also have the right to dismiss these officials unilaterally. Currently, the president appoints prime minister and other officials, and parliament endorses appointment of prime minister and can vote no-confidence in cabinet as a whole.

5. The parliament, upon submission of the prime minister, will appoint other members of the cabinet of ministers, the head of the antimonopoly committee, the head of the state committee on television and radio broadcasting,

and the head of the state property fund. The parliament would also have the right to dismiss these officials unilaterally. Currently, president appoints these officials upon submission from the prime minister.

6. The parliament would approve appointment to office of the prosecutor general. Currently, the parliament endorses the presidential appointee and vote no-confidence, but no dismissal mechanism exists.

7. The cabinet of ministers would create, reorganize, and liquidate ministries and other bodies of executive power. Currently, the president has this power.

8. The cabinet of ministers, upon submission from the prime minister, appoints to offices and dismisses from offices: heads of central executive agencies which are not members of the cabinet of ministers. Currently, the president has this power.

9. The authority of the state prosecutor will be expanded to include the right of supervision of the observance of human and citizens' rights and freedoms and the fulfillment of laws by bodies of executive power and local self-government.

10. A member of parliament's mandate would be terminated on his or her leaving, or not joining the parliamentary faction from which he or she was elected.

We perceive the impact of these reforms to be quite significant for Ukraine's democratic stability. However, whether the impact will be positive or negative will depend in part on the changes in the political dynamics as a result of the presidential election.

The Supreme Court's invalidation of the vote results of the first presidential runoff election on the grounds that true results of the election could not be affirmed due to widespread violations and fraud, and the parliament's passage of a bill dealing specifically with procedural matters of the repeat vote of December 26 to curb fraud provided a big step forward for the rule of law in Ukrainian elections.

On December 26, 2005, the repeat vote was conducted in largely free and fair manner, due in part to the bill regulating the election procedure and in part to a very large number of international and domestic observers that came to Ukraine from the United States, Canada, Poland, and many other democracies.

The changes in the institutional framework of the election process discussed above were intended to provide for a more procedurally specific way to ensure free and fair conduct of elections. Changes that were made specifically in the presidential election law could very well lead to changes in the parliamentary election law moving Ukraine towards securing international democratic standards in conduct of elections.

The move to a pure proportional representation system coupled with the changes in allocation of powers to the parliament would seem to move Ukraine to more of a parliamentary system in keeping with systems in Western Europe. This could serve to further consolidate and strengthen the party system and focus the attention of voters on the parties' policy positions thus establishing a tighter substantive link between citizens and the government. Whether this will happen or not depends on some other factors.

Proliferation and fragmentation of the parties in parliament has been a problem in Ukraine as it has been in other countries of Eastern Europe and the former Soviet Union. The effective number of electoral parties in Ukraine has been the highest in all post-communist states (Bielasiak, 2002, p. 205). With so many parties in parliament, illustrated by continual shifting of party memberships by deputies and extreme volatility of parties from election to election, citizens find it difficult to identify the parties and what programmatic positions they represent. The proliferation has made it difficult for voters to perceive that their choice has resulted in a real direction in government. A particular problem has been that several factions have not been founded on the basis of clear ideology, representation of a social group, or policy program, but on the basis of the relationship between the faction leader with the president who had extraordinary power to affect the member's business interests.

After the election, there are already indications that members of traditionally pro-Kuchma factions have defected, moving to support Yushchenko. If Yushchenko's Our Ukraine coalition is strengthened in the parliament as a result of his victory, and he is able to enact a real reform program, the citizenry may soon come to see the connection between their votes and real change. The propensity from the previous parliamentary election for citizens to cast their votes for a few electoral groups may continue to strengthen.

However, the move to a 3% threshold could make it more difficult for any one party to gain a majority of seats and could lead to even more proliferation making the formation of a workable majority even more problematic. The new proportional threshold could also make it easier for various "clans" to use their resources to buy or coerce their way into parliament making the formation of the majority once again an agreement among insider oligarchic groups whose focus is control of various economic/industrial assets rather than programmatic directions for the country. In this respect, Ukraine's move to lower the threshold is quite the opposite of reforms made in other Eastern European countries that have instead moved to raise their thresholds, in the majority of instances from 4 to 5% (Bielasiak, 2002, p. 196). With the next parliamentary elections conducted wholly on the basis of party lists, the number of parties represented in parliament may even increase.

In addition to changing the election system for the national parliament, the parliament also changed the election law for sub-national governments. On April 6, 2004, the parliament voted to change the elections to oblast, city district, city councils, and the Crimean Autonomous Republic parliament from a district based system to one of proportional representation. The election threshold for parties to enter the assemblies was also set at 3%. This changed framework for regional and local assemblies will likely have differential effects regarding parties. In some eastern regions, oligarchic parties will likely gain majority control of assemblies. In the southern and northeastern regions and possibly Crimea, the Left will gain majorities. In the west and center, the Right will gain majorities. With the president retaining control of the appointment of the heads of local state administrations, the potential for significant conflict exists between the appointed heads of the local state administrations and the elected assemblies, particularly in the eastern and southern oblasts where the oligarchic parties could dominate.

The question at this point is whether the changes in the Ukrainian institutional governance structure are likely to be sufficient to move Ukraine out of the transition "grey zone" toward becoming a consolidated democracy. The change to full proportional representation transforms the system into one that more closely resembles those existing in Eastern Europe. As discussed below, the effect of this change is likely to be mitigated either positively or negatively by other factors including changes in the institutional structure of government and President Yushchenko's policy priorities.

The constitutional changes as a whole will result in a sizable shift of governmental power to the parliament providing it with a much larger role in the appointment and dismissal of executive officials. Such appointment powers extend beyond the cabinet of ministers to other administrative officials. For example, the parliament will now have power to appoint and dismiss the head of the antimonopoly committee, the chair of the state committee on television and radio broadcasting, and the head of the state property fund. The parliament will also appoint and dismiss the head of the state security service upon submission by the president. Further, under the new constitutional provisions the parliament will have to affirm a president's decision to dismiss the prosecutor general.

Given the parliament's expanded role in the appointment of ministers, a real potential exists to increase the accountability of the ministries to parliament and to develop a strengthened relationship between the ministries and the respective legislative committees for the development of legislation. This will be important, because there is now a prohibition on ministers also holding a parliamentary seat, so ministers will not also be sitting in parliament. Parliament has more leverage now to insist on meaningful oversight mechanisms and will need to put stronger measures in place. If this is done, democratic responsiveness could be significantly enhanced. The shift in power to parliament could serve to provide a much more equal executive-legislative balance which is a characteristic of more consensual democracies. With the current tensions between east and west Ukraine, the promise of representation in a strengthened parliament could serve to quiet the fears of domination by President Yushchenko and dampen demands for autonomy or secession that had been voiced during the presidential campaign.

A potential for conflict remains, however, between a somewhat weakened president and strengthened prime minister, and cabinet of ministers. The president retains the authority to appoint and dismiss heads of local state administrations, whereas one of the primary Cabinet of ministers' responsibilities will be to implement government policies in regions. Any future policy conflict between the president and the parliament could be diverted to the regions. In the short run, this could exacerbate conflicts in the eastern and southern oblasts if councils there become bastions of opposition to Yushchenko.

As a result of the constitutional changes, a new institutional actor will appear in parliament: the parliamentary majority coalition. With specific responsibilities assigned by the amended constitution to this entity, clearer procedural and legislative provisions delineating the framework for the majority functioning will have to be adopted by the parliament. In addition, Ukraine's parliamentary political parties will have to modify their free wheeling ways of deciding issue by issue what programs they will support and develop a majority program for which they can sustain coalition support. If a conflict between different political actors prevents them from joining into a coalition in parliament within thirty days, then the president will dismiss the parliament thus throwing the country into a political deadlock. To obviate this possibility, the president will have to negotiate with the majority coalition over his nomination for prime minister.

Thus, the new structure, places a high priority on Ukraine's political parties exercising responsibility for the government's program – a responsibility they have not exercised thus far. If a coalition can come together and do this, then an essential linkage between the voters' decision and those of government will be forged. If they cannot, further political instability is likely. The amendment that deputies elected from party lists can be deprived of their parliamentary mandates if they do not join the faction from which they were elected can serve to increase party discipline and together with proportional representation contribute to party responsibility and parliamentary stability. This effect will, of course, be mediated by whether or not the move to full proportional representation results in even more parties entering parliament and increases party fragmentation.

The new constitutional arrangements require amending many acts. In case the local government bill is passed as law in spring 2005, the parliamentary-presidential reform bill will be enacted on September 1, 2005. The question is whether parliament will have enough time to amend those acts.

The foregoing analysis is based on the presumption that the constitutional changes will go into effect in either September 2005 or January 2006.

Given that Yushchenko opposed the amending of the Constitution during the heat of the presidential campaign, there is some possibility that he or his supporters will challenge the constitutionality of the amendments in the Constitutional Court on grounds that the bill passed was essentially identical to the one defeated in April 2004, and the Constitution requires that one year must pass before a defeated amendment to the Constitution can be voted on again. If the Constitutional Court were to decide to invalidate the constitutional reforms, changes in the institutional framework would be limited to the election law changes that call for full proportional representation. If this becomes the case, the combined effect of institutional change and electoral law change – to produce more responsible political parties in control of the legislative agenda – will be substantially reduced. Clark and Witt rock's (2005, p. 186) findings lend support; in their most recent study they conclude that "highly fragmented party systems are the consequence of institutional designs [and that] strong presidents [in particular] undermine the rationale for the formation of parties seeking to control over the policy and government control functions of the legislature." It is the interaction of the institutional structure and the electoral rules that affect the outcomes that matter for legislative representation.

The implication of such a political dynamic would be quite different than the democratic stability we perceive as the result of the Orange Revolution. In such a case we would expect that the debate over the amendments to the Constitution would begin anew. On the other hand, President Yushchenko may decide that a predictable parliamentary preoccupation over a renewed institutional debate may distract from consideration of his policy reform program and lead him to forgo the appeal to the Constitutional Court.

Conclusion

Taken together, the move to proportional elections, a shift of power from the presidency to the parliament, and the advent of an institutional parliamentary majority will cause Ukraine's institutional governance structure to look more like those of Eastern Europe. This new institutional configuration moves Ukraine more in the direction of Lijphart's consensual democracy. However, we caution against Lijphart's oft-interpreted dichotomous prescription for democratic stability (majoritarian vs. consensual). We remind readers that the perceived present result of the Orange Revolution – a seeming spike in democratization – is not without precedent in Ukraine. Whether Ukraine will slip towards autocracy (as it did after the democratic peak in 1994) or progress towards consolidated democracy is dependent on how these institutional changes interact with the social, economic, and political dynamics that have been discussed above.

The Orange Revolution would seem to suggest some societal consensus supporting the institutional reforms on the basis of principle, rather than short term political gain. However, we have also discussed events which suggest that one can account for the institutional changes, at least in part, on the bases of powers seeking to align themselves with the most likely victor of the 2004 presidential candidate. In the past, we have observed that changes made on the basis of short-term political gain are changes that have led to repeated scrutiny and contestation over the basic structure of power – resulting in limited stability. The advent of a reform president coupled with institutional changes moving Ukraine toward a more consensual model may serve to break the cycle. If so, Ukraine's political elites will move from a preoccupation with repeated elite clashes over the structure of power to competing with each other over policy alternatives and votes among the electorate. This development would be positive for the development of democratization in Ukraine.

This article has highlighted some of the more important institutional factors (e.g., constitutional and electoral) that will play a significant role in determining whether these macro-institutional changes will, in the end, have the desired results of stabilizing Ukraine's democracy. Together, these factors should remind government reform advocates that it is necessary to go beyond the basic institutional framework of proposed governmental changes and also examine key intervening factors, political, economic, and historical, in order to obtain a more fulsome picture of the likely effects of institutional change.

References

Åslund, A. 2003. "Left behind: Ukraine's uncertain transformation." *The National Interest*, 107-116.
Baylis, T. 1996. "Presidents vs. prime ministers: shaping executive authority in Eastern Europe." *World Politics*, 48: 297-323.
Bielasiak, J. 2002. "The institutionalization of electoral and party systems in post-communist states." *Comparative Politics*, 34 (2): 189.
Birchfield, V., Crepaz, M.M.L. 1998. "The impact of constitutional structures and collective and competitive veto points on income inequality in industrialized democracies." *European Journal of Political Research*, 34: 175-200.
Blais, A., Carter, K. 1990. "Does proportional representation foster voter turnout?" *European Journal of Political Research*, 18: 167-181.
Carothers, T. 2002. "The end of the transition paradigm." *Journal of Democracy*, 13 (1): 5-21.
Clark, T., Wittrock, J. 2005. "Presidentialism and the effect of electoral law in post-communist systems: regime type matters." *Comparative Political Studies*, 38 (2): 171-188.
D'Anieri, P. 2001. "Democracy unfulfilled: the establishment of electoral authoritarianism in Ukraine." *Journal of Ukrainian Studies*, 26 (1-2): 13-35.
D'Anieri, P. 2003. "Leonid Kuchma and the personalization of the Ukrainian president." *Problems of Post-Communism*, 50 (5): 58-65.
D'Anieri, P., Kravchuk, R.S., Kuzio, T. 1999. *Politics and society in Ukraine*. Westview, Boulder, CO.
"Declaration by the EU presidency on behalf of the European Union on proposals for constitutional change in Ukraine." 2004. Brussels.
Diamond, L. 2002. "Thinking about hybrid regimes." *Journal of Democracy*, 13 (2): 21-35.
Frye, T. 1997. "A politics of institutional choice – post-communist presidencies." *Comparative Political Studies*, 30 (5): 523-552.
Geddes, B. 1996. "Initiation of new democratic institutions in Easter Europe and Latin America." In: Lijphart, A., Waisman, C.H. (eds.), *Institutional design in new democracies: Eastern Europe and Latin America*. Westview, Boulder, CO, pp. 15-41.
Horowitz, D. 1990. "Comparing democratic systems." *Journal of Democracy*, 1: 73-79.
Jackman, R.W., Miller, R.A. 1995. "Voter turnout in the industrial democracies during the 1980s." *Comparative Political Studies*, 27 (4): 467-492.
Lijphart, A. 1984. *Democracies: patterns of majoritarian and consensus government in twenty-one countries*. Yale University Press, New Haven and London.
Lijphart, A. 1999. *Patterns of democracy: government forms and performance in thirty-six countries*. Yale University Press, New Haven and London.

Lijphart, A. 2004. "Constitutional design for divided societies." *Journal of Democracy*, 15 (2): 96-109.
Linz, J.J. 1990a. "The perils of presidentialism." *Journal of Democracy*, 1 (1): 51-59.
Linz, J.J. 1990b. "The virtues of parliamentarism." *Journal of Democracy*, 1 (4): 73-91.
Linz, J.J. 1994. "Presidential or parliamentary democracy: does it make a difference?" In: Linz, J.J., Valenzuela, A. (eds.), *The failure of presidential democracy*. Johns Hopkins University Press, Baltimore.
Linz, J.J., Stepan, A.C. 1996. *Problems of democratic transition and consolidation: Southern Europe, South America, and Post-communist Europe*. Johns Hopkins University Press, Baltimore.
Luong, P.J. 2000. "After the break-up: institutional design in transitional states." *Comparative Political Studies*, 33 (5): 563-592.
Mainwaring, S. 1993. "Presidentialism, multipartism, and democracy: the difficult combination." *Comparative Political Studies*, 26: 198-228.
Mainwaring, S. 1997. "Presidentialism in Brazil: the impact of strong constitutional powers, weak partisan powers, and robust federalism." Latin American Program, Woodrow Wilson International Center for Scholars, Washington, DC.
Mainwaring, S., Shugart, M.S. 1997. "Presidentialism and democracy in Latin America: rethinking the terms of the debate." In: Mainwaring, S., Shugart, M.S. (eds.), *Presidentialism and democracy in Latin America*. Cambridge University Press, New York.
Maksymiuk, J. 2004. "Our Ukraine seems to be losing sway over constitutional reform." *RFE/RL Belarus and Ukraine Report* (February 10).
"Moroz says political reform voting must take place November 16-17, 2004." *Interfax Ukrainian News* (Russia, November 15).
O'Donnell, G.A. 2002. "In partial defense of an evanescent 'paradigm'". *Journal of Democracy*, 13 (3): 6-12.
O'Donnell, G.A., Schmitter, P.C. 1986. *Transitions from authoritarian rule: tentative conclusions about uncertain democracies*. Johns Hopkins University Press, Baltimore, MD.
Pigenko, V., Wise, C.R., Brown, T.L. 2002. "Elite attitudes and democratic stability: Analyzing legislators' attitudes towards the separation of powers in Ukraine." *Europe-Asia Studies*, 54 (1): 87-107.
Polityuk, P. 2002. "Ukraine parliamentary poll to decide Kuchma's fate." *Reuters News* (March 27).
Powell, B.G. 2000. *Elections as instruments of democracy*. Yale University Press, New Haven, CT.
Power, T.J., Gasiorowski, M.J. 1997. "Institutional and democratic consolidation in the third world." *Comparative Political Studies*, 30 (2): 123-155.

Protsyk, O. 2003. "Troubled semi-presidentialism: stability of the constitutional system and cabinet in Ukraine." *Europe-Asia Studies*, 55 (7): 1077-1095.

Przeworski, A., Alvarez, M., Cheibub, J., Limongi, F. 2000. *Democracy and development: political institutions and well-being in the world, 1950-1990*. Cambridge University Press.

Roberts, A. 2003. "What type of democracy is emerging in Eastern Europe?" Paper read at Midwest Political Science Association Conference, Chicago, IL.

Shin, D. 1994. "On the third wave of democratization." *World Politics*, 47: 135-170.

Shugart, M.S., Carey, J.M. 1992. *Presidents and assemblies: constitutional design and electoral dynamics*. Cambridge University Press, Cambridge, UK and New York.

Stepan, A.C., Skach, C. 1994. "Presidentialism and parliamentarism in comparative perspective." In: Linz, J.J., Valenzuela, A. (eds.), *The failure of presidential democracy*. Johns Hopkins University Press, Baltimore, pp. 119-136.

"Ten Ukrainian parliament factions reach agreement." 2004. News from *Inside Ukraine* (February 19).

"Ukraine's parliament votes on proposed election law." 2004. *Inside Ukraine* Newsletter, (March 8).

"Ukrainian president agrees to step down in 2004." 2003. *Dow Jones International News* (April 15).

Vickery, T. 2003. "Ukrainian opposition asks court to rule on third term for Kuchma amid heated debate over political reforms." *Associated Press Newswires* (June 24).

Wise, C.R., Brown, T.L. 1999. "The separation of powers in Ukraine." *Communist and Post-Communist Studies*, 32 (1): 23-44.

Wise, C.R., Pigenko, V. 1999. "The separation of powers puzzle in Ukraine: sorting out responsibilities and relationships between president, parliament, and the prime minister. " In: Kuzio, T., Kravchuk, R.S., D'Anieri, P. (eds.), *State and institutional building in Ukraine*. Macmillan, Bloomsburg, PA, pp. 25-55.

The Last Hurrah: The 2004 Ukrainian Presidential Elections and the Limits of Machine Politics

Paul D'Anieri, University of Kansas

Abstract
This paper considers Ukrainian politics from 1994 to 2004 (the term of Leonid Kuchma's presidency) from the standpoint of "machine politics." Many authors have argued that Ukraine and other post-Soviet states have combined elections with partly authoritarian regimes. The concept of machine politics, applied in this paper, helps explain how they do it. The paper then considers how and why the Kuchma machine collapsed in the "Orange Revolution" of 2004, and the comparative lessons of the Ukrainian experience.

The pattern of politics that has developed in Ukraine since 1994 has been labeled "competitive authoritarianism" (Levitsky and Way, 2002), "delegative democracy" (O'Donnell, 1994; Kubicek, 2001) and "machine politics" (D'Anieri, 2003) by various authors. While the labels differ, the gist of the arguments is the same. The Kuchma administration in Ukraine has been able to use methods that are at least nominally democratic to achieve ends similar to those of authoritarian rule. In other words, he and his supporters, the so-called "party of power" have been able to erode the link between elections and genuine political competition. As a result, Kuchma's power continued to grow from 1994 to 2004, to the point where it was not clear whether a challenge to his appointed successor could possibly succeed.

However, the 2004 election campaign has made clear that this model is no longer tenable in Ukraine. While it remains unclear at the time of this writing (January 2005) exactly what arrangement will exist following the contested election, it is clear that the status quo will not hold. The election is widely seen as a watershed between two alternatives: a more democratic future in which political competition is more firmly established; and a more authoritarian future, in which the façade of democracy is dropped for a more overtly authoritarian political model.

This article seeks, above all, to answer the question: why did this happen? Why has the model of "machine politics" (the term I prefer) proven unsustainable in Ukraine? Several other questions are related to this one: How has the application of "political technology" altered the practice of politics in the former Soviet Union? How is the use of such "technology" limited? How has the international context influenced the erosion of machine politics in Ukraine? We begin, however, with a discussion of machine politics, in general and in Ukraine.

What is a political "machine?"

The study of machine politics has had two "upswings" in the last century. The first occurred when American political scientists sought to understand the political machines that dominated US urban politics in the early 20th century. The second occurred in the late 1960s, when comparativists sought to understand the party machines that were emerging in newly decolonized states. In both waves of study, the problem attracted some of the leading scholars of the time, such as V.O. Key, Charles Merriam, and Walter Dean Burnham on the US case and Joseph Nye, James Scott, and Aristide Zolberg on the post-colonial cases (Key, 1935; Merriam, 1929; Burnham, 1967; Nye, 1967; Scott, 1969; Zolberg, 1966). Machines are defined as "one-party systems in formally democratic states... Nonideological in nature, machines serve as an alternative distributional networks to the market, dispensing material benefits to the party's supporters" (Erie, 1993: 719). The basic idea was that a dominant party organization could maintain control for long periods of time by using a combination of patronage, favoritism, and intimidation to skew elections decisively in its favor. This led essentially to single-party rule in many US cities, despite ostensibly democratic institutions.

It is this combination – democratic institutions somehow leading to uncontested elections and single party rule – that makes the concept potentially useful for the analysis of contemporary Ukraine. Related to the concept of the political machine is that of patron-client politics, of which political machines are viewed as one manifestation (Clapham, 1993: 687; see also Eisenstadt and Lemarchand, 1991). James Scott states that "the basic pattern is an informal cluster consisting of a power figure who is in a position to give security, inducements, or both, and his personal followers who, in return for such benefits, contribute their loyalty and personal assistance to the patron's designs."[1]

Not every corrupt party or government is a machine, and not every machine is corrupt. What characterizes the political machine from other kinds of parties or governments is the "glue" that holds it together. The machine is based on exchange rather than on ideology, class, or other broadly based identity factor (Scott, 1969: 1142). Whereas the typical party maintains loyalty by appealing to voters' ideological preferences or class interests, the machine party gathers votes through the offer of particularistic rewards. "It is the predominance of these reward networks – the special quality of the ties between leaders and followers – that distinguishes the machine party from the non-machine party" (Scott, 1969: 1144).

The concept of machine politics here is not intended to contradict the formulations of "electoral authoritarianism" or "delegative democracy," but rather to refine them. Machine politics includes an explanation of why we see patterns of politics that can be characterized by those other labels.

Machine politics in Ukraine: Leonid Kuchma's political machine

What did Kuchma's political machine look like? There were two main goals: winning elections and controlling the parliament afterwards. Obviously to the extent the machine was successful in winning elections, controlling the parliament was simple. But, as we have seen since 2002, it was possible to control the parliament even without winning the election outright, or at least to hamstring it so that it did not challenge the President.

Crucially, Kuchma's was not a fully authoritarian regime. Winning votes still mattered, and elections were still contested, if not fairly. Maintaining power could therefore be viewed as a three-step process. The first step was to make Kuchma (or his parliamentary party, if referring to parliamentary elections) as popular as possible. This was pursued primarily through control over the press. To the extent such efforts were successful, Kuchma's group could win elections without any further intervention (this has not been the case). Therefore

---

1   Scott emphasizes that patron-client relationships exist primarily on a face-to-face level. What distinguishes machine politics, and makes this concept more applicable to Ukraine, is the ability to vertically link many patron-client relationships to create a single organization connecting the head of a very large organization with a great

considerable effort was expended to sway votes in the actual election through a variety of techniques, including patronage and coercion. In a presidential election, this was used in two ways: in the first round it was determined who the second-round opponent would be; while the second round could tip the vote decisively. Thus, in 1999, the crucial event was not Kuchma's defeat of Symonenko in the second round, which was a foregone conclusion, but Symonenko's defeat of Moroz in the first round, eliminating the candidate most likely to defeat Kuchma. Within the parliament itself, even if groups loyal to Kuchma would not have won a majority in the elections (for example, 1998, 2002), a majority could still be formed by using various means to entice or coerce deputies to the President's side. At a minimum, formation of an opposition coalition could be foiled this way. The significant point for understanding Ukraine's politics is that none of these tools were used in isolation, and therefore none of them were required to succeed by itself.

The essential resources that the Ukrainian executive had at his disposal were control over law and administrative enforcement, control over large sectors of the economy, and patronage. To some extent, the former two categories overlapped, because one way of controlling the economy was through selective law and administrative enforcement. These basic resources were highly fungible, meaning that they could be used to influence actors and to pursue goals in a wide variety of spheres. This was mostly true of selective law and administrative enforcement, which could be used to ensure the defection of a politician from an opposition party, to close down a troublesome newspaper, or to give crucial business advantages to an ally, who in turn would contribute money for reelection efforts.

The goal in machine politics is to use de facto power to overcome institutional design and popular sentiment. The ostensible goal of the design of a post-Soviet constitution, electoral system, and legal system is to provide for several key components of democratic theory. These include rule by the governed, the accountability of elected officials, and limited government power. Elections, the separation of powers, and the rule of law are means to these ends. Elections provide for consent by the governed, and also create, through alternation of leaders in power, a check on the abuse of government authority.

---

number of individuals at the bottom level.

Other elements of the constitution are intended both to maintain the powerful role of elections, and to curb the abuse of power in many other ways. Rules maintaining freedom of the press allow any government misdeeds to be publicized, so that the governed can act on them. Together, these institutions should compel the government to govern in the interests of the people. Even in the most democratic society, these goals are only approximately obtained.

The goal of Kuchma and other Ukrainian elites has been to use various tactics to break these links, because they seek to remove the checks on their power: Where institutional design created a separation of powers, they have sought to subject both the judiciary and the legislature to the influence of the executive. Where the laws provided for free and fair elections, Ukraine's elites have sought to make elections unfair, so that they did not make the government more accountable, and especially so that continuation in power of the ruling group, rather than alternation in power, become the norm. They sought to curb freedom of the press, both to keep the public ignorant about the government's misdeeds, and also as a means of winning elections.

These goals were not unique to politicians in Ukraine. On the contrary, we can find attempts to do all of these things in every liberal democracy. The difference is in how far such attempts went, in how they could be countered, and in how much success they met. Above all, what concerns us here is the level of organization of such efforts. Ukraine's ruling political group constructed an organized system of distributing patronage, collecting votes, and coercing opponents which was both vertically integrated from the central to the local level and horizontally integrated, with different tactics being used in a coordinated fashion to achieve key goals. It is in that sense that it can be called a "machine," rather than just another corrupt government.

Winning elections

As Roeder asserts, the central problem for the would-be authoritarian is "control of accountability" (Roeder, 1994: 65). The single most important goal for Leonid Kuchma and the group of elites around him is to maintain control of the executive branch. As has been shown, and will be elaborated below, control of the executive branch is central to holding both political and economic power in Ukraine. Because Ukraine has institutionalized the practice of elections, this channel of accountability remains relevant, so Kuchma and his supporters have strived to control it. This is why the 2004 elections were rightly seen as crucial for the country's future. Parliamentary elections are also important, though less so, for Kuchma found that he could achieve many of his goals by sidelining parliament rather than controlling it. It is essential only to prevent opposition control of parliament, and if a pro-presidential majority can be obtained that is even better.

The goal is to achieve these things while preserving a semblance of fairness of elections, from which immense legitimacy, both at home and abroad, is maintained. Kuchma and his supporters developed an integrated set of techniques and tactics to ensure that elections contribute to their legitimacy but do not challenge their accountability. Many of these tactics have been commented on, but it is essential to see that they are not the assorted measures of a disorganized group of authoritarians, but rather a single, integrated, strategy for maintaining power.

Control of the media

Efforts to win elections began long before the election day, and even before the campaign started, in efforts to control media (Human Rights Watch, 2003a). The simplest way to win an election, independent of any direct coercion, was to make the voters want to vote for you. That requires either good government, or control over information, or preferably both. Since Kuchma and his supporters had limited interest in good government, they had to build their electoral support through control of the media. By ensuring that Ukraine's voters received a steady supply of positive information about the President, that they knew little of opposition leaders, and what they did know of opposition leaders was negative, Kuchma and then Yanukovych hoped to achieve the popularity that would make winning elections easier. Many of the tactics he has adopted have been honed in Russia, where they succeeded in providing Boris Yeltsin an unlikely win in 1996, and gave Vladimir Putin an overwhelming victory in 2004. A four-pronged strategy was used to control the media.

Selective law enforcement

Selective law enforcement is used to shut down or to intimidate media outlets that create problems for the President. These problems can arise either because these outlets directly criticize the President, or because they support other political groupings, or simply because they expose the darker side of politics in Ukraine, even without directly attacking Kuchma. Often, these things go together. While there remained a fair number of non-state newspapers in Ukraine, almost all of them were linked to one political grouping ("clan") or another, and therefore presented a latent threat to the President.

Intimidation of journalists

In addition to efforts aimed at intimidating or suppressing media organizations deemed dangerous to the President, efforts have also been aimed directly at individual journalists. Of the many attacks on journalists in Ukraine in recent years, it is difficult to say for certain which were perpetrated by the state or by people linked to the state, and which might have been carried out for more private purposes, by business organizations or individuals. However, the fact that several of the journalists attacked have been known primarily for their criticism of the government raises the suspicion that official forces are at work. Even if some cases are privately motivated, the state has sent a powerful signal by its failure to bring to justice anyone for most of these crimes. By its inactivity, the state has helped create an atmosphere of intimidation of journalists.

Temnyki

In October 2002, a new, more activist type of media control emerged, known as the "temnyk" in Ukrainian (Human Rights Watch, 2003b). Used in limited measure prior to the 2002 parliamentary elections, and more widely as attention shifted to the 2004 presidential elections, the temnyki appear to be the work of Viktor Medvedchuk, since their expanded use directly followed his installation as head of the Presidential Administration in mid-2002 and the formation of the Department for Information Policy. The temnyk was a roughly 8-10 page daily bulletin sent, presumably from the Administration of the President,[2] to major news outlets, indicating which stories were to receive prominent coverage that day, and what slant was to be given them. In substance, there may not have been anything new here: news editors and re-

---

2 Because the temnyki were unsigned and sent on blank paper, there was no absolute proof that they came from the Presidential Administration. But all evidence pointed in this direction, and there was no other plausible source.

porters generally had a good idea of what the authorities wanted to see covered and how, as well as what they did not want to see. But those general notions still left a great deal of leeway to individual news organizations. Apparently, this was seen as problematic by the administration of the President. The temnyki gave very precise instructions about news coverage, leaving little room for interpretation. Editors were clearly under pressure to conform, lest they be subject to the measures described above, or simply fired by their owners, who by this time were almost all controlled by Kuchma.

Ownership

A fourth method of state control of the media in Ukraine was ownership of key outlets, either directly by the state, or by key allies of the executive. State ownership was not necessary to control the news, as long as private owners could be counted on to support the administration. Media outlets deemed too critical could be harassed into closure, using the methods described above. In addition to removing troublesome sources, this practice led many others to practice self-censorship. This tool was wielded with increasing power as Kuchma's time in office progressed. Virtually all major media owners depended on state ties for survival and were thus subject to censorship.

Ukrainian television, where over 75% of Ukrainians get their news (OSCE/ ODIHR, 2002: 14), was prior to the 2004 elections effectively controlled by Kuchma and his supporters. While Ukraine has a vast number of small and largely irrelevant local TV and radio stations, there are six national television stations. Of these, one (UT-1) is owned by the state. Three others (Novyy Kanal, STB, and ICTV, are controlled financially by Kuchma's son-in-law, Viktor Pinchuk, who also controls the country's largest daily newspaper, Fakty I Komentarii. Leading figures in the pro-presidential SDPU(o) party, including Oleksandr Zinchenko, control the other two, Inter and Studio 1C1(Human Rights Watch, 2003b: 9). It has been used extensively during election campaigns to support Kuchma (in 1999) and the pro-Kuchma electoral bloc Za Yedinu Ukrainu in 2002.

In 2004, Ukrainian television was skewed very heavily in favor of Viktor Yanukovych. He received a hugely disproportionate share of coverage, which was highly favorable. In contrast, Viktor Yushchenko was nearly invisible, and when his campaign was covered, it was covered in an unfavorable light. For example, on October 29, two nights before the first round of the presidential election, viewers could choose between live coverage of the "Za Yanukovycha" (for Yanukovych) pop music concert from Kyiv's European Square and a "news" program consisting of a glowing biography of Yanukovych.

Summary: media control
By itself, however, control of the media cannot reliably achieve the results Kuchma and his colleagues seek, in large part because the Ukrainian public is widely skeptical of the news media. Because there is little recent tradition of a truly free and activist press in Ukraine, Ukrainians do not believe everything they read or hear. After decades of total state media control, a short period of free press in the 1990s has not been enough to undermine public skepticism. That period did not create an environment of independent objective media, but rather one of partly independent partisan media. Control of the media is an immensely powerful tool, but is probably not sufficient by itself to decide elections. To ensure success, Kuchma's team relied on other measures as well.

Patronage
A second major means of controlling elections, much more direct than media control, is control over patronage. By patronage we mean the ability of an actor to use control of jobs or government entitlements to control votes. In Ukraine, the largest source of patronage is government jobs, but state control over university places, pensions, and the quality of life for soldiers, prisoners, and hospital patients is also important.

The basic technique of patronage is to exchange jobs for votes: if an individual votes for the incumbent, he or she either receives a job, or simply keeps the one he or she has. This has been a widespread phenomenon around the world. Sometimes this practice is rather indirect, in which many government employees know that a change of leadership will result in the new leader's supporters getting many jobs, thus endangering the jobs of existing government workers, regardless of how they vote. In Ukraine, it appears to be more direct, and is based on a presumption that it is known how people vote.

How many votes can the executive branch garner this way? It is hard to determine for certain, for two reasons. First, obtaining exact figures concerning the number of government employees is difficult. Second, we cannot assume that 100% efficiency is possible, so we really do not know the percentage of government employees, students, and others whose votes could be controlled due to patronage (Yurchyshyn, 2001; UCIPR, 2001:2-3). It varies across category, with those most dependent or vulnerable most likely to vote for the authorities. That lack of precision should not obscure a more important point: the number of votes subject to patronage is enormous compared to what would be necessary to fight a reasonably closely contested election.

In the case of the 2004 elections, we know that government employees of various types (at national and local levels) were told whom to vote for. We also know that pressure was put on university rectors to threaten students with sanctions if they did not vote "correctly."

It is not necessary to perfectly monitor individuals' votes to coerce them. If there is only a reasonable chance that their vote will be known, the cautious person may find it best to cast their vote as requested. Nonetheless, several procedures have increased the machine's monitoring abilities. First among these is the use of absentee ballots. Unlike regular ballots, these are filled out away from regular polling places. If a factory's workers, for example, can be compelled to apply for absentee ballots, they can then be asked to show them to a supervisor before turning them in. Or the supervisors can distribute and collect such ballots, if extras can be obtained.

Another favorite mechanism is "carousel voting" in which one worker for the machine gets a ballot at the polling place, and smuggles it out rather than depositing it. Then that ballot can be "correctly" filled out, and given to a new voter. The voter, in return for a payment, smuggles that ballot in, deposits it, and brings the new blank ballot he or she has obtained out. This method allows the machine to reliably monitor the votes it is buying.

Tax/law enforcement threats

If the number of votes available through government employment and related dependence on the government were not enough, there is an even broader tool available to Kuchma to collect votes in society: enforcement policy. As noted above in the discussion of the press, tax inspectors, fire inspectors, or a variety of other executive branch authorities can, as often as they like, inspect any firm they want, and shut it down with near impunity. The complexity and self-contradictory nature of the Ukrainian tax and legal codes make perfect compliance nearly impossible.

Fraud

If all else fails, a final method of tipping election results is outright fraud. In Ukraine it is relatively difficult to simply falsify election returns, because the provisions for giving opposition candidates access to monitoring polling stations and vote counting are relatively stringent and are generally enforced. Fraud did not begin in 2004 in Ukraine. There were credible reports in 2002 of voters, especially soldiers, being bussed from one district to another in order to vote en masse (OSCE/ODIHR, 2002: 18). This practice was widespread again in 2004.

Because of the key role of local election commissions in monitoring fraud, there was a concerted effort by Kuchma and Yanukovych to control the composition of those commissions. This was done by entering a large number of "extra" candidates in the presidential election. The individuals were allies of the Kuchma/Yanukovych team, and had no chance of winning. But because they were officially registered, they obtained the right to have members in the electoral commissions. This greatly diluted the proportion of commission members from opposition parties. Then, when actual assignments were made from this bloated pool, the Central Election Commission, controlled by the Kuchma machine, distributed those posts unevenly, so that in some districts where the machine was hoping to commit fraud, there were only commission members from candidates that supported Yanukovych. To use an American term, the commissions were "gerrymandered," to facilitate fraud.

The exact amount of fraud committed in the 2004 presidential elections may never be known, but it was undoubtedly massive. In two of the eastern Ukrainian oblasts, for example, second round voter turnout in excess of 95% was reported (compared to turnout under 80% in the first round). Such figures are implausible, and, since those oblasts voted overwhelmingly for Yanukovych, this one aspect of fraud alone provided a major part of his alleged margin of victory.

The fall of the Kuchma machine

Why has the model of "machine politics" proven unsustainable in Ukraine? To put the question in context, we should note that in both the US cases and in the post-colonial cases, the same has been the case. While in some cases, machine politics has been replaced with a more fully competitive system that, is not the automatic result. In many of the post-colonial cases, the machine politics model has eroded not because it failed, but because leaders have been able to move toward full authoritarianism, which they find more convenient. This is what we have seen throughout the former Soviet Union. In countries which had reasonable democratic credentials in the mid-1990s, such as Russia, Kyrgyzstan, and Kazakhstan, powerful leaders have been able to increasingly limit the relevance of elections, shifting toward an authoritarian model.

In Ukraine, prior to the 2004 presidential elections, the existing model was widely perceived as unsustainable. This election, most observed, would either lead to a genuine democratization, or to the end of any hope for democratization for the foreseeable future. We can identify a single broad factor that led to this watershed: the unpopularity of the Kuchma administration and the "party of power" associated with it. Machine politics relies on skewing vote counts, but still requires collecting enough votes to win. In Ukraine, this became exceedingly difficult for the machine.

The party of power in Ukraine ran into both general and immediate problems in the run-up to the 2004 election. The general problem was the increasing venality of Kuchma's administration, and the contempt that this engendered within significant portions of the population. The protests that followed the murder of the journalist Georgii Gongadze in 1999 helped galvanize a group of opposition movements that hitherto had been famously unable to join forces. By 2004, the rightist forces of Yushchenko were allied with the socialists of Moroz and the populist leftists of Tymoshenko by a single shared goal: to get rid of Kuchma's group. The Kuchma machine was widely perceived in society to be corrupt, and had little in the way of achievements to offset this shortcoming. In short, both its popularity and legitimacy were minimal.

The more specific problem for the authorities in 2004 was the candidate selected to represent them in the election, Viktor Yanukovych. Yanukovych was the sitting Prime Minister and former Governor of Donetsk Oblast' in eastern Ukraine. He managed to alienate both elites and masses. Many elites mistrusted Yanukovych because he and the "Donetsk clan" from which he came appeared to want to seize as much as they could get their hands on, rather than splitting the spoils with others.

For the broader voting public, the biggest problem with Yanukovych was that he was widely perceived to be a political hack of the worst sort. It was widely known, despite the efforts of government controlled media, that Yanukovych had two criminal convictions in the 1970s, and he occasionally used rather crude prison slang in public speeches. Among much of the population, to have such a person as President would simply be an embarrassment. Moreover, there was genuine fear that Ukraine's already weakened democracy would be snuffed out altogether.

The party of power could hardly have picked a less electable candidate, and the choice of Yanukovych remains one of the great mysteries of this process. We do not know exactly why he was chosen, but two factors seem to have contributed. First, the power of the Donetsk clan may simply have been undeniable. The Donetsk "machine" was one of the most effective vote-gathering forces in Ukraine, and the Donetsk economic group was the most powerful economic group. It is possible that this group could have threatened to run its own candidate separately if Yanukovych were not chosen by the party of power.

At the same time, the choice of Yanukovych shows something of the mindset of the "party of power" and the presidential administration. They simply did not believe that, given the resources they controlled and the "technologies" they were prepared to deploy, they could possibly lose. It apparently did not seem important to Yanukovych's supporters to choose a popular candidate, because they chose the least popular one they could find. As we shall explain below, this tactic showed a fundamental misinterpretation of the nature of their previous ability to win elections. It may also have been based on a misreading of the "lessons" of controlled elections in other post-Soviet states, especially Russia. The mistake was to believe that "political technologies" were enough to win an election all by themselves, when in fact they are only enough to skew a portion of the vote.

The emergence of civil society

A related miscalculation was one that Kuchma and his supporters perhaps shared with many western observers and reform-minded Ukrainians: the belief that Ukraine had little in the way of "civil society." Clearly Kuchma and Yanukovych believed that they could steal the election and that no one would care very much. Moreover, they seemed to believe that by generating the expectation that the election was controlled, people would become reconciled to the idea. Therefore their tactics in the election campaign were heavy-handed and transparent, in the sense that no one could have believed that this campaign was fair. For example, coverage of the campaign on Ukraine's television stations was so thoroughly one-sided that even unsophisticated voters were able to see that it was manipulated. Apparently, the goal was to create a sense of inevitability that would promote acquiescence.

Instead, we saw a well-organized and financed opposition movement spring up. Prior to 2004, the conventional wisdom was that rightist forces could not unite, and that the vast majority of Ukrainians simply did not care enough to actively oppose the government.

The most dramatic aspect of this election, and the least anticipated, was the size and organization of the movement to defeat Yanukovych. We knew, of course, that Yushchenko would be the standard bearer. But we did not anticipate the number of people who would put aside their daily work to organize and agitate on his behalf. While the media attention focused on the demonstrations that took place following the second round, the "real story" was in the organizational effort that made those protests possible and kept them going. For months before the elections, various groups, among whom student groups were most prominent, were organizing for three purposes: to build electoral support for Yushchenko, to foil government attempts at rigging the election, and to prepare a protest movement. Without the first two, the third would never have mattered.

This election demonstrated not only the large numbers of Ukrainians willing to become politically active, but the organizational capacity within society. It required considerable logistical preparation to organize people to register as poll watchers, to get trained, and to cover as many stations as possible. At the same time, we saw an impressive ability for spontaneous action: only a week before the first round, the idea of silently showing one's support for Yushchenko by wearing orange began to spread. By the second round (three weeks later), orange ribbons, scarves, and banners were ubiquitous, in an incredibly effective statement that opposition to Yanukovych was widespread. All of the state control over the media could not do anything to counter the message sent by all this orange.

There were regional limits to much of this activity. This election showed that Ukraine's regional cleavages are still incredibly salient. The voting differences between western oblasts, where over 90% voted for Yushchenko, and eastern areas where a similar proportion voted for Yanukovych, are as large today or even larger than they were in 1991. In part, however, this was due to a concerted effort on the part of Yanukovych, abetted by Vladimir Putin, to inflame regional differences to his advantage.

The shift in Ukraine's regional balance

In 1991, 1994, and 1999 presidential elections, the candidate who carried the eastern regions of Ukraine won the election. This is not surprising, since Eastern Ukraine is more heavily populated. In 2004, however, we witnessed a tectonic shift in the geography of electoral politics. The oblasts of so-called "left-bank Ukraine," lying to the immediate east of the Dnipro river, voted heavily for Yushchenko rather than Yanukovych. In electoral terms, these oblasts' left the East and joined the West. This does not appear to have been predicted by anyone.

A definitive explanation of this shift is not yet available, but we might focus on two factors. First, despite the obvious continued salience of the regional divide, it is possible that civic Ukrainian nationalism is strengthening. This might lead those in left bank Ukraine to reject the heavy-handed pro-Russian policies of Yanukovych, not out of ethnic or linguistic grounds, but out of loyalty to the Ukrainian state and Ukrainian independence, which Yanukovych appeared to regard with limited enthusiasm.

Second, Yushchenko himself is a native of one of these oblasts (Sumy). It may be that this was more a result of voting for the native son than of any secular change. However, the lopsidedness of Yushchenko's win in this region, and the fact that it occurred far more widely than his native Sumy, indicates a more secular change. This should be a subject for further research.

"Political technology" and elections in the Soviet Union

In both the Russian and Ukrainian presidential elections, much attention has been paid to what has been labeled "political technology," and to the "political technologists" who implement such methods (Wilson, 2005). We might define "political technology" as the various methods with which elections can be skewed.

Some of these are blatantly illegal, others are completely legal. We can think, for example, of a variety of "technologies" applied in the recent US presidential elections, concerning figuring out which votes are up for grabs and how best to win them. Voter mobilization efforts also fall into this category.

In many respects, this technology is not new. Controlling media, extorting financial support from businesspeople, using the government payroll to gain votes, and controlling the counting of votes, are all time-honored methods of machine politics (and other variants) going back over a hundred years. The difference in the former Soviet Union is that the weak legal climate makes it possible to apply a much broader range of techniques than students of politics in the advanced western democracies are used to seeing.

The lesson of this election, for both political scientists and for politicians in the region, is that such tactics are neither omnipotent nor foolproof. The Ukrainian "party of power," along with some outside analysts, tended to overestimate the effect of such methods. The tools of machine politics can no doubt influence votes, though the exact influence is unclear and will obviously vary from case to case.

In a close election, which will be tipped by a small percentage of the votes, such methods could be decisive if they were available much more extensively to one side than to the other, as is the case throughout the former Soviet Union, where control of the state apparatus conveys huge advantages.

However, such tactics cannot by themselves create a winner, regardless of how unpopular he or she is. This seems to have been the misconception driving the Ukrainian party of power. They seemed to assume that their huge advantages in "political technology" would automatically deliver them the election. They may have been encouraged in their belief by the ease of Vladimir Putin's victory in Russia, where such tactics were employed extensively. The crucial difference, which seems to have gone unnoticed, is that Putin had immense personal popularity, and almost certainly would have won the election even if it were fair. In other words, "political technology," while widely applied in Russia, was probably irrelevant to the result of the election.

In Ukraine, such technology easily could have been much more influential. There is no doubt that control of the media, patronage, and so on, could be used to influence a substantial number of votes. The results of the 2002 parliamentary elections indicated the same. Moreover, "administrative resources" do not require falsifying results, rather they influence the actual vote (a distinction that will be given more attention below). Thus, to the extent that they change votes, it is very difficult to measure their effects.

The problem for Yanukovych was that he had to make up a much bigger gap than machine politics and political technology could overcome. Had the party of power selected a more popular candidate, they could likely have swung the 5-10% of the vote needed to change the outcome of the election without resorting to outright and obvious fraud and intimidation. Picking such an unpopular candidate made the gap too big to cover. Therefore, they had to move from "machine politics" to outright falsification, indicating a move toward full authoritarianism.

Not only was Yanukovych too unpopular to begin with for "political technology" to carry the day, but his extensive reliance on it seems to have backfired, convincing many voters to support Yushchenko, and galvanizing both the domestic opposition and the international community.

In order to understand what happened in Ukraine, we need to distinguish between the application of the two types of "political technology." The first contains all the standard techniques of machine politics intended to sway whom people choose to vote for. This includes differential access to the media, use of the government budget to build voter support, and patronage. All of these are present to some extent in every democracy in the world. By influencing how people vote, these methods play into the legitimacy of the democratic process. Candidates who can win with these techniques can claim democratic legitimacy, even if the process is not fair. For Yeltsin in 1996, Kuchma in 1999, and Putin in 2000, the application of substantial "administrative resources" did not substantially undermine the perception of legitimacy, either domestically or among the international community, where complaints about problems were undermined by overall support for the elections and the Presidents themselves.

When one is required to actually falsify the voting, however, it becomes easier to undermine the legitimacy of the results. Alternate vote counts and exit polls both can provide evidence that the election was stolen. The widespread perception among Ukrainians that the election was fixed was a result of an abundance of clear evidence to that effect. Without such evidence of fraud, it is unlikely that post-election events would have developed as they did.

In sum, we need to recognize the limitations of "political technologies." That they can tip a close election is obvious. They can skew a certain percentage of the vote without leaving enough clear evidence to undermine the legitimacy of the elections. But they cannot make an unpopular candidate popular, and they are not a replacement for political skill, which was rarely discussed in the Ukrainian election, but was perhaps the deciding factor. The ineptitude with which Yanukovych and his supporters exploited their considerable advantages is remarkable.

Yanukovych used his advantages so heavy-handedly that he scared off millions of voters and unified a previously fractured opposition. It would appear that neither he, nor the main strategists of the party of power, understood that they were operating in an imperfectly democratic system. Instead, they behaved as if they were already in an authoritarian system in which people would simply vote for whomever they were told to.

Division among the elites

Among the intense focus on common Ukrainians gathering in Kyiv's Maidan Nezalezhnosti to protest the falsified elections, the role of the elites in that process has been largely overlooked. Apart from a lengthy analysis of the security services by C.J. Chivers of The New York Times, the behavior of elites has received insufficient attention (Chivers, 2005; for a contrasting view, see Kuzio, 2005). Several points deserve further scrutiny.

The most visible point is that the security services never attempted to disperse the protesters in central Kyiv. This fact alone, however, does not necessarily imply a split in the elite: it might simply mean that the elite, facing a situation that escaped their control, decided against massive bloodshed. However, at earlier stages in the crisis, key parts of the elite eased the job of protest organizers, both by what they did and what they refused to do.

First, there were no efforts to block access to central Kyiv. This contrasts substantially with efforts that were taken during earlier protests during the "Ukraine Without Kuchma" campaign in 2002. In that instance, state authorities used several means to squelch these protests, while almost always avoiding direct coercive repression. These meant, as I have already mentioned, blocking access to central Kyiv, and into Kyiv from other parts of the country. Additional means not used then, but presumably available in 2004, would have included shutting down the cell phone networks and internet on which the protestors relied so heavily to coordinate their activity. Just weeks before the protests broke out, the ability to shut off central Kyiv was demonstrated clearly during the parade celebrating the 60th anniversary of the liberation of Ukraine in World War II. That the level of repression of protests declined in 2004 to nearly zero indicates that decisions were made to allow the protests to grow.

Second, unmistakable signals were sent to potential protestors that the protests would be allowed, that they would not be repressed, and that they would succeed. The most important such signal may have been the announcement, immediately after the second round of the elections, that the Kyiv City Council rejected the legitimacy of the announced results. Kyiv's Mayor, Oleksandr Omelchenko, had appeared previously to support Yanukovych. His immediate defection sent clear signals that at least some of the elite would support protests, and more important, that Kyiv would be "open for protest." Later, high-ranking figures in the Security Service of Ukraine (SBU) appeared on the stage at the Maidan Nezalezhnosti to announce that force would not be used against the protestors. All of these moves encouraged the wavering to join the protests, ensuring they would reach a tipping point, at which growing confidence in success would yield ever increasing turnout.

As the crisis proceeded, the elite did not merely divide; rather most of it defected to Yushchenko, so that Yanukovych became the isolated politician. On November 29, Yanukovych's campaign manager, Serhiy Tyhypko resigned, admitting that large-scale election fraud had taken place (Interfax November 29, 2004; BBC Monitoring International Reports, November 29, 2004). On the same day, President Kuchma himself announced support for a rerun of the second round of the election, destroying what remained of Yanukovych's position (*Financial Times*, November 30, 2004).

The positions of the various military and paramilitary forces (the military, the Security Service of Ukraine, and the Interior Ministry) were more ambiguous, but overall served to encourage protests as well. The Interior Ministry, assumed to be most willing to use force against protestors, had done nothing to prevent their assembly in Kyiv. Rumors that a crackdown was imminent ebbed and flowed during the crisis, but there was never any show of strength. The Army was almost neutral, but this neutrality clearly played into the hands of the opposition as it guaranteed that the Army would not suppress the demonstrations. Most significantly, the SBU seemed to encourage the protestors, and ensured them that they would be safe.

It is hard to determine conclusively the role of these elites in the Orange Revolution, but it is very reasonable to suppose that a serious effort to prevent the protestors from gathering might have kept the protests to a level where they could have then been dispersed. Evidence that this was possible is provided by the example set in 2002.

International support

Both sides in the Ukrainian election sought to use external allies to strengthen their position. For Yanukovych, this meant a heavy reliance on Russia, which overtly supported him. For Yushchenko, it meant the slightly more restrained, but still unmistakable, support of the European Union, the US, Poland and Lithuania.

Russia supported Yanukovych, and saw in him the potential to make major progress on a goal Russia has held since 1991: the economic, political, and cultural reintegration of Ukraine into Russia. Russia, like others, saw a stark difference between the two candidates. While Yanukovych was seen as helping Russia achieve major goals, Yushchenko, it was feared, would put those goals beyond reach. He was identified with a pro-West, pro-NATO, and anti-Russian perspective attributed to western Ukrainian nationalists.

These perceptions may have had more to do with propaganda than with reality. In economic terms, Yanukovych had recently supervised the rigged privatization of the Kryvorizhstal company, which had excluded leading Russian firms from participation. In contrast, Yushchenko's commitment to more open trade might work to the advantage of powerful Russian firms. But it is probably the case that Yushchenko views the country's future primarily in terms of its relationship with the European Union.

We might speculate on a further reason for Putin to oppose the election of Yushchenko, and the turning of Ukraine toward Europe: the example that such a development would set for Russian politics. Just as Georgia and Yugoslavia were seen as examples for Ukraine, the development of a vibrant democracy with meaningful elections in Ukraine might cause Russians to question the stifled "controlled democracy" with which they now seem fairly content.

The numbers are difficult to confirm, but it is widely believed that Russia contributed approximately $300 million to Yanukovych's election campaign, roughly half of the total (which was comparable to spending by George Bush's 2004 campaign spending in a country with 50 times the GNP of Ukraine).

Putin's own political team, led by Gleb Pavlovsky, played a major role in advising Yanukovych, and many attributed to Pavlovsky many of the "political technologies" and "dirty tricks" that materialized in the campaign. It is difficult to assess how much weight he had; the evidence we have indicates that the Kuchma and Yanukovych team had plenty of internal capacity to manipulate elections, to intimidate their opponents, and to provoke conflict.

What remains rather unclear is how successful all of this assistance was. Obviously, it was not enough to prevent Yanukovych and his supporters from resorting to obvious fraud in order to claim he had won the election. In the aftermath, Russian analyst Sergei Karaganov argued that Russia's support had backfired:

> We ... had the right to prefer one of the candidates. But we made almost all of the imaginable mistakes. Our campaigning took the form of a brazen commercial operation, which was bound to irritate even Russia's supporters in Ukraine. Moreover, political specialists managed to involve in their games even the top Russia leaders, who took a stand and hence weakened their long-term ability to influence the situation in Ukraine (Karaganov, 2004).

By siding so decisively with Yanukovych, Russia placed a high stakes bet. If Yushchenko were to win, either through the ballot box or through protests, any potential for him to adopt a conciliatory policy toward Russia was likely destroyed. That made it even more important for Russia that he would not triumph. With Yuliya Tymoshenko, who is under indictment in Russia, appointed as Ukrainian Prime Minister, it is hard to foresee how a constructive relationship will be salvaged in the near future.

The United States and the European Union were also involved, and although their governments carefully avoided stating which candidate they preferred, it was not hard to see that they hoped for a Yushchenko victory. Rather than supporting him directly, however, they argued repeatedly that their only interest was that the elections be held freely and fairly. In the months leading up to the election they expressed increasing concern over the increasing control over the media.

However, because the efforts to skew the election were so one-sided, it was difficult to oppose those efforts without seeming to support Yushchenko. Despite the care taken by western diplomats, the perception was widespread that they supported Yushchenko. By the time of the election, the efforts to rig the election were so thorough that it would be impossible to say whether, if Yanukovych won the election, he had won fairly. Hence a Yushchenko victory became the de facto standard in many people's eyes for a fair election. The assumption that Yushchenko would definitely win the election if it were fair, and that a Yanukovych victory was prima facie evidence of fraud, contributed to the notion that the West took sides.

Conclusion

In 2004, Ukrainian reformers sought to initiate the political revolution that did not occur in 1991.Throughout the 1990s, political change was evolutionary, in which the terms of new arrangements were worked out by the existing elite within existing Soviet legal and political structures.

The dominant pattern of politics in Ukraine from 1994 to 2004 can variously be labeled "electoral authoritarianism," "delegative democracy," or "machine politics," the label we have used here. For those in power, the goal of "machine politics" is to gain the legitimacy provided by democratic elections without being subjected to the checks on power that competitive elections can provide. The "problem" with machine politics is that it does not guarantee fool-proof results. The leader seeking reelection (or the new aspirant seeking to replace a retiring or dead leader) must be able to gain enough votes so that the election can be decisively skewed without resort to outright fraud.

The problem for Kuchma's machine in 2004, in trying to pass the presidency to Viktor Yanukovych, was that it had a very unpopular candidate, while the opposition had a very popular candidate. While that gap could be narrowed by the techniques of machine politics, they were applied so brazenly in this case that they alienated more voters than they were able to win over or compel.

By the day of the runoff election, therefore, continuing machine politics was no longer an option: it simply would not work anymore. The choice was between either shifting to more democracy (and losing the election) or moving to a more fully authoritarian system (by overtly fixing the election and suppressing the ensuing dissent).

In comparative perspective, Ukraine fits well within the range of outcomes we have seen in other countries in recent years. In several important cases, machine politics has proven unsustainable, and these countries moved via evolution or revolution into more democratic systems. In Georgia and Serbia, this occurred through revolution in the streets, but in Slovakia, Vladimir Meciar accepted electoral defeat, declined to overturn the results, and continued to play the game within the new rules.

In other cases, the opposite has occurred, and such cases are unfortunately more numerous. Throughout the former Soviet republics turned into newly independent states, and further abroad (Venezuela and Zimbabwe are examples) we have seen leaders deliberately move their systems from something resembling machine politics to outright authoritarianism, while in other cases (Turkmenistan, Uzbekistan), there was never much deviation from authoritarianism to begin with.

The implications of the Ukrainian case for Russia are already being examined (Latynina, 2004; for a very skeptical view, see Lippman, 2005). A very different range of expectations will appear for the future of politics in that country. Will the example of Ukraine convince Russians at both the elite and mass levels that they can achieve a different kind of politics? This remains to be seen, but the energy which Putin invested in supporting Yanukovych indicates that he is concerned.

A key question that must remain for another analysis is what politics in Ukraine will be like after the Orange Revolution. Western analysts have tended to assume that the ejection of Kuchma and Yanukovych puts the country on a straightforward path to liberal democracy. Yet there are many complications ahead. Most important among these is the implementation of constitutional reforms agreed to as part of the deal to rerun the second round of the elections. The story of democratization in Ukraine is, at best, at a midpoint.

References

Burnham, W.D. 1967. "Party systems and the political process." In: Chambers, W.N., Burnham, W.D. (eds.), *The American party system: stages of political development*. Oxford University Press, New York.

Chivers, C.J. 2005. "How top spies in Ukraine changed the nation's path." *The New York Times* (17 January).

Clapham, C. 1993. "Patron-client politics." In: Krieger, J. (Ed.), *The Oxford companion to politics of the world*. Oxford University Press, New York, P. 687.

D'Anieri, P. 2003. "Machine politics in Ukraine: reconstructing the circular flow of power." Paper presented at the Annual Meeting of the American Association for the Advancement of Slavic Studies.

Eisenstadt, S.N., Lemarchand, R. (eds.) 1991. *Political clientalism, patronage, and development*. Sage, Beverly Hills.

Erie, S.P. 1993. "Political machine." In: Krieger, J. (ed.), *The Oxford companion to politics of the world*. Oxford University Press, New York, p. 719.

Human Rights Watch. 2003a. *Human Rights Watch world report 2003: Europe & Central Asia: Ukraine*.

Human Rights Watch, 2003b. "Negotiating the news: informal censorship of Ukrainian television."

Karaganov, S. 2004. "Lessons of the Ukrainian crisis." *RIA Novosti* (25 November).

Key Jr., V.O. 1935. *The techniques of political graft in the United States*. University of Chicago Libraries, Chicago.

Kubicek, P. 2001. "The limits of electoral democracy in Ukraine." *Democratization*, 8: 117-139.

Kuzio, T. 2005. "Did Ukraine's security services really prevent bloodshed during the Orange Revolution?" *Eurasia Daily Monitor* (24 January).

Latynina, Y. 2004. "Moskva postavila na chernen'kogo A Kiev ves' oranzhevyi." *Novaya Gazeta* (25 November).

Levitsky, S., Way, L.L. 2002. "The rise of competitive authoritarianism: elections without democracy." *Journal of Democracy*, 13: 51-63.

Lippman, M. 2005. "Russia is not Ukraine: the closing of Russian civil society." *Carnegie Endowment Policy Outlook*, January/February.

Merriam, C.E. 1929. *Chicago: a more intimate view of urban politics*. New York: Macmillan.

Nye, J.S. 1967. "Corruption and political development." *American Political Science Review*, 61: 417-427.

O'Donnell, G. 1994. "Delegative democracy." *Journal of Democracy*, 5 (1): 55-79.

OSCE/ODIHR. 2002. *Final report, Ukraine parliamentary elections*. (31 March).

Roeder, P.G. 1994. "Varieties of post-Soviet authoritarian regimes." *Post-Soviet Affairs*, 10: 61-91.

Scott, J. 1969. "Corruption, machine politics, and political change." *American Political Science Review*, 63: 1142-1158.
UCIPR, 2001. "Political season's blocking sublimation." *UCIPR Research Update*, 2-3 (23 July).
Wilson, A. 2005. *Virtual politics: faking democracy in the post-soviet world*. New Haven, Yale University Press.
Yurchyshyn, V. 2001. "Investment future of regions will depend on administrative resource's functioning." *PART.ORG.UA* – Political Network Edition (12 October).
Zolberg, A. 1966. *Creating political order: the party states of West Africa*. Rand McNally, Chicago.

Ukrainian Political Parties and Foreign Policy in Election Campaigns: The Parliamentary Elections of 1998 and 2002

Anna Makhorkina, Old Dominion University

Abstract
The foreign policy agendas of Ukrainian political parties participating in parliamentary elections are among the important factors of influence on Ukrainians voting in favor or against. There is a positive correlation between the preferences of Ukrainian voters and the foreign policy orientations of the political parties as expressed in their electoral platforms. Even if it is not likely that in general foreign policy plays a dominant role in the average citizen's voting decisions, it is, nevertheless, very relevant in the context of Ukrainian politics. In this article it is demonstrated that the use of foreign policy issues is a part of the overall electoral strategy of Ukrainian political parties.

Introduction

Democratic responsiveness of official state policies to its citizens' preferences has been at the center of scholarly debate for the past several decades. Does public opinion matter when it comes to foreign policy orientations of a state? To answer this question positively is problematic even in the context of well-established liberal democracies, where the public pressures concerning foreign policy issues take place within a certain democratic institutional framework. Their presence guarantees that the public wishes and preferences will be transferred to the official foreign policy makers, taken into consideration and implemented into the policy. Societies in democratic transition usually lack such institutional mechanism, which leaves the popular attitudes outside the officials' attention. The prospects for the public playing any significant role in a state's foreign policy orientation in societies undergoing democratic transition, therefore, seem extremely weak. Consequently, in Ukraine, as one scholar has observed, "public opinion influences nothing. If the executive can get away with Kuchmagate then he or she can get away with anything."[1]

In any democratic society the time when public opinion and preferences have to be taken into account by state officials and politicians is during the elections. The democratic election process, as Tocqueville observed back in 1835, is a time of increased influence of the masses, when the politician's main concern becomes not about the rule "in the interest of the state, but rather in the interest of his own reelection." (de Toqueville, 1969, p. 135).

By all accounts, elections are an important time in the political life of any democracy, when different political parties as well as independent candidates are trying to attract voters. In Ukraine, which has been described as a "delegative democracy" where citizens remain passive between the elections and only become involved in politics and civic activism during elections, this seems especially true (O'Donnell, 1994; Kubicek, 1994).[2] During the parliamentary elections of 1998 and 2002 three major issues at the core of Ukrainian political parties' electoral agendas included: first, economic and social reform; second, Ukraine's relations with Russia; and third, Ukraine's relations with Europe. Both domestic and foreign policy issues were essential. These three major areas seemed to correlate with the general preferences of the Ukrainian public. Thus, according to public opinion polls conducted by SOCIS-Omnibus, among the major issues that concerned Ukrainians were economic and social well-being, Ukraine's relations with Russia, and related to it, the question of Ukraine's integration into European structures.[3]

This leads us to the assumption that there is a positive correlation between the preferences of Ukrainian voters and the foreign policy orientations of the political parties as expressed in their electoral platforms. In other words, the foreign policy agendas of Ukrainian political parties participating in parliamentary elections are among the important factors influencing Ukrainians' voting in favor or against it. Even if it is not likely that, in general, foreign policy

---

[1] Taras Kuzio, conversation with the author, 7th Annual Convention of the Association for the Study of Nationalities (ASN), April 12th, 2002.
[2] Some scholars, however, believe that this definition can only be applicable to the Eastern and Southern Ukrainian public, since Central and Western Ukrainians remains active both between and during elections (Chudowsky and Kuzio, 2003).
[3] "SOCIS-Omnibus" public opinion poll analysis in Stegniy (2002).

plays a dominant role in the average citizen's voting decisions, it is, nevertheless, very relevant in the context of Ukrainian politics.

In this article it is demonstrated that the use of foreign policy issues is a part of the overall electoral strategy of Ukrainian political parties, and the changes in this strategy over time are presented and explained.[4] For this purpose, the foreign policy orientations of the political parties partaking in Ukraine's parliamentary elections in 1998 and 2002 are evaluated and compared, and the connections between foreign policy orientations of the parties and the preferences of Ukrainian voters are established.[5]

Political parties and factors influencing the voters: theoretical and contextual framework

The general consensus in Western democratic literature is that the electoral period is the time when public policy should come as close to the most prominent preferences of the voters as possible. There is a whole range of studies of factors influencing the voting behavior. Among the main categories of influence are party identification, voter's feelings about a candidate's stand on issues, and a candidate's personality and character (Niemi and Wiesberg, 1984; Hughes, 1978; Rosenau, 1965, 1974; Piper and Terchek, 1983; Stokes, 1966).

A standard model of the relationship between political parties and their electorate maintains that the public votes along party identification lines, where identification is characterized as a stable psychological orientation of the individual toward the political party. One research based on the study of electoral

---

4 The question of whether public opinion matters when it comes to foreign policy orientations in Ukraine is not at the center of this project. On public opinion and its influence on Ukrainian foreign policy see Chudowsky and Kuzio (2003) and Chudowsky (2001).

5 Abbreviations of party names used in the text: Batkivshchyna, All-Ukrainian Association Batkivshchyna; CPU, Communist Party of Ukraine; SPU, Socialist Party of Ukraine; NRU, People Movement of Ukraine, or Rukh; CUN, Congress of Ukrainian Nationalists; FU, Party "Forward, Ukraine!"; UNA, Ukrainian National Assembly; R&O, Reforms and Order Party; LPU, Liberal Party of Ukraine; the Greens, the Green party of Ukraine; SDPU(u), Social Democratic Party of Ukraine (united); Solidarity, Party "Solidarity"; PDP, Popular Democratic Party; PSP, Progressive Socialist Party; NDP, People's Democratic Party; UNR or Rukh, Ukrainian People's Movement; RCP, Republican Christian Party; ChPU, Christian People's Union; YPU, Youth Party of Ukraine; PIEU, Party of Industrialists and Entrepreneurs of Ukraine; DemPU, Democratic Party of Ukraine; DU, Party "Democratic Union".

behavior in the United States showed that the difference in political preferences of American voters significantly influenced the level of support for one or another political party (Campbell et al. 1960). Thus, a voters' opinion on a particular political issue was primarily shaped by that individual's loyalty to a particular party. And although partisanship was considered "firm but not immovable," the "identification with political parties, once established, is an attachment which is not easily changed."[6] The evidence was provided that party identification developed in childhood under parental influence, and that change in party identification was possible mainly due to changes in a voter's personal circumstances, rather than resulting from an impact of political events.

It is not realistic to apply the same model to the situation in Ukraine. First, the party identification among Ukrainians has been historically preconditioned to be low relative to that in the developed Western democracies. The Ukrainian multiparty political system started to develop since 1990, with the adoption of the law that legalized the creation of alternative parties.[7] These newly legalized parties, however, did not have to compete for votes until the parliamentary elections of 1994. As the elections were still based on the old Soviet-era majoritarian electoral system, the political parties were not given much chance to start playing a mobilizing role in Ukrainian society. Only with the introduction of the new semi-proportional electoral law for the parliamentary elections of 1998, did Ukrainian political parties start to mobilize the Ukrainian public. The electoral law adopted in 1997 stated that half of the members of the Ukrainian parliament were to be elected on a majoritarian basis. The other half of the seats (250) was to be won by proportional representation. In the latter case votes were cast for parties and seats were allotted on the basis of the nation – lists according to the percentage of votes that each party received during elections, with the cut-off margin being 4%. It was then that "Ukraine can be said to have possessed anything resembling a national party system that was

---

6 Campbell et al. (1960, pp. 148-149).
7 The law was passed in the fall of 1990, requiring that a party had to have 3000 members to register. Although it was reduced later to 300, it significantly slowed down the development of the new Ukrainian party system. According to Sarah Birch, the proof of weakness of the new party system was that neither of the candidates in the 1991 presidential elections was affiliated with a political party, and in 1994 only one serious presidential contender – the Socialist Moroz – was a party member (see Birch, 2000, p. 14).

capable of mediating between the preferences of the electorate and the structure of parliament." (Birch, 2000, p. 15).[8]

Second, the overall level of trust towards political parties is low among the Ukrainian public. Many Ukrainians feel that their interests are not represented by political parties. When asked, "which party best represents your own views and interests?" 42% answered "none", and 21% said they don't know (Ferguson, 1999). The public believes that parties do not advance the interests of the voters, but rather promote some other interests (Table 1).

Table 1: Whose interests are advanced by Ukrainian political parties (%)?

	1997	1999
Interests of the leader of the political party	26	24
Interests of the government apparatus	10	13
Interests of financial structures	13	10
Interests of the citizens of Ukraine	7	12
Interests of criminal structures	4	8
Interests of specific groups	4	4
Interests of voters in my region	4	1
Interests of the intelligentsia	2	1
Other	2	5
Do not know/refused to answer	27	22

Source: Ferguson (1999).

Finally, a characteristic of the Ukrainian party system is its structure around well-known popular personalities and its recognition-vote orientation

---

[8] In March 2004 the new electoral law was adopted postulating a fully proportional party-list system for parliamentary elections. According to this law 450 deputies to the Ukrainian Parliament will be elected in 225 constituencies from the lists of those parties that win at least 3% of the national vote, instead of the existing before 4% voting threshold.

(which is also reflected in public attitudes shown in Table 1).[9] A vivid example of this is the naming of major electoral party blocs in parliamentary elections in 2002 after their leaders rather than based on their party affiliations, such as the Victor Yushchenko Bloc "Our Ukraine" and the Juliya Tymoshenko election bloc.

There is another model of the relationship between political parties and their electorate which claims that the nature of a person's attachment to a certain party is determined mainly by his or her position on certain political issues (Fiorina, 1981). According to this model, party identification is used by citizens to make sense of the political reality in the short-term. However, "citizens constantly evaluate their political environments and adjust their views of the political parties accordingly. They alter their own partisan attachments as their comparative judgments of the parties' merits change over time" (MacKuen et al. 1989). A citizens' vote in favor or against a particular party is affected not by party identification but rather by voters' issue positions. The closer the positions of the person and the party on a certain issue the better the probability of that person voting for the party.

Usually there is more than just one political issue involved in the decision of whom to vote for. Evaluation of the perceived economic situation is among the main factors that influence the electorate's opinion on overall effectiveness of the candidate (MacKuen et al. 1989; Sanders, 1996). Thus, it has been noticed that during economic stagnation citizens are more concerned with issues of employment, and wellbeing, and, therefore, are more likely to vote for the parties of the left hoping that the policy will be focused on those particular issues. Foreign policy issues, while not being at the forefront of citizens' political agendas, cannot be ignored either. This is especially true for societies where opinions on major issues are highly polarized, and especially when following definite territorial lines. For example, a set of findings based on surveys carried out in Ukraine in 1995 and 1997 demonstrated the strong east-west polarization on a series of issues relevant to the support of political parties. Among the strongest influences on Ukrainians in identifying with a political party was a foreign policy issue – their attitude towards the Russian question (Hesli et al. 1998).

---

9   The latter proves to be not uncommon for the electoral politics in the West either (see

This model of electorates' support for a political party as based on citizens' issue preferences rather than pure party identification may not exactly be applicable in the setting of Ukrainian politics. However, it can provide a basis for analysis of voting behavior of the Ukrainian people during the parliamentary elections of 1998 and 2002, when in order to win seats in the parliament, political parties had to offer Ukrainian voters a program that would reflect the major public concerns as closely as possible.

Foreign policy preferences of Ukrainian voters

In day-to-day life, foreign policy issues usually are not at the center of public attention. During election campaigns, economic and social needs of the population have to be addressed first, because it is expected that public appraisal of economic indicators is the major source of influence on voting behavior.

However, in the case of the Ukrainian voter, economic concerns are not the only factor defining the political party choices. Although the interest of the Ukrainian public towards foreign policy issues decreased over the past decade to a certain degree (see Table 2), it still remains a significant factor in voting considerations. Thus, according to a public opinion poll conducted by Razumkov Center during the election campaign in 2002, the foreign policy orientations of political parties had to play a certain role for a majority (65.7%) of the Ukrainian population during their voting at parliamentary elections (almost 20% out of which said that foreign policy position of a party will play a crucial role).

---

above).

Table 2: Problems that concern Ukrainian voters

	1994	1995	1996	1997	1998	1999	2001
Living standards	74	72	66	79	83	89	76
Crime	49	55	50	42	45	37	43
Ukraine's security	25	23	20	16	15	10	16
Relations with Russia	29	28	23	21	16	9	21
Revival of Ukrainian nation	11	9	7	9	4	4	8
Russian language	5	5	6	5	4	2	5
Crimea and Black	9	5	7	3	4	1	e
Sea fleet							

Source: Chudowsky (2001, p. 314).

The explanation of this continuous presence of foreign policy in the list of the Ukrainian public's concerns is twofold. Initially, the interest was provoked by the emergence of Ukraine as an independent state. That is when the preservation of Ukrainian statehood and related external influences appeared on Ukrainian voters' agenda. Having celebrated 13 years of Ukraine's independence, however, the need to worry about external threats somewhat diminished.

Secondly, regionalism, which is often quoted to be an important determinant of voting behavior in Ukraine, is primarily expressed in differing geopolitical orientations of the Ukrainian people. As one author observes, "modern Ukraine is a deeply divided society with a pronounced pattern of regional diversity" (Wilson, 1997, p. 1). Different notions of national identification among Ukrainians, depending on whether it is Eastern or Western Ukraine, produced different visions of Ukraine's "other": the Eastern Ukrainians look towards Russia, the Western Ukrainians strive towards the West (Prizel, 1998).

Several studies on the voting behavior of Ukrainian public demonstrated that these regional differences between Eastern and Western Ukraine had significant influence on the voting pattern during the parliamentary and presidential elections in 1994 and the parliamentary elections of 1998 (Harasymiv, 2002; Khmelko and Wilson, 1998; Birch, 1995, 2000; Hesli, 1995; Kubicek, 2000). As Sarah Birch observed, the 1994 parliamentary elections revealed "a sharpening of the regional polarization of the country, with the nationalist, anti-Russian West pitted against the more socialist-minded, pro-Russian East" (Birch, 1995, p. 93). In 1997 the place of residence of Ukrainian voters was still considered the primary factor explaining issue positions of the electorate, before ethno-linguistic group factor (Hesli et al. 1998). And while regional differences do not manifest themselves in positions of one's satisfaction with the quality of life or economic situation, as well as the attitudes towards a free market, it is foreign policy orientations that distinguish a region as the most-important factor of political preferences. As seen from the Table 3, the foreign policy priorities of the Ukrainian population has clear regional specificity. The fundamental differences are the positions of residents of Eastern and Western regions.[10]

Table 3: Regional distribution of the respondents by the parameter "priorities of Ukrainian foreign policy orientations" (%), 2002

	West	Center	East	South
Relations with Russia	9.4	27.8	45.1	34.3
Relations with EU countries	56	31.3	21.9	24.0
Relations with CIS countries	13.1	21.4	21.7	25.7
Relations with USA	9.4	3.7	1.5	3.7
Relations with other countries	1.1	4.7	1.1	1.0
Difficult to answer	11.0	11.1	8.7	11.3

Source: Based on survey conducted by Razumkov Center (Pashkov, 2002a).

---

10 The definition of regions, as presented in the Table 4, is taken from Pashkov (2002a). The regions include: West, Volyn, Zakarpattia, Ivano-Frankivsk, Lviv, Rivne, Ternopil, and Chernivtsi oblasts; Center, Vinnytsia, Zhytomyr, Kirovograd, Poltava, Khmelnytsk, Cherkasy, Chernigiv oblasts, and Kiev, the capital; East, Dnipropetrivsk, Donetsk, Zaporizzhia, Lyhansk, Sumy, and Khrakiv oblasts; South, Crimea, Odesa, Kherson, and Mykolaiv oblasts.

The Ukrainian public seems to be confused over the issue of Ukraine's integration into the European structures and its cooperation within the CIS: while 58% think that Ukraine should join EU in the next 5 years, 45% favor Ukraine's union with Russia and Belarus (Pashkov, 2002a). Again, the most drastic differences on these questions are between positions of Ukrainians from Western and Eastern regions of Ukraine: while pro-European attitudes are dominant in the West, the East gives priority to relations with Russia.

It thus becomes evident that when analyzing the Ukrainian public's preferences on different social and political issues, one should address not only the economic concerns of the electorate but also foreign policy preferences. The major foreign policy issue that interests the Ukrainian electorate is the "Russian question," and the issue of Ukraine's integration into European and trans-Atlantic structures.

Therefore, given the preferences of Ukrainian voters, almost all parties that registered for participation in parliamentary elections in 1998 and 2002, along with the economic and social agendas of the electoral platforms, provided their foreign policy positions as well.

Foreign policy in political parties' programs: parliamentary elections of 1998

The parliamentary elections of 1998 could be considered as the beginning phase in the process of formation of the all-national party system in Ukraine, when the Ukrainian voters started slowly but steadily to identify themselves with certain political parties and give their votes correspondingly. According to Ferguson's study, in 1998 a plurality of Ukrainian voters (41%) did recognize the differences between the political parties and their agendas and could identify with them (Ferguson, 1999, p. 38).

Characteristic of the Ukrainian political parties during this time period was their distinct placement along the left-right spectrum. Although several different views on the classification of Ukrainian parties exist, the most general one follows the simple right-center-left classification (Huber and Inglehart, 1995; D'Anieri et al. 1999; Birch, 2000; Harasymiv, 2002). The left – generally characterized as anti-reformist and pro-Russian – traditionally included the Communist Party of Ukraine (CPU) and the Socialist Party of Ukraine (SPU); the right – the pro-reformist national democrats and anti-Russia Westernizers –

comprised of most prominently – the People's Movement of Ukraine (NRU or Rukh),[11] Congress of Ukrainian Nationalists (CUN), the Ukrainian National Assembly (UNA), the "Reforms and Order" party (R&O), and the Greens; and the emerging center – pro-reformist Westernizers and multi-vectorists – was represented by the Social Democratic Party of Ukraine-united SDPU(u), the Popular Democratic Party (PDP), and the Hromada. The support that these three major "families" of Ukrainian political parties enjoyed tended to be regionally biased. And, as was established earlier, while economic concerns were more or less equally spread throughout the whole of Ukraine, it had to be foreign policy issues that helped to distribute public loyalties between at least the three parties that won most seats in the elections.

Out of eight parties that obtained seats in the parliament in 1998, the CPU with its 24.5% of the votes was by far the most popular. The third biggest winner in the elections was the bloc of the Socialist and Peasant parties, which obtained 8.6% of the party list vote. Running under the common banner of "For Truth, For the People, For Ukraine!", the joint foreign policy position of Socialists and Peasants was to strengthen "brotherly" relations with Russia and Belarus, facilitate Ukraine's integration into CIS, and strongly oppose Ukraine's prospects for membership in NATO. The main support for the Communists and the Socialists came from the Eastern and Southern regions of Ukraine.[12]

The second most popular party in 1998 was Rukh, which gained 9.4% of the party list vote. Its foreign policy platform was Ukraine's integration into Europe and enhancing the country's security by overcoming the energy crisis and upgrading the equipment of the armed forces. Rukh was the most popular in Western oblasts.

The remaining five parties that crossed the threshold of 4%, showed more or less evenly distributed support in all of the regions of Ukraine. Four of them were running on centrist positions – the PDP, the Hromada party, the SDPU(u), and the Greens; and one had a clearly leftist platform – the Pro-

---

11   In 1999 the original Rukh split into two factions. One, People's Movement of Ukraine, or Narodnyi Rukh Ukrainy (NRU), was first headed by Hennadiy Udovenko and now by Borys Tarasyuk. The second faction, Ukrainian People's Movement, or Ukrains'kyi Narodnyi Rukh (UNR) with its leader, Yuriy Kostenko, was renamed Ukrainian People's Party.

gressive Socialist Party (PSP). All of them had clearly distinct foreign policy orientations.

The pro-presidential PDP (5%) promoted the importance of Ukraine's economic independence and was eager to see Ukraine becoming a leading European state. For this, the PDP advocated a multi-vector foreign policy for Ukraine, one directed at both friendly relations with Russia and other CIS states and development of closer relations with the European communities, while participating in NATO transformation into a collective security system.

The Hromada party (4.6%) listed among its foreign policy priorities a course towards Ukraine's integration into European institutions, development of a strategic partnership with the United States, and improvement of relations with CIS countries, Russia in particular. Its main support came from one oblast in the East, Dnipropetrivsk.

The SDPU(u) (4%) ran on a very statist platform, supporting Ukraine's independence and sovereignty, and a multi-vector foreign policy of cooperation with Russia and the West, integration into European and world institutions, and building of security community together with the countries of the Western, Eastern and Central Europe, and Russia. It received the majority of its 4% from the Zakarpattia oblasts in Western Ukraine.

The Green party of Ukraine (5.4%) with an ecological emphasis on politics built its foreign policy on the need for demilitarization and condemnation of the arms sales abroad, while advocating a global system of ecological security.

Finally, the PSP, with its campaign slogan "We shall build a Soviet and Socialist Ukraine!" advocated Ukraine's strategic partnership with Russia and Belarus while denouncing any partnership with NATO. It was least popular in Western regions, and enjoyed somewhat higher support in the South.

The regional cleavages, therefore, still remained important determinants of voter's behavior, although they were not openly confrontational. The most prominent regional differences could be observed among the voters for the clear left and right political parties. At the same time, it is clear that the voting for or against a certain political party was based not only on voter's economic considerations, but also (and mainly so) on foreign political preferences. The

---

12   The analysis of the political parties' platforms and the election results is based on information from the Ukrainian Central Electoral Committee web-site: http://www.cvk.gov.ua.

factor that consistently and predictably influenced the nature of voting preferences of the Ukrainian public was the "Russian question" and the relations with Europe.[13]

Foreign policy in the programs of political parties: parliamentary elections of 2002

On the eve of Ukrainian parliamentary elections of 2002 the basic structure of the Ukrainian party system remained generally based on three main camps: the left-wing camp dominated by the Communists and the Socialists; the right-wing camp gathered under the umbrella of the Victor Yushchenko bloc "Our Ukraine" (OU) and center represented by various business interests mostly patronized by the president, such as the pro-presidential coalition "For a United Ukraine" (FUU).[14] There were other comparatively smaller although very active parties such as the Yuliya Tymoshenko bloc, the SDPU(u), the extreme-left Nataliya Vitrenko bloc, and the pro-presidential All-Ukrainian political association "Women for the Future." Several of the remaining political groupings – the so-called "spoiler" parties – were believed to be created to divert support away from forces opposed to the president.[15]

While all of the political parties and blocs in their election programs gave priority to economic and social issues, practically every one of them addressed foreign policy issues as well. Common for all candidates were declarations of peaceful foreign policy based on the rule of international law and national interests of Ukraine. Although there were differences as to the definition of Ukraine's national interests based on party political affiliation, it was clear that most parties based their electoral platforms on a distinctively statist position. Where platforms of political parties differed was in the realm of international relations of Ukraine, such as Ukraine's participation in international and regional structures (specifically questions of Ukraine's integration into European organizations), and setting priorities in its cooperation between East and West (in particular, Ukraine's relations with Russia and the West).

---

13 Another characteristic of the election campaign of 1998 was the clear cut positions of Ukrainian political parties along the left-right continuum, with the consequent foreign policy programs.
14 The leader of "For a United Ukraine" was Volodymyr Lytvyn, a head of a president's administration.
15 Those were such parties as the Communist Party (Renewed), and the Rukh for Unity.

It is notable that almost all parties participating in the electoral campaign realized the importance of Ukraine's economic integration into the European Union and a decrease in its foreign economic dependence.[16] The opinion polls of political party and bloc leaders revealed the broad consensus on the European choice of Ukraine (Pashkov, 2002b). Neither party rejected Ukraine's participation in European integration processes. Even the Communist Party acknowledged the importance of the European vector in Ukraine's international relations, although the priority was still given to the development of relations with Russia and the CIS.

At the same time, none of the parties stood against establishment of mutually advantageous, pragmatic relations with the Russian Federation. The differences on this issue were only observed in terms of the proposed extent and mechanisms of cooperation. Thus, for the left and center-left parties (CPU, SPU) and almost all members of the FUU relations with Russia were a priority. From right-wing parties, only one declared the importance of a high level of relations with Russia (Batkivshchyna), while others often saw relations with Russia as secondary, and usually stipulated by specific demands to the Russian Federation.

The most common foreign policy concept in the programs of the centrist parties was that of "multi-vector" foreign policy. People's Democratic Party (NDP) wrote: "Our state has to conduct multi-vector foreign policy." The program of the Democratic Union Party proclaimed that the party "will conduct multi-vector foreign policy based on the principles of neutrality and non-alignment." The SDPU(u) declared "Ukraine in Europe," while simultaneously emphasizing the importance of Ukraine's relations with the countries of the Baltic Sea-Black Sea region (Belarus, Lithuania, Latvia, and Estonia) and the Danube basin, and pointing out the significance of solving common problems with Russia.

---

16 The parties pointed out the following concrete tasks in this direction, such as strengthening of Ukraine's competitive positions, growth of exports, diversification of markets, protection of the interests of domestic manufacturers on foreign markets, preservation and strengthening of Ukraine's role as a transit country, diversification of sources of energy resources, harmonization of the legislation with the norms and standards of the European Union, observance of international norms of protection of intellectual property rights, and Ukraine's accession to the WTO.

Therefore, while Ukraine's political center was faithful to its traditions in foreign policy orientations, slight overlap emerged on both extremes of the party center. Leftists no longer were adamant opponents to Ukraine's pro-Western politics, as long as it was in the national interests of Ukraine. Similarly, rightists ceased to discard Russia as a possible strategic partner.

Another important characteristic of the parliamentary elections campaign of 2002 was the large number of broad coalitions of political parties created for the purpose of consolidating the chances for winning seats in parliament. This resulted in a lack of clearly defined electoral platforms. The long-term electoral programs of political parties comprising such coalitions did not always fully coincide. Consequently, a coherent electoral program of a party coalition was a matter of compromise, and mainly at the expense of foreign policy statements of the political parties (Chalyj, 2002, p. 26).

For example, the electoral bloc, "For United Ukraine," included five parties.[17] Two out of the five clearly pronounced the priority of European orientation of Ukraine's foreign policy (NDP and "Labor Ukraine" party). One party – the Party of the Regions (PR) – saw Ukraine's integration into Europe only in cooperation with Russia. The other two – the Agrarian Party of Ukraine (APU) and the Party of Industrials and Entrepreneurs (PIEU) – clearly declared the multi-vectored foreign policy. At the same time, while the APU supported Ukraine's non-aligned status, the NDP and the PR strived for Ukraine's deepening cooperation with NATO. As a result, the common foreign policy orientation of the electoral program of the "FUU" bloc turned out clearly balanced and consensual, containing provisions of both strengthening ties with the CIS countries (particularly Russia) and Ukraine's integration into Europe.

The situation was similar in the electoral bloc of the Democratic Party of Ukraine (DemPU) – Party "Democratic Union" (DU). The DU abides by Ukraine's multi-vectored policy, while the DemPU is oriented towards cooperation with the West, and as a result the section of the electoral program of the Bloc containing foreign policy principles included a general statement of the subordination of Ukraine's foreign policy to the interests of Ukrainian citizens and the people of Ukraine.

---

17 Five political parties that formed the electoral bloc "For United Ukraine" are the APU, PIEU, PDP, PR and Party "Labor Ukraine".

The bloc "Our Ukraine" comprising ten political parties, encountered comparable dilemma.[18] The majority of political parties of the Bloc, such as the CUN, the NRU (Tarasyuk), the R&O, the Republican Christian Party (RCP), the Ukraine's People's Movement (UNR, Kostenko), and the Christian People's Union (ChPU), promoted Ukraine's orientation towards NATO. The Youth Party of Ukraine (YPU) adhered to multi-vector foreign policy. The UNR and NRU pointed out the importance of solving problematic relations with Russia, while UNR simultaneously proclaimed the US to be the main strategic partner of Ukraine. Three parties were advocating Ukraine's immediate accession to the EU (RCP, UNR, R&O), while four of them demanded immediate exit of Ukraine from the CIS (CUN, NRU, UNR). The resulting electoral program, however, omitted most of the specific foreign policy positions of the parties, and in its foreign policy section it declared Ukraine's foreign policy goal to be Ukraine's active participation in international security, promotion of new regional structures of security and co-operation with neighboring countries, and promotion of closer co-operation with the Ukrainian diaspora and formation of a united influential Ukrainian community in the world. As far as regional priorities of Ukraine were concerned, the electoral program chose cooperation in the region (with European states and Russia) and with the US.

At the same time, the Yuliya Tymoshenkos' bloc, which united four political parties with similar pro-European foreign policy orientations, did not hesitate to declare in its electoral program that the goal of Ukraine's foreign policy was the "removal of a humiliating question: whom to join?" and pursuing the policy "for the benefit of the nation, on the basis of peaceful, equitable relations with all states with which Ukraine has common interests."[19]

Out of 33 political parties and blocs registered for participation in the parliamentary elections of 2002, only six were successful in gaining seats in the parliament. Looking at a larger picture, no particular force had clearly "won" the elections. "Our Ukraine" bloc won 23.6% of the party list vote, which with 14.5% of total single-deputy seats provided the bloc with 24.8% of the total number of elected deputies. The CPU for the first time was moved to the second place with its total of 14.8% of the seats. "For United Ukraine" bloc

---

18　Ten political parties that constituted the electoral bloc "Our Ukraine" are the CUN, LPU, YPU, NRU, FU, R&O, Solidarity, ChPU, RCP, and UNR.
19　Yulia Tymoshenko personal web-site, http://www.tymoshenko.com.ua/.

gained fewer party seats than was predicted, but made up for it in 29.7% of the single-deputy seats.[20] Therefore, immediately after the elections the two biggest political forces in the new Ukrainian parliament were more or less equally positioned: "Our Ukraine" had 111 seats, and "For United Ukraine" had 101. The remaining two parties, the SPU and SDPU(u), and the Yuliya Tymoshenko's bloc gained 4.9%, 5.4%, and 4.9% respectively. Although it was much less than the leading three parties got, they still passed the 4% threshold very comfortably.[21]

All six found room to express their foreign policy priorities in the election programs. It should be kept in mind, however, that while priorities of single parties are relatively easy to identify, those of the election blocs were the result of a compromise between the not always identical positions of the political parties that comprised the bloc.[22] That is why it was possible to demonstrate the influence of foreign policy orientations of political parties participating in the parliamentary elections of 1998 on voters' decisions. In the case of the parliamentary elections of 2002 it was more difficult to do so.

First of all, as was discussed above, because of the participation of so many blocs in the election campaign, for the average Ukrainian voter the foreign policy priorities of contenders were difficult to discern. Some analyses of elections results point out that political divisions along regional lines still had certain influence on Ukrainian voters in 2002. Thus, Western and Central Ukraine voted for radical domestic reforms and pro-Western foreign policy orientation, while Southern and Eastern Ukraine voted for an "authoritarian-corporatist state."[23] However, while the distribution of votes for the winning political parties and coalitions among different regions of Ukraine does allow for such conclusions, it does not provide clear evidence of the foreign policy orientations of the Ukrainian public being a determinant factor in their choice.

---

20 The percentage of all-Ukrainian vote that different parties and blocs received does not add up to 100% because I only mentioned the political parties that passed the 4% threshold, while there were many other political parties participating in the elections that were not able to win seats in the parliament but did get a certain percentage of votes. If all those were added together, then it would come up to 100%.
21 All three received a "buffer" of comfortable more than 1% above the needed 4%.
22 Analysis is based on the political parties' and blocs' election programs, found at the web-site of the Central Election Committee (http://www.cvk.ukrpack.net).
23 Analysis is based on the political parties' and blocs' election programs, found at the web-site of the Central Election Committee (http://www.cvk.ukrpack.net).

At the same time, looking at the political parties with clear cut foreign policy agendas that were turned down by Ukrainian voters provides an interesting food for thought. For example, the two Russian nationalist blocs – the Russian Bloc and ZUBR ("For Ukraine, Belarus, and Russia") bloc – were promoting Ukraine's membership in the Russia-Belarus Union, Russian as a second language and Russians being constitutionally defined as second titular nation in Ukraine. The two blocs received 0.73% and 0.43%, respectively. The Russian bloc received its highest vote of 8.9% only in Sevastopol. Although the Ukrainian people are desirous of closer relations with Russia and CIS, at the same time they have more support for Ukrainian independent statehood (Table 4). Therefore, such foreign policy orientations of the political party or/and bloc appeared too radical as it was too resembling of Ukraine's not so distant Soviet past.

Table 4: Relations with Russia that are preferred by Ukrainians

	1994	1995	1996	1997	1998	1999	2001
Closed borders, visa and customs regime	15	14	18	13	11	10	9
Ukraine and Russia should be independent but friendly – open borders, no visa or custom regime	49	49	53	53	50	52	56
Ukraine and Russia should unite into a single state	34	31	25	30	36	35	32
Don't know or no answer	3	6	4	4	3	3	2

Source: Victor Chudowsky and Taras Kuzio (2003, p. 286).

Foreign policy as a determinant factor of influence on a Ukrainian voter's choice

The role of foreign policy considerations in voters' choice during elections and its use by political parties during elections campaigns is not always clear. In the parliamentary elections of 1998 foreign policy seemed to be among the major concerns of the Ukrainian public and it was convenient and important for political parties to use it in their electoral programs. Because the political parties preferred to "run it alone" (which in turn produced more clear-cut electoral programs with more clear-cut foreign-policy agendas, directed at a particular voter, usually on a regional basis), it is easier to see that foreign policy had a significant influence on voters' choice of political party to vote for.

By 2002, while foreign policy remained on the Ukrainian public's priority list, the political party spectrum became less discernible, with a bigger number of party coalitions, emergence of opposition as a valid political force competing for public recognition with the traditional favorite Communist party and the "party of power," and the resulting confusion regarding the international orientations in electoral platforms. Therefore, it seems more difficult to establish the connection between a political party's (or bloc's) foreign policy orientation and a voter's choice.

Nevertheless, it is clear that the importance of the Ukrainian public's foreign policy preferences have been recognized by political parties and their leaders. The regional differences at the core of the voting pattern have also been taken into consideration. In order to gain more votes throughout Ukraine (not just in a particular region) and to gain all-national support, the common electoral programs of a bloc did not include the extreme foreign policy issues from the agendas of separate political parties comprising this bloc. This was done in order to avoid the controversial effects it could have provoked among Ukrainian voters, and therefore decrease the chances of being (re)elected. The same was true for separate political parties, which had to somewhat soften their traditionally firm positions along the East-West foreign policy spectrum.

In lieu of conclusions: so what?

To study how the foreign policy orientation of political parties determines the voter's choice is essential for a general understanding of factors that influence the Ukrainian public's identification with a certain political party and the consequent vote for it. While it was established that foreign policy positions of various parties during election campaigns do play a role and are used by parties to influence the voting behavior, there remains the question of significance and implications of such a connection.

The Ukrainian reality is that the major foreign policy decisions are made by a very small circle of officials surrounding the president, or the so-called "central ruling elites." Given the level of corruption in Ukraine, "it seems highly unlikely that there has been no attempt by economic interest groups to alter the government's foreign policy." (D'Anieri et al. 1999, pp. 227-228) Also, given the state of democratic development in Ukraine, there have been serious doubts that public opinion on a variety of foreign policy issues has had any effect on what the leaders decide to do. Therefore, although the parliament does seek a role in foreign policy, more often it is not in formulating concrete foreign policy plans, but rather in opposing the official policies put forward by the government. The most recent examples of this could be seen in the parliament's inability to significantly influence Ukraine's participation in EEC, or from analyzing its behavior during the Ukrainian-Russian Tuzla conflict.

Potentially, however, knowing the foreign policy positions of the political parties can help predict the possible changes in the foreign policy course of Ukraine with a new parliamentary convocation. Although according to the national law of Ukraine, the President and the Foreign Ministry are in charge of Ukraine's foreign policy,[24] the parliament of Ukraine also plays an important role in shaping and carrying out foreign policy of the state. Or at least, it is so prescribed in the Basic Law. According to the Constitution of Ukraine, its parliament defines the main principles of foreign policy and makes decisions about ratification of international documents that regulate the directions, mechanisms and principles of Ukraine's relations with other countries. And although the role of the political parties' elites in the parliament in foreign policy decision-making is very modest,[25] it does not mean that there is no hope (or even potential) for improvement. In an expert opinion poll only 8.5% of the polled acknowledged the role of political parties in shaping Ukraine's foreign policy. At the same time, however, the desired level of influence by these institutions is seen differently by the Ukrainian population: Ukrainians would prefer the parliament and political parties to play a more significant role than they do in reality – 64% and 32.9% respectively (Pashkov, 2002a, pp. 44-45).

---

24 In addition, there is the National Security and Defense Council, which coordinates foreign and security policy decision-making.
25 Among the elites that influence foreign policy of Ukraine, the experts pointed out the dominance of the Presidential administration (90%). The deputies to the parliament received only 15.6%. "Foreign policy interests and resources of Ukrainian party elites" Center for Peace, Conversion and foreign policy of Ukraine. Report No 28, August 2001.

Besides realizing that foreign policy is an essential factor in influencing voters' behavior, political parties can use it more wisely and rationally in future election campaigns, or simply for gaining wider support among Ukrainians, which can in turn help them to become more consolidated, based on a nation-wide electorate. That is not, of course, to say that foreign policy issues outshadow the more imperative economic and social issues of everyday life. However, the above analysis suggests that foreign policy should not be discounted by politicians in defining and promoting their political agendas.

References

Birch, S. 1995. "The Ukrainian parliamentary and presidential elections of 1994." *Electoral Studies*, 14 (1): 93-99.

Birch, S. 2000a. "Interpreting the regional effect in Ukrainian politics." *Europe-Asia Studies* 5: 1017-1041.

Birch, S. 2000b. *Elections and democratization in Ukraine*. Macmillan, London.

Campbell, A., Converse, P., Miller, W., Stokes, D. 1960. *The American voter.* New York.

Chalyj, V. 2002. "Foreign policy sphere in election programs of parties and blocs." *National Security and Defense*, 26: 22-26.

Chudowsky, V. 2001. "Ukraine's climate of opinion and the political problem of the 'Western Vector.'" *Journal of Ukrainian Studies*, 26 (1-2): 309-324.

Chudowsky, V., Kuzio, T. 2003. "Does public opinion matter in Ukraine? The case of foreign policy." *Communist and Post-Communist Studies*, 36: 273-290.

D'Anieri, P., Kravchuk, R., Kuzio, T. (eds.) 1999. *Politics and society in Ukraine*. Westview, Boulder, CO.

Ferguson, G. 1999. "Public opinion in Ukraine 1999." *Voices of the Electorate Series*. International Foundation for Election Systems.

Fiorina, M. 1981. *Retrospective voting in American national elections*. Yale University Press, New Haven.

Harasymiv, B. 2002. *Post-Communist Ukraine*. Canadian Institute of Ukrainian Studies, Toronto.

Hesli, V. 1995. "Public support for the devolution of power in Ukraine: regional patterns." *Europe-Asia Studies*, 47: 91-121.

Hesli, V., Reisinger, W., Miller, A. 1998. "Political party development in divided societies: the case of Ukraine." *Electoral Studies*, 17 (2): 235-256.

Hughes, B. 1978. *The domestic context of American foreign policy*. Freeman and Company.

Huber, J., Inglehart, R. 1995. "Expert interpretations of party space and party locations in 42 societies." *Party Politics*, 1 (1): 73-112.

Khmelko, V., Wilson, A. 1998. "Regionalism and ethnic and linguistic cleavages in Ukraine." In: Kuzio, T. (ed.), *Contemporary Ukraine*. M.E. Sharpe, Armonk, NY, pp. 60-80.

Kubicek, P. 1994. "Delegative democracy in Russia and Ukraine." *Communist and Post-Communist Studies*, 27 (4): 443-461.

Kubicek, P. 2000. "Regional polarization in Ukraine: public opinion, voting and legislative behavior." *Europe-Asia Studies*, 52: 273-294.

MacKuen, M., Erikson, R., Stimson, J. 1989. "Macropartisanship." *American Political Science Review*, 83 (4): 1125-1142.

Niemi, R., Wiesberg, H. 1984. *Controversies in voting behavior*. CQ Press, Washington, DC.

O'Donnell, G. 1994. "Delegative democracy." *Journal of Democracy*, 5 (1): 55-69.

Pashkov, M. 2002a. "Foreign policy of Ukraine: positions and assessment of citizens." *National Security and Defense*, 2: 34-45.

Pashkov, M. 2002b. "Foreign policy of Ukraine: positions of party and bloc leaders." *National Security and Defense*, 2: 27-33.

Piper, D., Terchek, R. (eds.) 1983. *Interaction: foreign policy and public policy*. American Enterprise Institute for Public Policy Research.

Prizel, I. 1998. *National identity and foreign policy: nationalism and leadership in Poland, Russia, and Ukraine*. Cambridge University Press, Cambridge.

Rosenau, J. (Ed.), 1965. *Domestic sources of foreign policy*. The Free Press, New York.

Rosenau, J. 1974. *Citizenship between elections: an inquiry into the mobilizable American*. The Free Press, New York.

Sanders, D. 1996. "Economic performance, management competence and the outcome of the next general election." *Political Studies*, 44: 203-231.

Stegniy O. 2002. "Public opinion and foreign policy orientations in Ukraine." *Colloque CERI*, (1 July), http://www.ceri-sciences-po.org.

Stokes, D. 1966. "Some dynamic elements of contests for the presidency." *American Political Science Review*, 60: 19-28.

de Toqueville, A. 1969. *Democracy in America, 1835*. Reprint. Doubleday & Co, Garden City, NY.

Wilson, A. 1997. *Ukrainian nationalism in the 1990s: a minority faith*. Cambridge University Press.

The European Union and Democratization in Ukraine

Paul Kubicek, Oakland University

Abstract
The European Union (EU) has encouraged democratic development in a number of post-communist states. This article examines the extent of EU involvement in Ukraine and its results. It notes that there has been a substantial disconnect between the rhetoric of Ukraine's "European Choice" and authoritarian trends in the country. Ukraine signed a series of agreements with the EU, but membership in the organization was never offered. The EU's interest in Ukraine, however, was rather meager and it never gained means to have much leverage. As authoritarianism became more pronounced, the EU began to disengage from the country. The article argues that part of the problem was that the EU never applied political conditionality to Ukraine as it had with other states. The "Orange Revolution" opens up new possibilities and challenges, and the EU now must come to grips with a more democratically and Western-oriented leadership.

Ukraine merited scant attention from the European Union (EU) when the latter added ten new members in May 2004. If anything, that expansion led many to believe that the EU had cemented its eastern border, and that Ukraine, despite its once-ballyhooed "European choice," was destined to be left out of the organization. By the end of 2004, however, as the "Orange Revolution" swept Kyiv, Ukraine was at the center of the EU's concerns, and the denouement of the crisis surrounding the Ukrainian presidential elections would prove to be a success both for nascent Ukrainian democracy and for European diplomacy. With Ukrainians now asserting their newfound European credentials, the prospect of eventual Ukrainian membership in the EU may yet appear on the table. Before reaching that stage, however, there is much work to be done to further and consolidate political and economic reforms in Ukraine.

More than ever Europe has a stake in them and seems poised to redouble efforts to have a positive effect on their outcome.

This article examines the role of the EU as an external agent for democratization in Ukraine. Obviously, the events of 2004 have given new urgency and salience to this issue, but one should also remember that the EU has been engaged as a "partner" with Ukraine for over a decade, albeit, heretofore, with only modest success. Drawing upon that experience as well as on the broader literature on democratization, this article will assess the various tools at the disposal of the EU, their use and shortcomings in the past decade, and prospects for EU influence under the presidency of newly elected Viktor Yushchenko. Drawing in part upon the EU's experience in east-central Europe, it argues that the EU could and should do more to encourage reforms in Ukraine.

The EU and democracy promotion

The EU's interest in democratization is hardly confined to Ukraine. Indeed, the EU's efforts to promote democracy in Europe and beyond is a prominent feature in European foreign policy. Recently, EU expansion has been touted as not only offering economic benefits to new members but also as a means to promote and safeguard democracy in states that have had limited experience with liberal, participatory political systems. In the words of one writer, the EU can act as a "powerful catalyst" for change by providing "an elaborate structure of economic and social incentives" so that the strategies of political elites are "strongly shaped by the pressure of externally designed rules and structures." (Whitehead, 1996, p. 261).

However, despite the obvious policy appeal of the link between EU expansion and democratization, this nexus is, in the words of some observers, "undertheorized" and "more assumed than proven." (Whitehead, 2001, p. 415; Pridham, 1994, p. 7). Indeed, despite the correlation between EU expansion and democratization in Southern Europe (Spain, Portugal, and Greece) in the 1980s and in Central Europe (Poland, Czech Republic, Hungary, and Slovenia) in the 1990s, one could argue that these cases of successful democratization were over-determined and that these states were well on their way to democracy before the EU offered membership as a carrot for political liberalization. More interesting have been the cases of what might be labeled "reluctant democratizers," (Kubicek, 2003a) the states with leaders, structures, and/or cultural traditions that did not eagerly embrace democracy and in which EU policies to promote democracy, at least initially, produced minimal or mixed results. Among all the states of Eastern Europe, Ukraine, for well-known reasons elaborated in other articles in this volume, must rank as one of the most "reluctant" democratizers. Suffice to note that when queried in September 2003, only 22% of Ukrainian respondents in a national survey stated that they considered their country a democracy − a figure lower than that of surveys reported in previous years (IFES, 2003).[1]

The EU, of course is not the only international actor that seeks to influence Ukrainian domestic politics. One might include discussion of NATO and the US, not to mention Russia. But the EU is, arguably, the one with the most explicit priority for democratization.[2] The question, however, is: what can the EU do to promote democracy in Ukraine?

Before venturing into the specifics of the Ukrainian case, it might be useful to review briefly theories and perspectives on democracy promotion by external actors and the spread of international norms. This is an issue of great importance in contemporary international relations theory, and several propositions have been put forward to explain when and how external actors can shape outcomes in target states. A partial list of approaches would mention numerous terms and factors: contagion, sometimes called diffusion or a demonstration effect, incorporation, consent, adaptation, complex interde-

---

[1] This was a survey of 1200 individuals. Notably, 30% in a similar survey in September 2001 considered Ukraine a democracy. Moreover, in 2003 over 70% expressed not much or no confidence in the president and legislature and only 14% thought people could influence the government.

[2] As stated in the 1993 Copenhagen Criteria, democracy, rule of law, and respect for human rights are explicit conditions of membership in the EU. On the other hand, the US, while giving rhetorical support to democracy and backing the call for new elections in 2004, has also had other strategic goals vis-a` -vis Ukraine and NATO, as a military bloc, has other concerns besides democracy and has not always abided by its professed commitment to democracy for its members (see Reiter, 2001). Russia, one might note, makes no claim of preference to work with or aid democracies, and, as is now well known, has aided Ukrainian politicians implicated in electoral corruption and criminal activity.

pendence, international zeitgeist, convergence, socialization, learning, and conditionality.[3]

Among competing theories, several could have relevance to the Ukrainian case. These would include the following.

Contagion

One notion that is widespread in much of the literature on democratization is democratic contagion. The essence of this idea is that events or systems in one country or group of countries, to the extent that they are seen to be attractive or achievable, can spread across borders. This is captured by the language of a democratic wave (Huntington, 1991). Since democracy has spread to Ukraine's western neighbors – in part, perhaps, due to EU efforts – one might contend that Ukraine will become "infected" with democracy from sheer proximity and interaction with these states or as part of a plan to emulate their (and the other EU member states') perceived success (Kopstein and Reilly, 2000).

While this notion may have certain logic, it is apparent that it has had real difficulties working in the Ukrainian case. While democracy was consolidated in the 1990s in countries such as Poland and Hungary, Ukraine slid further and further into an authoritarian morass. The problem with contagion and its various correlates is that it is a supply-side theory and overlooks the demands/preferences of human agency (especially those of elites who may have no interest in democracy), aside perhaps from a simple psychological drive to copy a successful neighbor. It also ignores the role of historical memory or how local conditions may filter foreign influences, and it neglects the agency and intent of international actors, which can vary from case to case. Thus, it would be a mistake to assume that international factors act uniformly through some sort of contagion effect. Instead, we need to look more closely at actor-based theories to determine under what conditions democratic norms might spread.

---

3   Some useful sources are Whitehead (1996, 2001), Cortell and Davis (1996, 2000), Crawford (1997), Smith (1998), Risse et al. (1999), Grugel (1999), Checkel (1999, 2001), Pridham (2000, 2001), Cooley (2003), and Kubicek (2003a).

Convergence of norms

The idea of convergence can be viewed as a refinement on the more simple notions of contagion. Pridham (2000, p. 296) offers that it is "gradual movement in system conformity based upon established democracies with power to attract and assist regimes in transition," and that the EU may be the "most ambitious example" of convergence. Democratic principles may converge due to socialization through the growth of transnational networks, involvement of EU agencies in political, legal, and economic reform efforts, and more impersonal changes fostered by globalization. Unlike conditionality, discussed below, convergence is more a constructivist idea, predicated above all else on the internalization of democratic norms by elites and publics in targeted states. Unlike contagion, it suggests that norms are spread through the activities of a democracy "promoter" such as the EU. Evidence of its presence – insofar as it tries to ascertain the internal motives of actors – is often hard to find, but one can put forward a few notions of when democratic convergence is more likely.

One common-sense principle would be that the salience and attractiveness of the norm will affect the status of the state or organization trying to promote the norm. In other words, to the extent that the EU is seen as an authoritative and successful actor by Ukrainians, the more likely that EU norms of democracy will take hold. On a somewhat related note, one might also argue that the norm must have some sort of cultural resonance in the target state – in other words, the acceptance of externally promoted norms depends upon their interaction and compatibility with local norms and practices, at both the mass and elite level (Mendelson and Glenn, 2002). Regarding the EU, one might note that on the broadest level the EU is more likely to be successful if the target state claims to be "European."

A competing set of hypotheses concerns special circumstances in new states or states with new elites, what Checkel (2001) calls "novice agents." One argument would be that new states and elites – to the extent that they may be less burdened with legacies of the past or ingrained beliefs – would be more susceptible to outside influence. This could clearly apply – at least in theory – to Ukraine, where there was the potential to chart a new course with new ideas after its separation from the Soviet Union. The counter-hypothesis, however, would be that new states, in need to foster nationalism to establish the state's legitimacy and establish claims for the state's uniqueness, may be less likely to accede to demands – particularly those with an integrative logic – from outside actors. Nationalism can therefore be invoked to defend the state from foreign influence and deny the legitimacy of "foreign" norms.

Two other notions capture some aspects of the dynamics of norm adoption. One set of arguments focuses on what might be called rhetorical spillover, meaning that repeated invocation of the norm, even if it is just lip-service, will boost the norm's resonance and lead to greater chances for norm internalization. Risse and Sikkink (1999, p. 16) suggest that the more elites "talk the talk" the more they "entangle themselves in a moral discourse which they cannot escape in the long run." An important corollary to this argument is that external agents need to find allies within the state (groups of state elites, political parties, non-governmental organizations) and form "transnational networks" to transmit the norm and spread its acceptance. Risse and Sikkink (1999) suggest that norm promotion works best in a "spiral model" with a "boomerang effect" in which external agents join together with domestic opponents of the status quo, whose very ties to foreign actors help empower them domestically and help them press for concessions from the established authorities. Of course, the success of these networks will be conditioned on a number of factors enumerated above (for example, status of the external actor, cultural resonance), as well as the resources – political and financial – that the external actor is willing to devote to its agenda.

Conditionality

This is perhaps the most developed of all approaches relating to international aspects of democratization and can also be considered the most visible and pro-active of policies explicitly designed to promote democratic convergence. By conditionality, one refers to the linking of perceived benefits (political support, economic aid, membership in an organization) to the fulfillment of a certain program, in this case the advancement of democratic principles and institutions in a "target" state. Conditionality is most clearly enshrined in the EU's Copenhagen Criteria for membership, but one can point to a number of EU foreign policies built around the notion of democratic conditionality, particularly observance of human rights (Smith, 1998). Conditionality is used to exert direct leverage on others, and "carrots" and "sticks" are employed to persuade, induce, and at times coerce states into adopting the desired policy. Conditionality thus works on a cost/benefit analysis, and democracy results from a rational calculation; it is apt to produce, at least initially, instrumental adaptation of policy and not (as in the case of convergence) an internalization of norms.

Under what circumstances might conditionality succeed? A couple of obvious points are that the carrots must be viewed as valuable enough for elites in the target state to embark upon a potentially risky change in policy and that the sticks must be real enough that the elites know that there will be sizeable costs if they do not change course. Moreover, the target state should not have an alternative source of carrots or means to avoid the punishment of the sticks. In the case of Ukraine, this is very relevant to the extent that some Ukrainian leaders believe that they can always ally with Russia and then play Russia and the West off of each other in order to avoid real punishment and extract maximum concessions from each. Conditionality is also more likely to work if there are transnational networks that provide a domestic source of pressure on existing authorities and defuse any claims that outside demands are illegitimate or run against the interests of the country.

A final issue with applicability to Ukraine, especially under President Leonid Kuchma (1994-2004) is what Pridham (2000) calls the problem of "grey zone" democracies. By this, he means that states that are partially democratic may be able to avoid sanctions because external actors might not want to make matters worse and risk the limited democratic gains or wholly alienate the regime. This would be especially true in cases where the regime can plausibly claim some degree of democratic progress from a wholly authoritarian regime.[4] Ukraine – which had competitive elections and thereby qualified as an "electoral democracy" – had clear shortcomings on wider questions of liberal or substantive democracy, clearly fit in this "grey zone." To the extent that one can argue that the glass is "half-full" as opposed to "half-empty," Ukrainian leaders may have felt less pressured to push through more reforms to consolidate democracy. The issue, at least until 2004, was how far can conditionality be pushed against a state like Ukraine that is partially democratic

---

4   Levistsky and Way (2002) label this system "competitive authoritarianism," and they include Ukraine as an example. See also Way's article in this volume for more as applied to Ukraine.

and whose leaders profess to be (in rhetoric at least) generally supportive of democratic ideas.

Ukraine's European choice

In the first years of its independence, Ukraine was treated almost as an international pariah, due to its possession of Soviet-era nuclear weapons, slow progress in political and economic reform, and international support given to Boris Yeltsin in Moscow. This would begin to change in 1994 with the election of Leonid Kuchma as President of Ukraine. Breaking with some expectations, Kuchma quickly positioned himself as a champion of reform and of a "multi-vector" foreign policy and won Western support by pushing ratification of the Non-Proliferation Treaty through the Verkhovna Rada in the fall of 1994. As Ukraine expressed greater interest in trans-Atlantic and European structures – actively participating in NATO's Partnership for Peace, joining the Council of Europe, signing a Charter with NATO in 1997, concluding agreements with the EU – its stock rose in Western capitals. It assumed a new geopolitical importance, with one analyst famously dubbing the country the "keystone in the arch" of European security (Garnett, 1997).

Early on, however, it was clear that the European Union had a special priority for Kyiv. The foundation for Ukraine's current relationship with the EU dates from the June 1994 Partnership and Cooperation Agreement (PCA), the first such accord signed with any CIS country. The PCA established an institutional framework for relations, including an annual Ukraine-EU summit, ministerial level meetings, and exchanges between the Verkhovna Rada and the European Parliament. Working committees were established to tackle issues such as trade and investment, customs, energy, nuclear issues, crime, technology, education, and economic development. The PCA also included a provision allowing for a free trade area in the future. The PCA helped open the door further to EU assistance through the TACIS (Technical Assistance to CIS) program, which will be discussed below.

While one could have seen the PCA as a means to promote Ukrainian-EU contact and thus convergence of democratic norms, in practice the PCA focused on efforts to facilitate trade by helping to bring Ukraine up to WTO standards. While it does specify 27 areas of cooperation, it is best viewed as a roadmap to assist in the economic reform process. Technical economic questions are pre-eminent among its provisions, and while it does allow for the relationship between the two parties to evolve to a more advanced stage, it falls far short of the Association Agreements concluded with states in the queue for EU membership. Moreover, a decade after its signing and 6 years after being ratified, many of its provisions have yet to be implemented, with both sides accusing the other of not sticking to the Agreement, particularly on trade and investment barriers (Wolczuk, 2003). One official with the European Commission lamented that Ukraine's compliance was "at most hesitant and at times even ebbing," as Ukraine was "in breach of virtually all key provisions on trade in goods." (Schneider, 2001, p. 71) Ukrainians, for their part, felt that restrictions on the importation of Ukrainian steel and textile products (which are covered under special protocols), undermined the notions of fairness and partnership in the PCA.

Frustration with the PCA, however, did not lead either side to abandon the relationship. On the Ukrainian side, despite the admission that much needed to be done to fulfill the PCA, the rhetoric vis-a` -vis Europe began to be ratcheted up by 1996. In February of that year, Kuchma sought to link his country with Europe, claiming that "the cradle of Ukrainian culture is European Christian civilization. That is why our home is, above all, Europe." (Solchanyk, 2001, p. 92) In April, in front of the Parliamentary Assembly of the Council of Europe, Kuchma announced that its strategic goal was integration into European structures, with priority on full membership in the EU. Despite the fact that the EU did not even entertain the prospect of Ukrainian membership, a European and Transatlantic Integration Department was set up in the Ministry of Foreign Affairs, and the National Agency of Ukraine for Reconstruction and Development became the National Agency for Development and European Integration. In 1998, prior presidential statements became manifest in state policy with the issuance of the presidential decree "Strategy of Ukraine's Integration in the European Union." In August 2000, another presidential decree created a National Council on the Issues of Adapting Ukraine's Legislation to the Legislation of the European Union, a body chaired by Kuchma himself. Ukrainian officials were emphatic about the importance of the European vector in Ukrainian foreign policy. Then-Foreign Minister Boris Tarasiuk proclaimed in 1999 that the "European idea has become Ukraine's national idea and a consolidating factor for its society" (Solchanyk, 2001, p. 94).

The motives behind this "European Choice" are fairly easy to discern. The EU is seen as a guarantor of political stability and economic prosperity, and membership, if obtained, would be proof of Ukrainian success in the post-Soviet period. The EU would also be a source of aid, and membership would prevent a new "Eurocurtain" being drawn along the Polish-Ukrainian frontier, a fear of many Ukrainians today. Ties to the EU may also provide additional security against possible Russian threats to Ukrainian independence.

While Ukraine's "European Choice" was prominent in the rhetoric of state officials, what can one say about the views of the public? The evidence on this score is generally supportive of EU membership. When queried in 2002, for example, 57% of Ukrainians supported the goal of EU membership for Ukraine, and only 16% were opposed.[5] (Wolczuk, 2003, p. 6) Pro-integration opinions in Ukraine were thus higher than they were in the 1990s in several Central European countries (Grabbe and Hughes, 1999). However, at least until 2004, this did not mean that there was substantial movement "from below" to integrate Ukraine with the EU. Mass public and organized interests appeared to know little about the EU and did not constitute an active force in Ukrainian foreign policy (Pavliuk, 2001a; Wolczuk, 2003). Indeed, one pair of authors suggested, in a statement that may need some revision that on foreign policy questions public opinion has little importance since "passivity is the essential characteristic of the Ukrainian public." (Chudowsky and Kuzio, 2003, p. 276).

Moreover, one should stress that the "multi-vector" approach of Ukrainian foreign policy did not give way to a singular focus on Brussels. Russia remained very important for Ukraine, the largest single trading partner,[6] it is the source of most Ukrainian energy, and for cultural and historical reasons a source of attraction to many in Ukraine. Indeed, surveys have consistently shown strong support for better ties with Russia – especially in the more Russophone southern and eastern regions of Ukraine – and obviously Prime

---

5 One might note as well that, according to Wolczuk (2003) EU membership is much more supported in Western Ukraine (75%), than in Southern Ukraine (47%), and that these regional differences do much to color Ukrainian policy on a number of questions.

6 In 2003, for example, 18.7% of Ukrainian exports went to Russia and Russia was the source of 37.6% of its imports, mostly energy. Russia is also the largest investor in a

Minister Viktor Yanukovych believed that playing the "Russian card" (dual citizenship, making Russian a state language, campaigning with Russian President Vladimir Putin) would be a winning strategy in the 2004 elections. This should not, however, mean that Ukrainians are unequivocally pro-Russian, only that many apparently believe that Ukraine can and should integrate with both the EU and the CIS (Wolczuk, 2003). However, the fact that the EU has yet to open the door of membership to Ukraine also made some question the wisdom of putting most energies and hopes in the EU, and many Ukrainian officials were not happy with what they saw as the EU's "throwing European CIS countries out of the framework of integration processes in Europe." (*Uriadovyi Kur'ier*, Kyiv 1998).

After 2000, as Kuchma's various political shenanigans provoked criticism in the West, he noticeably turned toward Moscow, since Putin did not treat him as a pariah or criminal (Arel, 2001). Viktor Chernomyrdin, named ambassador to Kyiv in May 2001, also promised to bring greater prospects of Russian-Ukrainian economic integration (especially in energy), and Kuchma in turn let Putin know that Russia would be the top priority. In 2003 Kuchma controversially agreed to a Russian demand to reverse the Odessa-Brody oil pipeline for Russia's benefit and, in an even more dramatic development, Ukraine joined with Russia, Belarus, and Kazakhstan in a "Single Economic Space" in fall 2003. Some were concerned, at least before the 2004 elections, that Western pressure on Ukraine would do little but drive the country further into the embrace of Russia. The EU, as well as other Western actors, was thus been put in a difficult position about how to respond to Ukraine's democratic shortcomings.

Europe's response

Although the stated European concerns in Ukraine – implementation of meaningful economic reform, political and economic transparency, and creation of democracy and the rule of law – have been a constant since Ukraine gained independence, European policy has evolved over time. Pavliuk (2001b) divided the policies into four phases: neglect (1991-1993); support

---

number of key industries (e.g. energy) in Ukraine. Data from report of Vienna Institute for International Economic Studies, 6 December 2004, at http://www.wiiw.ac.at.

(1994-1996); frustration and fatigue (1997-1999); and disengagement (2000-2004?).

From 1991 to 1993, Ukraine received scant attention from Western capitals. Kuchma, then Prime Minister, suggested, "On the map of world leaders, Ukraine does not even exist. They are indifferent to whether Ukraine is independent or not" (*The Economist*,1993).

As noted, this would change in 1994. The EU's motives for engaging Ukraine are not hard to identify. Instability or protracted economic difficulties in Ukraine – a state that by 2004 would border the EU itself – would be a threat to the EU. Ukraine is also a large potential market for European trade and investment. Ukraine independence is also seen by some as a guarantor against a revival of Russian imperialism, although US policymakers have been quicker to recognize Ukraine's strategic importance than their European counterparts (Moroney, 2001). However, since Ukraine was not in queue for membership, the European investment in Ukraine was not nearly the same as in Poland, Hungary, or other candidates for membership. As Pavliuk (2001a, p. 81; 2001b, p. 15) noted, "The EU's stake in Ukraine is certainly not as high as Ukraine's stake in the EU," as well as the fact that relations with Ukraine were not a "self-sufficient goal" for the West but instead a means for pursuing other goals: nuclear disarmament, NATO enlargement, good relations with Russia, and the closure of Chernobyl. This fact does much to explain shortcomings in EU policy.

What have been the general results of EU engagement with Ukraine? Aid has been dispersed primarily through the TACIS program. From 1991 to 2002 (with most of this after 1994), total TACIS assistance to Ukraine totaled almost €600 million, and total EU assistance in these years topped €1 billion (http://www.europa.eu.int/comm./external_relations/Ukraine/intro/gac.htm).

This aid includes technical, macroeconomic, and humanitarian assistance, and considerable emphasis has been given to nuclear safety and assistance to Ukraine in the closing of the Chernobyl power station. As a whole, TACIS in Ukraine manages nearly 60 programs, many of which are designed to enhance transportation, border control, the natural environment, legal reform, and education.[7] While much of the money is dispersed to the government, there are some programs that seek to foster nongovernmental organizations. Assessment of TACIS's impact is, in the words of one EU official, "mixed," in part because resources have been spread too thin in a variety of sectors (Cameron, 2000, p. 83). Moreover, one could add that many of TACIS's aims and tactics – particularly in Western-style education, professional training, and NGO development – will take time to pay off and can reach only a small fraction of Ukrainian society. Moreover, TACIS's ability to address the most politically sensitive questions (as opposed to ensuring compliance with technical elements of the PCA) may be limited and it can also do little to restructure the overall oligarch-dominated political economy of the state. Finally, one should note that the TACIS program does not operate under conditions of conditionality or with well-defined incentives for the Ukrainian state. Programs that are judged a failure are unlikely to be renewed, but the overall consequences to the state are not clearly laid out. Thus, unlike in Central Europe, where the Copenhagen Criteria and adoption of the acquis communitaire provide an easy scorecard for progress with high incentives for compliance, aid to Ukraine operated with far more ambiguous environment. This limited the effectiveness of EU engagement with Ukraine.

As for trade, there has been growth in EU-Ukraine trade – the overall volume of exports and imports has risen from V3.79 billion in 1995 to V9.67 billion in 2002.[8] While trade with the EU is now 20% of Ukrainian trade, trade with Ukraine is only 0.3% of total EU trade and is far less than trade with Central European countries. This is yet another indication that ties with Ukraine are on an entirely different level than the EU's ties with its immediate eastern neighbors.

Perhaps sensitive to some Ukrainian concerns and looking to push reforms ahead in Ukraine, Brussels upgraded its relationship with Kyiv by promulgating a Common Strategy on Ukraine in December 1999. Notably, this was a "consolation prize," given in lieu of offering potential membership to Ukraine, whose candidacy had been not been entertained in any prior EU de-

---

7   For more on TACIS and other EU activities, see data from the EU Delegation in Kyiv at http://www.delukr.cec.eu.int/en/eu_and_country/data.htm.
8   From European Union website: http://www.delukr.cec.eu.int/en/eu_and_country/data.htm.

cision. This document also fell short of offering Ukraine Associate Membership, a halfway-house measure that Kyiv considered a realistic alternative to an invitation to full membership. Overall, the Common Strategy pays homage to the "shared values and common interests" of the EU and Ukraine while outlining several broad goals for the EU (furtherance of democratic and economic transition, ensuring peace and stability). It "acknowledges Ukraine's European aspirations and welcomes Ukraine's pro-European choice," while noting that full implementation of the PCA is a "prerequisite for Ukraine's successful integration into the European economy."[9] For our purposes, one should note that the Strategy, in addition to a host of economic, environmental, and security concerns, specifically notes EU support for the "consolidation of democracy and good governance." While the document is often high on rhetoric and short on detail, it does list some specific democratization efforts, including supporting Ukraine's efforts to sign and observe international human rights obligations, encouraging an ombudsman-institution in Ukraine, and contributing to the development of free media in the country. However, the Strategy duly notes "the main responsibility for Ukraine's future lies with Ukraine itself."

What have been the results of this Strategy? While a typical scholarly assessment is that "internal stagnation threatens to unravel the hard-fought gains of Ukrainian foreign policy" (Garnett, 1999, p. 124) some official EU statements presented a far brighter picture. Javier Solana, the EU's High Representative for its Common Foreign and Security Policy, wrote in a Ukrainian paper in 2000djust before the Kuchmagate scandal broke – that "over the years, Ukraine has committed itself to moving towards a fully functioning democracy, and the results are already very clear to see" (*Zerkalo nedeli*, Kyiv 2000). A joint statement from the EU-Ukraine Summit in September 2001 did not mention the murdered journalist Georgii Gongadze by name, while noting Kuchma's own commitments to the rule of law, human rights, and democracy.[10] A report from the Council of the EU in December 2001 was worded a bit stronger, with the EU emphasizing "profound concerns" about violence against journalists, and noted that Ukraine also needed to make

---

9   European Council Common Strategy of 11 December 1999 on Ukraine, Document 1999/877/CFSP, found in Official Journal of the European Communities, 23 December 1999.

more efforts to ensure judicial independence. However, the EU also noted it was '"encouraged by Ukraine's resolve to pursue its policy of reform and to comply with European standards."[11] Notably, a recommendation by the Parliamentary Assembly of the Council of Europe to expel Ukraine from the Council of Europe – adopted in April 2001 in the wake of Kuchmagate – was never adopted. Instead, in 2001 at its Gothenburg Summit, the EU offered to include Ukraine in the European Conference, an informal gathering of European states. While one cannot say for sure what was discussed behind the scenes, members of the EU delegation in Kyiv informed me in the summer of 2001 that there had been no discussion of a cut-off or curtailment in aid to Ukraine.

This is not to say that the EU has refused to criticize Ukraine in more specific ways. In 2001, the EU issued two declarations that revealed clear concerns. One was on Gongadze case and other was on reformist Prime Minister Viktor Yushchenko's dismissal. The statement on Gongadze expressed concern about the media environment, called for a full investigation into Gongadze's disappearance and an independent analysis of the tapes, and reminded Ukraine of its commitment to broader democratic freedoms. There was, however, no implicit or explicit threat of sanctions if the case was not resolved to the EU's satisfaction. The statement on Yushchenko was a bit stronger, as the EU stressed that progress with the reforms adopted by the Yushchenko government was "a pre-requisite for a deeper relationship with the EU."[12] In September 2003, the EU issued a stronger statement on the third anniversary of Gongadze's murder, noting its concern over lack of progress in the case and the deaths of other journalists in Ukraine, but, rather surprisingly, also expressed "satisfaction" with the willingness of Ukrainian authorities "o allow mass media in Ukraine to work according to European standards." (*Kyiv Post*, 2003).

10 Joint Statement of EU-Ukraine Summit, 11 September 2001, available at http://www.europexxi. ua/english/index.html.
11 Council Report to the European Council on the Implementation of the Common Strategy of the European Union on Ukraine, 15195/01, 11 December 2001.
12 See Declarations of the EU presidency, About working conditions for media and to remind about concerns regarding the Gongadze case, 5922/01, 5 February 2001, and On developments in Ukraine, 8082/1/01, 27 April 2001, available at http://europa.eu.int/abc/doc/off/bull/en/200101/p106046.htm and http://europa.eu.int/ abc/doc/off/bull/en/200104/p106023.htm.

Actions, of course, may speak louder than highfalutin diplomatese, and it is no doubt true that many European states saw Ukraine as a state on the fringe of Europe (like Turkey, at least prior to 1999), with little or no chance of really joining Europe. Garnett (1999, p. 128) opined, "In the chancelleries of Europe, little thought is given to Ukraine, except perhaps in regards to Chernobyl." In 2002, allegations over the sale of an advanced radar system to Iraq provoked the wrath of the Bush administration, a (temporary) suspension of US assistance to Kyiv, and risked turning Ukraine – again – into an international pariah (Kubicek, 2003b). As part of the fallout of this scandal, Kuchma was pointedly not invited to the 2002 NATO summit in Prague (he went anyway, much to the consternation of the US and UK). Ukraine tried to make up to the US by supporting US intervention in Iraq and sending a contingent of troops there, but, clearly, Ukraine did not repair the damage. Significantly, during the military standoff between Russia and Ukraine over the island of Tuzla and the Kerch Strait in the fall of 2003dan event that precipitated one Russian official to suggest (jokingly, he said) that if Russia bombs Ukraine – NATO refused to intervene, noting it was a bi-lateral problem between Russia and Ukraine (*Nezavisimaia gazeta*, 2003).

As for the EU, during the 2003 EU-Ukraine summit in Yalta, it again refused to approve Ukrainian Associate Membership and offered no timelines or clear indication that EU membership would ever be a possibility for Ukraine. Romano Prodi, then chair of the European Commission, suggested that Ukraine was as plausible a candidate for EU membership as New Zealand and put forward a "Neighborhood Policy" that grouped Ukraine with countries such as Morocco and Tunisia that were considered geographically unqualified for EU membership. Ukrainians lamented that the EU kept Ukraine waiting on the doorstep, but one might better suggest that Ukraine was sitting on the unwelcome mat.

In turn, with the still unexplained events surrounding Tuzla aside,[13] Ukraine drew closer to Russia. In February 2003, Kuchma, a former critic of the CIS, became the first non-Russian head of the CIS Council of State, despite the fact that de jure Ukraine is not even a member of the CIS. The aforementioned agreement on a Single Economic Space was met with great surprise in

European quarters, with the German Ambassador to Ukraine noting, "We have no clear-cut idea of Ukraine's purposes concerning the EU," and Ukraine was told by numerous actors that if the Single Economic Space does evolve into a customs union that it could seriously jeopardize its integration with both the World Trade Organization and the EU (Selyuk, 2003). For Ukraine's part, Kuchma suggested, "with the European markets closed to us ... it's better to have a real bird in hand than two in the bush" (Maksymiuk, 2003). Notably, this rather unexpected move provoked indignation among many in Ukraine – not just opposition leaders such as Yushchenko but also the Foreign Minister, Economy Minister, and Justice Minister. By 2003, it became clear that the EU expected little progress in its relations with Ukraine as long as Kuchma was in power, as he personally was seen as the main obstacle to democratization and in July 2004 even suggested that the ultimate goal of joining both NATO and the EU should be dropped from Ukraine's defense doctrine. Nonetheless there was some hope that the presidential elections in 2004 might produce change for the better. Of course, few expected events to turn out as they did, and certainly the election of the openly pro-EU Yushchenko as a president, together with the assertion of Ukrainian "people power," should bode well both for democratization and improved relations with Europe.

Lessons from the Kuchma years

What is to be made of EU-Ukrainian relations? Obviously, as of this writing, much is in flux, and there are good reasons to be quite hopeful for improvement. Before discussing the fallout from the recent Ukrainian elections, it would be useful to review some of the "lessons" that can be learned from the previous decade, as Yushchenko will not inherit a tabula rasa in terms of either domestic or foreign policy.

Until very recently, it was apparent that despite words from both Kyiv and Brussels to turn rhetoric of cooperation into concrete steps, little was accomplished. One Ukrainian report noted that the European idea became "mythologized in the Ukrainian political discourse and turned into a substitute of the late communist myth, with no firm connection with the reality (sic)" (Center for Peace, Conversion, and Foreign Policy, 2001, p. 2). Another observer went

---

13   There is much speculation that the incident was staged by Putin and Kuchma to

further, noting not only that Western influence "does not go very far," but also that:

> Ukraine's previous talk about integrating with the West was never matched by real action. Kiev has been happy to take Western money, but it was equally happy to take free Russian gas. Beyond that, it has never had much of a foreign policy (Bush, 2001).

This is not to say that nothing was done. In 1997, Ukraine adopted a moratorium on the death penalty – a requirement for membership in the Council of Europe – and finally banned it in May 2001. Checkel (2001) noted how the Council of Europe and other external actors were instrumental in encouraging Ukraine to adopt an inclusive, non-ethnic definition of citizenship, a decision that contributed to relative inter-ethnic harmony in the country. Due in part to EU pressure and promises of compensation, Ukraine closed the reactors at Chernobyl at the end of 2000.

However, disappointment has been marked on both sides, especially on the vexed question of democratization. Ukraine was not invited to join the European club, and the EU, despite using strained language not to sound too harsh, saw precious little progress on basic elements of political and economic reform. By 2004, a decade after the signing of the PCA, EU-Ukrainian relations were as ambiguous as ever, and Ukraine muddled along, with its "European choice" flagging as more action occurred on the Russian vector of its foreign policy. True, the OSCE and others sent observers for the 2004 elections, but with the levers of power and the media firmly in control of the existing elites, few believed the possibility of regime change in Kyiv. As the EU turned attention to the thorny issue of expansion to Turkey, few (aside from the Poles) were devoting much attention to Ukraine.

Why did relations with Europe reach this point? Why did the EU's democratization agenda have such clear shortcomings? Obviously, one can point fingers to Kuchma and his entourage, and no doubt the Gongadze and radar system scandals were a serious disappointment to foreign friends of Ukraine. Problems in EU-Ukraine ties, however, were evident before November 2000,

---

bolster their political standings.

when the first revelations of the tape scandals came to light. Some can be attributed to unrealistic or inflated expectations and simple misunderstandings. Pavliuk (1999, p. 4) noted the "frustration" on the Ukrainian side and "fatigue" on the part of Europe. He added:

> Despite several years of political dialogue and cooperation, each side still has little knowledge of the other, and the two see the future of their relationship quite differently. While Ukraine has declared its intention to become a EU associate member and its ambition to attain full EU membership in the future, the EU does not include it in either the 'fast track' or 'slow track' group of future members.

In particular, one might note that Ukraine's elites did not understand that the EU is much more interested in democratic development and economic performance than Ukraine's geo-political significance or its European heritage and that membership in the EU is qualitatively different from membership in the OSCE or Council of Europe. Moreover, one was often struck by the fact that while the mantra "return to Europe" flowed freely from the lips of Ukrainian policymakers and academics, there was little recognition that the Europe of today is far different than the one when Ukraine established its European roots. In other words, one witnessed merely "declarative Europeanization" (Wolczuk, 2003), or, to put it in Garnett's terms, the lofty rhetoric of Ukraine's "European choice" mixes with its troubled domestic politics like "oil and water" (Garnett, 1999).

Certainly, by 2001-2004, the situation was made even worse. While much of the blame is commonly put on Kuchma and the "party of power" in Ukraine that has dragged its feet on fundamental reforms, Ukrainians point to a lack of clear and inclusive strategy and perhaps even discriminatory treatment by Brussels, as the countries of the Western Balkans have the door of membership open to them whereas Ukraine, with clear claims to be a European state, has been denied the possibility of admission. In 2000, a joint statement by the French and German Foreign Ministries noted that "it is sufficient [for the EU] to content oneself with close cooperation with Kiev" and that the EU's mission was "not to unite the entire continent." Romano Prodi was equally dismissive, saying, "[membership for] Morocco, Ukraine, or Moldova? I see no reason for that." (Kuzio, 2003, pp. 10-11) The EU's "Wider Europe" Communication of 2003, which emphasized "integration, not accession" and was part of what Kuzio (2003) called the EU's "virtual policy" towards Ukraine, did little to assuage Ukrainians' concerns that they are doomed to be left outside of the EU and that a "Eurocurtain" designed to keep them out of Europe is descending on their western border. Even Chris Patten, Commissioner for Foreign Relations of the EU, acknowledged the weaknesses in the EU approach, noting "...we cannot supply the clear, unambiguous political will that is needed [to push forward reform in Ukraine]. There has been too much insistence in the past on the forms of our partnership, and too little on the groundwork to make that partnership a reality" (Patten, 2001).

These are crucial points, and help us to address many of the issues raised by the concepts and hypotheses put forward at the beginning of this piece. As noted, contagion has not occurred – Ukraine's western neighbors have made good progress, whereas Ukraine's has been patchy at best. As for convergence, we can note that there are few problems regarding the status of the EU, which is generally respected at both the mass and elite level, or "cultural match," to the extent that Ukraine aspires to be a European country and no leader – at least rhetorically – rejects democracy or Western political norms as incompatible with Ukrainian culture. Few, until recently, perhaps, would argue that the EU represents a "bad" role model or that the EU has no moral authority. In other words, the voice of the EU was not dismissed out of hand by Ukrainians. Indeed, the position of the EU received a lot of rhetorical support from many important Ukrainian political actors, and most of the main parties in Ukraine back eventual membership. However, EU norms – at least on important political questions – have yet to take hold, at least among the upper echelons of the elite. Superficial "declarative Europeanization" undermined any proposition of a rhetorical "spillover." By 2004, the abyss between the rhetoric of Ukraine's "European choice" and its domestic politics had become so wide that the European Parliament even referred to a "lack of shared common values" between the EU and the political establishment in Kyiv (*Ukrainska Pravda*, 2004).

Why then did convergence not occur? In order to answer this we should look at the hypotheses regarding new states and those on transnational networks. As for Ukraine being a new state, one might think this would make it more receptive to outside influence. On key questions of democratization, of course, this was not the case, at least for those holding power. The reason, however, was not Ukrainian nationalism. Indeed, the parties that are most associated with the so-called "nationalist" position in Ukraine – Rukh and Yushchenko's Our Ukraine – are the most pro-EU, and voters in Western Ukraine, often regarded as the center of the Ukrainian nationalism, are solidly pro-EU. Moreover, one hears little – with possible exceptions on economic protection of certain industries – to suggest that nationalism in any significant way is standing in the way of EU-Ukraine relations.

The point that is missed by hypotheses on the "newness" of states is that Ukraine, although a new state, was run by old leaders from the Soviet era that retained a "neo-Soviet political culture" (Kuzio, 2003, p. 10). In part, this contributed to a cultural disjuncture, since these elites, as opposed to Ukrainians as a whole, had little experience with or affinity for democracy. More to the point was the fact that since Ukraine did not have a "democratic breakthrough" until 2004, this communist past existed as a "residue" in the post-communist period. EU influence, such as it was, could not overcome the legacy of the past, and, with low levels of incentive for change (something addressed below), there was little reason to expect the leadership to suddenly become committed "democrats."

In addition, the EU was not very successful in creating transnational networks within Ukraine. In part this was because civil society in Ukraine remained rather weak. Although Rukh, Our Ukraine, and some other national-democratic forces were unequivocally pro-EU, they never constituted anywhere near a majority in the parliament. Pavliuk (2001a, p. 72) noted that the problem was that "real power" in the country was held by economic pressure groups that "have so far dictated the need for protectionism and preservation of the existing political and economic systems in Ukraine rather than their adaptation to European norms and principles." He added that "no large Ukrainian businesses have a strong stake in the EU market," which further limited the ability of the EU to team up with agents "from below" to pressure the government to change course.

This is not to say that the EU had no cards at all to play. However, it played them very conservatively, backing away, at least until the 2004 elections, from openly supporting opposition groups. As for the elite under Kuchma, it is hard to pinpoint how they would have benefited from making the reforms (for example, economic transparency) sought by the EU. As a consequence, the government machinery – contrary to the rhetoric of state officials – was "on the whole is largely ambivalent or even suspicious of the country's European integration" (Pavliuk, 2001a, p. 73). The result was rhetoric with the hope of receiving some type of assistance, but foot-dragging on many basic political and economic issues. The EU faced similar circumstances in other "reluctant democratizers" (Slovakia under Meciar), and progress was made only after the hard-line elites were ousted from office. The key point, again, was that the EU could not persuade obdurate anti-democrats, such as Kuchma, to change course, and consequently it would have to wait until there was some sort of regime change.

If there has not been convergence of norms – which might have been too much to expect – why has conditionality, implying a cost/benefit acceptance of norms, not worked? The simplest answer is that it has not really been tried. The carrot of membership – the crucial variable that has been assumed to help push reforms through potential bottlenecks in East Central Europe (Kubicek, 2003a) – was not on the table. Ukrainian membership, at best, was on the very distant horizon, and, as noted, some European leaders even dismissed this possibility. Ukraine and Moldova are the only two countries that expressed an interest in joining that are not in the membership queue, and Ukraine even lacks an Associate Membership, something granted with ease to Central European states in the early 1990s. While one can understand European reluctance to accept Ukraine under Kuchma, one can argue that without an endpoint, a target with clear and significant rewards, the incentive to follow EU dictates or preferences was low and that the EU did not have sufficient leverage to affect Ukrainian politics. Indeed, Cooley (2003), reviewing EU policy in a number of states, notes that EU aid only is "trivial" compared to the benefits of actual membership and that such assistance alone will have little impact in countries where elites do not have willingness to reform.

This problem was compounded by the lack of sticks. Sanctions were not employed or considered by the EU. Declarations were made on some issues, but these were not followed up by any actions. For example, it has been over four years since the tape scandal broke, and there has yet to be a full, impartial investigation demanded by the EU. Nonetheless, there were few consequences. Ukraine was not a pariah, and since November 2000 Kuchma has even welcomed leading EU political figures (and the Pope!) to Ukraine. Even the Council of Europe backed away from a recommendation to expel Ukraine for its failures to respect basic elements of democracy. In off-the-record discussions with EU officials in Kyiv in 2001, they told me that they put much more stock in engagement, dialogue, and policy change in small, incremental steps than in pushing a policy of "take it or leave it" conditionality (for example, fulfill the PCA now or else face this punishment). Their reasoning was that EU-Ukrainian relations had to be handled gingerly, and that Ukraine was, in essence, not far enough down the path to membership for the EU to make strong demands.

Of course, this begs the question of why Ukraine was treated so gingerly. One possible reason, as Pavliuk (2001a, b) suggested, was that the EU really did not care that much or have a really large stake in Ukraine, so it was willing to turn a blind eye to some developments and was reticent to risk conflict. Another reason was that the EU (and the West more generally) did not want to risk "losing" Ukraine. True, Ukrainian leaders argued that the country has no other choice but Europe, but they did not always act if this was the case. Russia lurked in the background, and Kuchma, after directing some accusatory barbs at Moscow in the wake of the tape scandal, made a number of significant overtures to bolster Ukrainian-Russian cooperation. This was done not only for its own merits, but also with an eye to the West, playing a Russia card to extract concessions and aid from the West, where acolytes of geo-politics fretted about a possible Russia – Ukraine re-union. Cynics might therefore suggest that the billions in aid from the US and the EU was used more to buy off Ukrainian elites than to promote political or economic change. The point is thus not that the West cared nothing for Ukraine, but cared only that it remains outside of Russia's sphere of control. Ukraine's "exit" option thus gave it the capacity to escape harsh demands of conditionality and, knowing this, the West chose to "ride softly" with Kyiv while forgetting about any "big stick."

Some of the preceding points to a final problem: the ambiguous nature of the previously mentioned "grey zone." Ukraine under Kuchma suffered from "competitive authoritarianism" (Levistsky and Way, 2002). Elections were held; competition was allowed; civic freedoms existed and were respected at least part of the time. True, there were significant lapses, but EU leaders could draft documents noting Ukraine's "democratic progress," something impossible in the case of other countries such as Belarus. Moreover, Kuchma would often invoke the rhetoric of reform and moving towards Europe, thus making it harder for the EU to pull away entirely. In short, one could suggest that the quasi-democratic nature of the Ukrainian state allowed each side to play a game. The EU (and other actors, to be sure), not willing to throw in the towel and admit, among other things, that years of effort and billions in aid did little to produce democracy, clung to the notion that Ukraine possessed some democratic elements, was not as bad as some of its neighbors, and could, with new elections, make a real breakthrough. Ukrainian elites, for their part, were able to present a democratic face to the world, while engaging in manipulation and behind the scenes maneuvers (occasionally not well hidden) to ensure they remain in power. It was better for both sides to act as if the emperor had clothes.

New leadership, new possibilities?

The momentous events in November-December 2004 brought significant changes to Ukraine and in all likelihood suggest that the EU will be more intimately involved with Ukraine than ever before. The main events surrounding the elections are generally well known and are covered elsewhere in this issue, most explicitly by Paul D'Anieri. While one cannot downplay the courage of the demonstrators in Kyiv and other cities who protested for free and fair elections, the EU and its supporting organizations played an important role. Europe had its eyes on these elections throughout 2004, and the OSCE (among other groups) sent thousands of observers to all three rounds of elections. The fact that these outside observers immediately called the first two rounds fraudulent and stated their refusal to recognize Yanukovych's "victory" was a crucial factor that bolstered the claims of Ukrainians who maintained the election had been stolen. After the crowds emerged, European officials, among them Javier Solana of the EU, Alexander Kwasniewski and Lech Walesa of Poland, and Valdas Adamkus of Lithuania played an important role in the mediation of the dispute. Although no one may be entirely happy with the final compromise t hat was reached, the fact that power was transferred from Kuchma to Yushchenko peacefully and with a stamp of democratic legitimacy ranks as Ukraine's most important achievement since the country gained independence.

The dispute over the election, of course, was often portrayed as a struggle between East and West Ukraine and, by extension, a struggle between Russia and the West over influence in the country. Of course, there was a discernable East/West divide in the election results, but, for many Ukrainians, the issue hinged less on regionalism or foreign policy than on democracy, the end of corruption, economic improvement, and establishing themselves as active, empowered citizens as opposed to subjects easily manipulated by the Soviet-style elite. With the new president proudly proclaiming that Ukraine is a European country – a statement that pays homage not only to geography or history but also of shared values of democracy, a crucial component that was missing under the previous administration – one should expect more overtures from Kyiv to Brussels, and, presumably, more attention from Brussels to Kyiv.

There are many reasons for renewed European interest in Ukraine. Most obviously, with the expansion of 2004, Ukraine now borders three EU members. Problems in Ukraine are thus not far away, and Ukraine's immediate neighbors, especially Poland, are prodding Brussels to engage more actively with Kyiv. Some in Europe fear the consequences of "losing" Ukraine to a more authoritarian and assertive Russia. Lech Walesa warned that either Ukraine becomes a democracy or "Russia will absorb it, as it has done with Belarus, and we will have the Soviet Union again, more dangerous this time." (*The Economist*, 2004). Obviously, the prospect of separatism and civil war in a major European country on Europe's doorstep pushed the EU to do what it could to promote a peaceful transfer of power to a new president.

Geo-political concerns aside, however, there is also a new feeling about Ukraine. It is, in the words of one observer, no longer "hopeless" and as such has been "discovered" by Europe (Lukyanov, 2004). Although Yushchenko will have a host of difficulties and Ukraine has much work to do to catch up with its western neighbors, there is a real prospect of both internal democratization and broader engagement with the Western world. Democratic convergence, which was a chimera under the Kuchma regime, is more of a possibility, and one would expect Western "transnational networks" to be encouraged rather than treated with suspicion. As one European observer noted, events in Ukraine may herald the "hour of Europe" and that a nation has arrived "gift-wrapped on our doorstep" (Stephen, 2004). Without question, one can expect more political, economic, and security assistance from Europe to Ukraine in coming years.

Clearly, there is cause for celebration. The "Orange Revolution" may be a case of democratic contagion, albeit one that was 13 years late. One might argue that the "idea" of Europe played a crucial role in motivating Ukrainians to act for democracy, not just in an abstract way but also in the fact that Europe was expanding and they did not want it to end at the Polish-Ukrainian border. Credit can be given as well to notions of convergence, as many of the protestors, especially the student core of the Pora movement, had benefited from contact with European colleagues, especially Otpor in Serbia.[14] Acceptance of democratic, "European" norms, fostered in part through diffuse socialization, as well as EU flags, were clearly on display in Maidan Nezalezhnosti and elsewhere in Ukraine. It is no coincidence that Viktor Yushchenko would announce that the world has seen a "genuinely different Ukraine ... a noble European nation, one that embraces genuine democratic values" (Yushchenko, 2004).

Obviously, one can consider the election of Yushchenko a "victory" for Europe – not only because he will preside over a more pro-European foreign policy than his erstwhile opponent, but also because his elevation to the presidency is a vindication of sorts to European diplomacy, norms, and the sheer attractive pull of the EU. However, the larger issue – Ukraine's place in Europe – is far from settled.

Many in Ukraine believe the time is ripe to offer Ukraine prospective membership in the EU. After all, if Turkey can qualify as a European country, they ask, why not Ukraine? If the EU is serious about partnership with Ukraine, why leave it outside the membership queue? After the momentous events at the end of 2004, many would assert that the refusal of the EU to reconsider membership for Ukraine and at least open the door to prospective membership would be a slap in the face to the millions of Ukrainians inspired by the values of Europe.

Indeed, it is a bit ironic that, given results in 2004 that far exceeded outside expectations, the debate on EU membership for Ukraine may move no-

---

14   One allegation was that Pora was financed by the CIA. If true, this may also qualify as a "transnational network," albeit not the type usually conceived by theorists of democratization.

where. Yes, Kuchma is gone, but, one could add, Ukraine is still far from meeting EU criteria: average monthly income is under $100; life expectancy of a Ukrainian male born today is 62 years; it is a conduit for drugs and illegal arms shipments; women destined for involuntary servitude are a big export; and the cost of modernizing its economy would be staggering. Tony Judt, recognizing that "This [Ukraine] is Europe," quickly adds, "Nonetheless, Ukraine is not part of the European Union, and it is not going to be" (Judt, 2004). Even before the crisis was finally resolved, EU officials were backing away from any pledge to put membership on the table, suggesting that "Membership is not our only resource." (*Wall Street Journal*, 2004). Part of European reticence can be explained by enlargement fatigue and that the EU already has Turkish accession on its agenda. Moreover, Yushchenko will have much to do to unite the country and to root out the corruption that was endemic during the Kuchma years. His success is far from assured. Ukraine is also a big, relatively poor country, and its historical ties to Moscow may also make Brussels reluctant to offer it membership. Many of these issues, of course, are unaffected by the "Orange Revolution." Timothy Garton Ash suggests that there is a rather ugly subtext to some European reservations and even criticism of developments in Kyiv: "Why won't all these bloody, semi-barbarian, East Europeans leave us alone, to go on living happily ever after in our right, tight, little West European [or merely British] paradise?" (Ash, 2004).

Obviously, Ukrainian membership would have costs, and, coupled with possible Turkish accession in the coming decade, one might fairly conclude that the bold vision of an "ever closer union" of European states would be jeopardized by including more countries. Of course, this did not prevent the 2004 expansion, and one could argue that if Europe's core identity is evolving into a "rights-based" community with universalistic appeal, then expansion to all geographically qualified candidates is required (Sjursen, 2002). Even granting the probable costs of expansion, however, one should add that Ukrainians are not asking for membership today – only the admission that Ukraine could be eligible for membership and will be treated like an aspiring member Turkey, Croatia), not Morocco or Algeria.

From the perspective of democratization and reform in Ukraine, such a development should be welcomed. First, the status quo is untenable. This was true before November 2004 and is even truer today. European officials cannot come to Kyiv repeating the same messages on human and civil rights, democracy, European values, and economic reform without offering Ukrainians something substantial. True, the EU can help Ukraine gain WTO membership, declare Ukraine a market economy (thus removing some trade barriers), and conclude an Association Agreement. However, expectations in Kyiv are much higher – anything less than the prospect of membership, which has been granted to Turkey, would be a disappointment. Second, Europe must recognize the changes ushered in by the 2004 elections. If, in the summer of 2004 at the EU-Ukraine Summit, observers could speak of a "clash of civilizations" between the two sides and that Ukrainian integration into EU structures was at a "dead end" (Kuzio, 2004), the EU must do something substantial to acknowledge the new situation and revive the integration process. Third, and most importantly, one must recognize that the success of democratization in Ukraine is far from assured. Parliamentary elections in 2006 will be important, all the more so in light of constitutional changes, and the expectations on Yushchenko and his allies are high. The country is very divided, and many Yanukovych voters believe their candidate was robbed of victory. Yushchenko must tread carefully and will face strong opposition, and outside support will be crucial, particularly on economic and legal reforms. As in other cases in Southern and Eastern Europe, the impetus for reform and change must come from within, but the EU can play an important role acting as a guardrail to insure that the reforms stay on track (Kubicek, 2003a). The fact that the EU Parliament voted 467-19 in January 2005 to give Ukraine a "clear, European perspective, possibly leading to EU membership" is a good first start, although the European Commission and Council of Ministers have to date been reluctant to make any similar statement.

  This is where conditionality comes into play, a strategy that has worked elsewhere but has not been employed with respect to Ukraine. True, circumstances were hardly auspicious with Kuchma, but, under Yushchenko, presumably one has a leader with whom Europe "can do business." "Declarative Europeanization" was a constant in Ukrainian policy for nearly a decade, and now there is a new elite that promises to make Europeanization a reality. In order for Yushchenko and company to be successful, Europe must help. Conditionality, in addition to providing a benchmark for reforms, offers the prospects of substantial rewards for embarking on a program that will be lengthy and difficult. To prevent backsliding, it is important that the EU – through use of conditionality – support reform efforts and offer tangible, material inducement for change.

At present, one witnesses a profound and rather disturbing paradox. On the one hand, the prospect of joining the EU has proven to be one of the most effective tools in persuading regimes to change institutions, laws, and even, perhaps, values. One has seen "reluctant democratizers" in Latvia, Slovakia, Romania, Croatia, and Turkey accede to EU demands if the stakes were high enough, which, typically, meant membership in the EU itself (Kubicek, 2003a). The change of leadership in Ukraine fits into the mold of these earlier cases. In other words, a regime that truly was "hopeless" and impervious to persuasion and blandishments is gone, and expectations of the new regime are quite, perhaps unrealistically, high. It will need help and incentives, ones that are easily understood and visible to voters. Yet, there are concerns that Ukraine will "lapse back into being a faraway country of which they [Westerners] know little" (*The Economist*, 2005). Perhaps it would be too much to hope for that Europe would immediately open the door to Ukraine when, for insistence, it took several iterations to do the same for Turkey. In the midst of the "Orange Revolution," the European Commission stressed that membership was not to be on the agenda for Ukraine.

However, the EU needs to recognize that Yushchenko's victory is less the ending and more the beginning for democratization in Ukraine. While Europe can congratulate itself on the outcome to date, the "hour of Europe" is not over. Europe has strong cards to play to help further democracy in Ukraine. It largely neglected Ukraine before. As recent events demonstrate, this is a country that Europe can neglect and exclude only at its own risk.

References

Arel, D. 2001. "Kuchmagate and the demise of Ukraine's geopolitical bluff." *East European Constitutional Review*, 10 (Spring/Summer): 54-59.

Ash, T.G. 2004. "Bitter lemons." *The Guardian* (2 December).

Bush, J. 2001. "Whither Ukraine?" *Business Central Europe Magazine* (June), available at http://www.artukraine.com/buildukraine/whitherukr.htm.

Cameron, F. 2000. "Relations between the European Union and Ukraine." In: Clem, J., Popson, N. (eds.), *Ukraine and its western neighbors*. Woodrow Wilson Center, Washington, DC, pp. 79-92.

Center for Peace, Conversion, and Foreign Policy of Ukraine (Kyiv), 2001. "The problem of changing the non-integration status of Ukraine in its relations with the European Union." *Occasional Report*, 31 (September).

Checkel, J. 1999. "Why comply? Social learning and European Identity change." *International Organization*, 55: 553-588.

Checkel, J. 2001. "Norms, institutions, and national identity in contemporary Europe." *International Studies Quarterly*, 43: 83-144.

Chudowsky, V., Kuzio, T. 2003. "Does public opinion matter in Ukraine: the case of foreign policy." *Communist and Post-Communist Studies*, 36 (3): 273-290.

Cooley, A. 2003. "Western conditions and domestic choices: the influence of external actors on the post-Communist transition." In: Freedom House. (ed.), *Nations in transit 2003*. Rowman and Littlefield, Lanham, MD, pp. 25-38.

Cortell, A., Davis, J. 1996. "How do international institutions matter? The domestic impact of international rules and norms." *International Studies Quarterly*, 40: 451-478.

Cortell, A., Davis, J. 2000. "Understanding the domestic impact of international norms: a research agenda." *International Studies Review*, 2: 65-87.

Crawford, G. 1997. "Foreign aid and political conditionality: issues of effectiveness and consistency." *Democratization*, 4: 69-108.

Garnett, S. 1997. *Keystone in the arch: Ukraine in the emerging security environment of Central and Eastern Europe*. Carnegie Endowment, Washington, DC.

Garnett, S. 1999. "Like oil and water: Ukraine's external westernization and internal stagnation." In: Kuzio, T., et al. (eds.), *State and institution building in Ukraine*. St. Martin's, New York, pp. 107-133.

Grabbe, H., Hughes, K. 1999. "Central and east European views on EU enlargement: political debates and public opinion." In: Henderson, K. (ed.), *Back to Europe: Central and Eastern Europe and the European Union*. London, UCL Press.

Grugel, J. (ed.), 1999. *Democracy without borders: transnationalization and conditionality in new democracies*. Routledge, London.

Huntington, S. 1991. *The third wave: democratization in the late twentieth century*. University of Oklahoma Press, Norman.

IFES (International Foundation for Electoral Systems). 2003. "Public opinion in Ukraine 2003." Report of national survey available at http://www.ifes.org/research_comm/ surveys/Ukraine_Survey_2003_ English.pdf.
Judt, T. 2004. "The eastern front, 2004." *The New York Times* (weekend section), (5 December): 13.
Kopstein, J., Reilly, D. 2000. "Geographic diffusion and the transformation of the postcommunist world." *World Politics*, 53 (1): 1-37.
Kubicek, P. (Ed.), 2003a. *The European Union and democratization*. Routledge, London.
Kubicek, P. (Ed.), 2003b. "U.S.-Ukrainian relations: from engagement to estrangement." *Problems of Post-Communism*, 50 (6): 3-10.
Kuzio, T. 2003. "EU and Ukraine – a turning point in 2004." European Union Institute for Security Studies (Paris), *Occasional Paper*, 47 (November).
Kuzio, T. 12 July 2004. "EU-Ukrainian relations hampered by clash of civilization." *Eurasia Daily Monitor*, 1 (49).
Levistsky, S., Way, L. 2002. "The rise of competitive authoritarianism." *Journal of Democracy*, 13 (2): 51-65.
Lukyanov, F. 2004. "Ukraine's European rebirth." *Gazeta.ru*, (2 December), available at http:// www.gazeta.ru.
Maksymiuk, J. 2003. "Kuchma signs accord on CIS single economic zone with 'reservations'." *RFE/RL Poland, Belarus, and Ukraine Report*, 5 (35) (23 September).
Mendelson, S., Glenn, J. (eds.), 2002. *The power and limits of NGOs*. Columbia University Press, New York.
Moroney, J.P. 2001. "Ukraine's European choice." In: Kis, T., Makayrk, I., Mychajlyszyn, N. (eds.), *Towards a new Ukraine III: geopolitical imperatives of Ukraine: regional contexts*. Ottawa University Ukrainian Studies, Ottawa, pp. 97-124.
Patten, C. 2001. Speech at the European Parliament, 14 March, available at http://europa.eu.int/comm./ external_relations/news/patten/speech_01_121.htm.
Pavliuk, O. 1999. *The European Union and Ukraine: the need for new vision*. East-West Institute, Kyiv.
Pavliuk, O. 2001a. "Ukraine and the EU: the risk of being excluded." In: Kempe, I. (ed.), *Beyond EU enlargement*. Bertelsmann Foundation, Gutersloh, pp. 65-84.
Pavliuk, O. 2001b. *Unfulfilling partnership: Ukraine and the West, 1991-2001*. East-West Institute, Kyiv.
Pridham, G. 1994. "The international dimension of democratization: theory, practice, and inter-regional comparisons." In: Pridham, G., Herring, E., Sanford, G., et al. (eds.), *Building democracy? The international dimension of democratization in Eastern Europe*. Leicester University Press, London, pp. 1-29.
Pridham, G. 2000. *The dynamics of democratization*. Continuum, New York.
Pridham, G. 2001. "Uneasy democratization: pariah regimes, political conditionality, and reborn transitions in Central and Eastern Europe." *Democratization*, 8 (1): 65-94.

Reiter, D. 2001. "Why NATO enlargement does not spread democracy." *International Security*, 25 (1): 41-67.
Risse, T., Sikkink, K. 1999. "The socialization of international human rights norms into domestic practices: introduction." In: Risse, T., Ropp, S., Sikkink, K. (eds.), *The power of human rights: international norms and domestic change*. Cambridge University Press, Cambridge, pp. 1-38.
Risse, T., Ropp, S., Sikkink, K. (eds.), 1999. *The power of human rights: international norms and domestic change*. Cambridge University Press, Cambridge.
Schneider, K. 2001. "The Partnership and Co-operation Agreement (PCA) between Ukraine and the EU – idea and reality." In: Hoffman, L., Mollers, F. (eds.), *Ukraine on the road to Europe*. Physica-Verlag, Heidelberg, pp. 66-78.
Selyuk, E. 2003. "Much ado about nothing." *The NIS Observed* (9 October).
Sjursen, H. 2002. "Why expand? The question of legitimacy and justification in the EU's enlargement policy." *Journal of Common Market Studies*, 40: 491-513.
Smith, K. 1998. "The use of political conditionality in the EU's relations with third countries: how effective?" *European Foreign Affairs Review* 3: 253-274.
Solchanyk, R. 2001. *Ukraine and Russia: the post-Soviet transition*. Rowman and Littlefield, Lanham, MD.
Stephen, C. 2004. "Will Ukraine finally be 'the hour of Europe'?" *The Scotsman* (3 December).
Whitehead, L. 1996. "Democracy by convergence: southern Europe." In: Whitehead, L. (ed.), *The international dimension of democratization*. Oxford University Press, Oxford, pp. 261-284.
Whitehead, L. 2001. "The enlargement of the European Union: a 'risky' form of democracy promotion." In: Whitehead, L. (ed.), *The international dimensions of democratization, expandeded*. Oxford University Press, Oxford, pp. 415-442.
Wolczuk, K. 2003. "Ukraine's policy towards the European Union: a case of 'declarative Europeanization'." Paper for the Stefan Batory Foundation Project, The Enlarged EU and Ukraine: New Relations.
Yushchenko, V. 2004. "Our Ukraine." *Wall Street Journal* (3 December).
The Economist. 1993. "You'd be nervous living next to a bear. 15 May," pp. 21-23.
The Economist. 2004. "Charlemagne: Another faraway country." 4 December, p. 54.
The Economist 2005. "The future is orange." 1 January, pp. 10-11.
Kyiv Post. 2003. "Statement by the European Union on Media Freedom and the Gongadze Case." 18 September.
Nezavisimaia gazeta. 2003. 21 October, p. 5.
Uriadovyi Kur'ier (Kyiv). 1998. 18 April.
Wall Street Journal. 2004. Ukraine Presents Membership Quandary for the European Union, 8 December, p. A11.
Ukrainska Pravda. 2004. 12 March.

Zerkalo nedeli (Kyiv). 2000. 19 September.

SOVIET AND POST-SOVIET POLITICS AND SOCIETY

Edited by Dr. Andreas Umland

ISSN 1614-3515

1   *Андреас Умланд (ред.)*
    Воплощение Европейской конвенции по правам человека в России
    Философские, юридические и эмпирические исследования
    ISBN 3-89821-387-0

2   *Christian Wipperfürth*
    Russland – ein vertrauenswürdiger Partner?
    Grundlagen, Hintergründe und Praxis gegenwärtiger russischer Außenpolitik
    Mit einem Vorwort von Heinz Timmermann
    ISBN 3-89821-401-X

3   *Manja Hussner*
    Die Übernahme internationalen Rechts in die russische und deutsche Rechtsordnung
    Eine vergleichende Analyse zur Völkerrechtsfreundlichkeit der Verfassungen der Russländischen Föderation und der Bundesrepublik Deutschland
    Mit einem Vorwort von Rainer Arnold
    ISBN 3-89821-438-9

4   *Matthew Tejada*
    Bulgaria's Democratic Consolidation and the Kozloduy Nuclear Power Plant (KNPP)
    The Unattainability of Closure
    With a foreword by Richard J. Crampton
    ISBN 3-89821-439-7

5   *Марк Григорьевич Меерович*
    Квадратные метры, определяющие сознание
    Государственная жилищная политика в СССР. 1921 – 1941 гг
    ISBN 3-89821-474-5

6   *Andrei P. Tsygankov, Pavel A. Tsygankov (Eds.)*
    New Directions in Russian International Studies
    ISBN 3-89821-422-2

7   *Марк Григорьевич Меерович*
    Как власть народ к труду приучала
    Жилище в СССР – средство управления людьми. 1917 – 1941 гг.
    С предисловием Елены Осокиной
    ISBN 3-89821-495-8

8   *David J. Galbreath*
    Nation-Building and Minority Politics in Post-Socialist States
    Interests, Influence and Identities in Estonia and Latvia
    With a foreword by David J. Smith
    ISBN 3-89821-467-2

9   *Алексей Юрьевич Безугольный*
    Народы Кавказа в Вооруженных силах СССР в годы Великой Отечественной войны 1941-1945 гг.
    С предисловием Николая Бугая
    ISBN 3-89821-475-3

10 *Вячеслав Лихачев и Владимир Прибыловский (ред.)*
    Русское Национальное Единство, 1990-2000. В 2-х томах
    ISBN 3-89821-523-7

11 *Николай Бугай (ред.)*
    Народы стран Балтии в условиях сталинизма (1940-е – 1950-е годы)
    Документированная история
    ISBN 3-89821-525-3

12 *Ingmar Bredies (Hrsg.)*
    Zur Anatomie der Orange Revolution in der Ukraine
    Wechsel des Elitenregimes oder Triumph des Parlamentarismus?
    ISBN 3-89821-524-5

13 *Anastasia V. Mitrofanova*
    The Politicization of Russian Orthodoxy
    Actors and Ideas
    With a foreword by William C. Gay
    ISBN 3-89821-481-8

14 *Nathan D. Larson*
    Alexander Solzhenitsyn and the Russo-Jewish Question
    ISBN 3-89821-483-4

15 *Guido Houben*
    Kulturpolitik und Ethnizität
    Staatliche Kunstförderung im Russland der neunziger Jahre
    Mit einem Vorwort von Gert Weisskirchen
    ISBN 3-89821-542-3

16 *Leonid Luks*
    Der russische „Sonderweg"?
    Aufsätze zur neuesten Geschichte Russlands im europäischen Kontext
    ISBN 3-89821-496-6

17 *Евгений Мороз*
    История «Мёртвой воды» – от страшной сказки к большой политике
    Политическое неоязычество в постсоветской России
    ISBN 3-89821-551-2

18 *Александр Верховский и Галина Кожевникова (ред.)*
    Этническая и религиозная интолерантность в российских СМИ
    Результаты мониторинга 2001-2004 гг.
    ISBN 3-89821-569-5

19 *Christian Ganzer*
    Sowjetisches Erbe und ukrainische Nation
    Das Museum der Geschichte des Zaporoger Kosakentums auf der Insel Chortycja
    Mit einem Vorwort von Frank Golczewski
    ISBN 3-89821-504-0

20 Эльза-Баир Гучинова
   Помнить нельзя забыть
   Антропология депортационной травмы калмыков
   С предисловием Кэролайн Хамфри
   ISBN 3-89821-506-7

21 Юлия Лидерман
   Мотивы «проверки» и «испытания» в постсоветской культуре
   Советское прошлое в российском кинематографе 1990-х годов
   С предисловием Евгения Марголита
   ISBN 3-89821-511-3

22 Tanya Lokshina, Ray Thomas, Mary Mayer (Eds.)
   The Imposition of a Fake Political Settlement in the Northern Caucasus
   The 2003 Chechen Presidential Election
   ISBN 3-89821-436-2

23 Timothy McCajor Hall, Rosie Read (Eds.)
   Changes in the Heart of Europe
   Recent Ethnographies of Czechs, Slovaks, Roma, and Sorbs
   With an afterword by Zdeněk Salzmann
   ISBN 3-89821-606-3

24 Christian Autengruber
   Die politischen Parteien in Bulgarien und Rumänien
   Eine vergleichende Analyse seit Beginn der 90er Jahre
   Mit einem Vorwort von Dorothée de Nève
   ISBN 3-89821-476-1

25 Annette Freyberg-Inan with Radu Cristescu
   The Ghosts in Our Classrooms, or: John Dewey Meets Ceauşescu
   The Promise and the Failures of Civic Education in Romania
   ISBN 3-89821-416-8

26 John B. Dunlop
   The 2002 Dubrovka and 2004 Beslan Hostage Crises
   A Critique of Russian Counter-Terrorism
   With a foreword by Donald N. Jensen
   ISBN 3-89821-608-X

27 Peter Koller
   Das touristische Potenzial von Kam''janec'-Podil's'kyj
   Eine fremdenverkehrsgeographische Untersuchung der Zukunftsperspektiven und Maßnahmenplanung zur Destinationsentwicklung des „ukrainischen Rothenburg"
   Mit einem Vorwort von Kristiane Klemm
   ISBN 3-89821-640-3

28 Françoise Daucé, Elisabeth Sieca-Kozlowski (Eds.)
   Dedovshchina in the Post-Soviet Military
   Hazing of Russian Army Conscripts in a Comparative Perspective
   With a foreword by Dale Herspring
   ISBN 3-89821-616-0

29   *Florian Strasser*
     Zivilgesellschaftliche Einflüsse auf die Orange Revolution
     Die gewaltlose Massenbewegung und die ukrainische Wahlkrise 2004
     Mit einem Vorwort von Egbert Jahn
     ISBN 3-89821-648-9

30   *Rebecca S. Katz*
     The Georgian Regime Crisis of 2003-2004
     A Case Study in Post-Soviet Media Representation of Politics, Crime and Corruption
     ISBN 3-89821-413-3

31   *Vladimir Kantor*
     Willkür oder Freiheit
     Beiträge zur russischen Geschichtsphilosophie
     Ediert von Dagmar Herrmann sowie mit einem Vorwort versehen von Leonid Luks
     ISBN 3-89821-589-X

32   *Laura A. Victoir*
     The Russian Land Estate Today
     A Case Study of Cultural Politics in Post-Soviet Russia
     With a foreword by Priscilla Roosevelt
     ISBN 3-89821-426-5

33   *Ivan Katchanovski*
     Cleft Countries
     Regional Political Divisions and Cultures in Post-Soviet Ukraine and Moldova
     With a foreword by Francis Fukuyama
     ISBN 3-89821-558-X

34   *Florian Mühlfried*
     Postsowjetische Feiern
     Das Georgische Bankett im Wandel
     Mit einem Vorwort von Kevin Tuite
     ISBN 3-89821-601-2

35   *Roger Griffin, Werner Loh, Andreas Umland (Eds.)*
     Fascism Past and Present, West and East
     An International Debate on Concepts and Cases in the Comparative Study of the Extreme Right
     With an afterword by Walter Laqueur
     ISBN 3-89821-674-8

36   *Sebastian Schlegel*
     Der „Weiße Archipel"
     Sowjetische Atomstädte 1945-1991
     Mit einem Geleitwort von Thomas Bohn
     ISBN 3-89821-679-9

37   *Vyacheslav Likhachev*
     Political Anti-Semitism in Post-Soviet Russia
     Actors and Ideas in 1991-2003
     Edited and translated from Russian by Eugene Veklerov
     ISBN 3-89821-529-6

38 Josette Baer (Ed.)
    Preparing Liberty in Central Europe
    Political Texts from the Spring of Nations 1848 to the Spring of Prague 1968
    With a foreword by Zdeněk V. David
    ISBN 3-89821-546-6

39 Михаил Лукьянов
    Российский консерватизм и реформа, 1907-1914
    С предисловием Марка Д. Стейнберга
    ISBN 3-89821-503-2

40 Nicola Melloni
    Market Without Economy
    The 1998 Russian Financial Crisis
    With a foreword by Eiji Furukawa
    ISBN 3-89821-407-9

41 Dmitrij Chmelnizki
    Die Architektur Stalins
    Bd. 1: Studien zu Ideologie und Stil
    Bd. 2: Bilddokumentation
    Mit einem Vorwort von Bruno Flierl
    ISBN 3-89821-515-6

42 Katja Yafimava
    Post-Soviet Russian-Belarussian Relationships
    The Role of Gas Transit Pipelines
    With a foreword by Jonathan P. Stern
    ISBN 3-89821-655-1

43 Boris Chavkin
    Verflechtungen der deutschen und russischen Zeitgeschichte
    Aufsätze und Archivfunde zu den Beziehungen Deutschlands und der Sowjetunion von 1917 bis 1991
    Ediert von Markus Edlinger sowie mit einem Vorwort versehen von Leonid Luks
    ISBN 3-89821-756-6

44 Anastasija Grynenko in Zusammenarbeit mit Claudia Dathe
    Die Terminologie des Gerichtswesens der Ukraine und Deutschlands im Vergleich
    Eine übersetzungswissenschaftliche Analyse juristischer Fachbegriffe im Deutschen, Ukrainischen und Russischen
    Mit einem Vorwort von Ulrich Hartmann
    ISBN 3-89821-691-8

45 Anton Burkov
    The Impact of the European Convention on Human Rights on Russian Law
    Legislation and Application in 1996-2006
    With a foreword by Françoise Hampson
    ISBN 978-3-89821-639-5

46 Stina Torjesen, Indra Overland (Eds.)
    International Election Observers in Post-Soviet Azerbaijan
    Geopolitical Pawns or Agents of Change?
    ISBN 978-3-89821-743-9

47   *Taras Kuzio*
      Ukraine – Crimea – Russia
      Triangle of Conflict
      ISBN 978-3-89821-761-3

48   *Claudia Šabić*
      "Ich erinnere mich nicht, aber L'viv!"
      Zur Funktion kultureller Faktoren für die Institutionalisierung und Entwicklung einer ukrainischen Region
      Mit einem Vorwort von Melanie Tatur
      ISBN 978-3-89821-752-1

49   *Marlies Bilz*
      Tatarstan in der Transformation
      Nationaler Diskurs und Politische Praxis 1988-1994
      Mit einem Vorwort von Frank Golczewski
      ISBN 978-3-89821-722-4

50   *Марлен Ларюэль (ред.)*
      Современные интерпретации русского национализма
      ISBN 978-3-89821-795-8

51   *Sonja Schüler*
      Die ethnische Dimension der Armut
      Roma im postsozialistischen Rumänien
      Mit einem Vorwort von Anton Sterbling
      ISBN 978-3-89821-776-7

52   *Галина Кожевникова*
      Радикальный национализм в России и противодействие ему
      Сборник докладов Центра «Сова» за 2004-2007 гг.
      С предисловием Александра Верховского
      ISBN 978-3-89821-721-7

53   *Галина Кожевникова и Владимир Прибыловский*
      Российская власть в биографиях I
      Высшие должностные лица РФ в 2004 г.
      ISBN 978-3-89821-796-5

54   *Галина Кожевникова и Владимир Прибыловский*
      Российская власть в биографиях II
      Члены Правительства РФ в 2004 г.
      ISBN 978-3-89821-797-2

55   *Галина Кожевникова и Владимир Прибыловский*
      Российская власть в биографиях III
      Руководители федеральных служб и агентств РФ в 2004 г.
      ISBN 978-3-89821-798-9

56   *Ileana Petroniu*
      Privatisierung in Transformationsökonomien
      Determinanten der Restrukturierungs-Bereitschaft am Beispiel Polens, Rumäniens und der Ukraine
      Mit einem Vorwort von Rainer W. Schäfer
      ISBN 978-3-89821-790-3

57 Christian Wipperfürth
    Russland und seine GUS-Nachbarn
    Hintergründe, aktuelle Entwicklungen und Konflikte in einer ressourcenreichen Region
    ISBN 978-3-89821-801-6

58 Togzhan Kassenova
    From Antagonism to Partnership
    The Uneasy Path of the U.S.-Russian Cooperative Threat Reduction
    With a foreword by Christoph Bluth
    ISBN 978-3-89821-707-1

59 Alexander Höllwerth
    Das sakrale eurasische Imperium des Aleksandr Dugin
    Eine Diskursanalyse zum postsowjetischen russischen Rechtsextremismus
    Mit einem Vorwort von Dirk Uffelmann
    ISBN 978-3-89821-813-9

60 Олег Рябов
    «Россия-Матушка»
    Национализм, гендер и война в России XX века
    С предисловием Елены Гощило
    ISBN 978-3-89821-487-2

61 Ivan Maistrenko
    Borot'bism
    A Chapter in the History of the Ukrainian Revolution
    With a new introduction by Chris Ford
    Translated by George S. N. Luckyj with the assistance of Ivan L. Rudnytsky
    ISBN 978-3-89821-697-5

62 Maryna Romanets
    Anamorphosic Texts and Reconfigured Visions
    Improvised Traditions in Contemporary Ukrainian and Irish Literature
    ISBN 978-3-89821-576-3

63 Paul D'Anieri and Taras Kuzio (Eds.)
    Aspects of the Orange Revolution I
    Democratization and Elections in Post-Communist Ukraine
    ISBN 978-3-89821-698-2

64 Bohdan Harasymiw in collaboration with Oleh S. Ilnytzkyj (Eds.)
    Aspects of the Orange Revolution II
    Information and Manipulation Strategies in the 2004 Ukrainian Presidential Elections
    ISBN 978-3-89821-699-9

65 Ingmar Bredies, Andreas Umland and Valentin Yakushik (Eds.)
    Aspects of the Orange Revolution III
    The Context and Dynamics of the 2004 Ukrainian Presidential Elections
    ISBN 978-3-89821-803-0

66 Ingmar Bredies, Andreas Umland and Valentin Yakushik (Eds.)
    Aspects of the Orange Revolution IV
    Foreign Assistance and Civic Action in the 2004 Ukrainian Presidential Elections
    ISBN 978-3-89821-808-5

67 *Ingmar Bredies, Andreas Umland and Valentin Yakushik (Eds.)*
    Aspects of the Orange Revolution V
    Institutional Observation Reports on the 2004 Ukrainian Presidential Elections
    ISBN 978-3-89821-809-2

68 *Taras Kuzio (Ed.)*
    Aspects of the Orange Revolution VI
    Post-Communist Democratic Revolutions in Comparative Perspective
    ISBN 978-3-89821-820-7

FORTHCOMING (MANUSCRIPT WORKING TITLES)

Stephanie Solowyda
Biography of Semen Frank
ISBN 3-89821-457-5

Margaret Dikovitskaya
Arguing with the Photographs
Russian Imperial Colonial Attitudes in Visual Culture
ISBN 3-89821-462-1

Stefan Ihrig
Welche Nation in welcher Geschichte?
Eigen- und Fremdbilder der nationalen Diskurse in der Historiographie und den Geschichtsbüchern in der Republik Moldova, 1991-2003
ISBN 3-89821-466-4

Sergei M. Plekhanov
Russian Nationalism in the Age of Globalization
ISBN 3-89821-484-2

Robert Pyrah
Cultural Memory and Identity
Literature, Criticism and the Theatre in Lviv - Lwow - Lemberg, 1918-1939 and in post-Soviet Ukraine
ISBN 3-89821-505-9

Andrei Rogatchevski
The National-Bolshevik Party
ISBN 3-89821-532-6

Zenon Victor Wasyliw
Soviet Culture in the Ukrainian Village
The Transformation of Everyday Life and Values, 1921-1928
ISBN 3-89821-536-9

Nele Sass
Das gegenkulturelle Milieu im postsowjetischen Russland
ISBN 3-89821-543-1

Julie Elkner
Maternalism versus Militarism
The Russian Soldiers' Mothers Committee
ISBN 3-89821-575-X

Alexandra Kamarowsky
Russia's Post-crisis Growth
ISBN 3-89821-580-6

Martin Friessnegg
Das Problem der Medienfreiheit in Russland seit dem Ende der Sowjetunion
ISBN 3-89821-588-1

Nikolaj Nikiforowitsch Borobow
Führende Persönlichkeiten in Russland vom 12. bis 20 Jhd.: Ein Lexikon
Aus dem Russischen übersetzt und herausgegeben von Eberhard Schneider
ISBN 3-89821-638-1

Martin Malek, Anna Schor-Tschudnowskaja
Tschetschenien und die Gleichgültigkeit Europas
Russlands Kriege und die Agonie der Idee der Menschenrechte
ISBN 3-89821-676-4

Andreas Langenohl
Political Culture and Criticism of Society
Intellectual Articulations in Post-Soviet Russia
ISBN 3-89821-709-4

Thomas Borén
Meeting Places in Transformation
ISBN 3-89821-739-6

Lars Löckner
Sowjetrussland in der Beurteilung der Emigrantenzeitung 'Rul', 1920-1924
ISBN 3-89821-741-8

Ekaterina Taratuta
The Red Line of Construction
Semantics and Mythology of a Siberian Heliopolis
ISBN 3-89821-742-6

Bernd Kappenberg
Zeichen setzen für Europa
Der Gebrauch europäischer lateinischer Sonderzeichen in der deutschen Öffentlichkeit
ISBN 3-89821-749-3

David Rupp
Die Rußländische Föderation und die russischsprachigen Minderheiten im "Nahen Ausland"
ISBN 3-89821-778-7

Tim Bohse
Die Transformation der postsowjetischen russischen Lokalpolitik am Beispiel der Stadt Kaliningrad
ISBN 3-89821-782-5

Julia Kusznir
Der politische Einfluss von Wirtschafts-eliten in russischen Regionen 1992 bis 2005
Eine Analyse am Beispiel der Erdöl und Erdgasindustrie
ISBN 978-389821-821-4

Alena Vysotskaya
Die Politik Russlands und Belarus hinsichtlich der Osterweiterung der Europäischen Union
Die Minderheitenfrage und das Problem der Freizügigkeit des Personenverkehrs
ISBN 978-389821-822-1

Siegbert Klee, Martin Sandhop, Oxana Schwajka, Andreas Umland
Elitenbildung in der Postsowjetischen Ukraine
ISBN 978-389821-829-0

Natalya Ketenci
The effect of location on the performance of Kazakhstani industrial enterprises in the transition period
ISBN 978-389821-831-3

Quotes from reviews of SPPS volumes:

On vol. 1 – *The Implementation of the ECHR in Russia*: "Full of examples, experiences and valuable observations which could provide the basis for new strategies."
Diana Schmidt, *Неприкосновенный запас*, 2005

On vol. 2 – *Putins Russland*: "Wipperfürth draws attention to little known facts. For instance, the Russians have still more positive feelings towards Germany than to any other non-Slavic country."
Oldag Kaspar, *Süddeutsche Zeitung*, 2005

On vol. 3 – *Die Übernahme internationalen Rechts in die russische Rechtsordnung*: "Hussner's is an interesting, detailed and, at the same time, focused study which deals with all relevant aspects and contains insights into contemporary Russian legal thought."
Herbert Küpper, *Jahrbuch für Ostrecht*, 2005

On vol. 5 – *Квадратные метры, определяющие сознание*: „Meerovich provides a study that will be of considerable value to housing specialists and policy analysts."
Christina Varga-Harris, *Slavic Review*, 2006

On vol. 6 – *New Directions in Russian International Studies*: "A helpful step in the direction of an overdue dialogue between Western and Russian IR scholarly communities."
Diana Schmidt, *Europe-Asia Studies*, 2006

On vol. 8 – *Nation-Building and Minority Politics in Post-Socialist States:* "Galbreath's book is an admirable and craftsmanlike piece of work, and should be read by all specialists interested in the Baltic area."
Andrejs Plakans, *Slavic Review*, 2007

On vol. 9 – *Народы Кавказа в Вооружённых силах СССР:* "In this superb new book, Bezugolnyi skillfully fashions an accurate and candid record of how and why the Soviet Union mobilized and employed the various ethnic groups in the Caucasus region in the Red Army's World War II effort."
David J. Glantz, *Journal of Slavic Military Studies*, 2006

On vol. 10 – *Русское Национальное Единство*: "A work that is likely to remain the definitive study of the Russian National Unity for a very long time."
Mischa Gabowitsch, *e-Extreme*, 2006

On vol. 14 – *Aleksandr Solzhenitsyn and the Modern Russo-Jewish Question*: "Larson has written a well-balanced survey of Solzhenitsyn's writings on Russian-Jewish relations."
Nikolai Butkevich, *e-Extreme*, 2006

On vol. 16 – *Der russische Sonderweg?:* "Luks's remarkable knowledge of the history of this wide territory from the Elbe to the Pacific Ocean and his life experience give his observations a particular sharpness and his judgements an exceptional weight."
Peter Krupnikow, *Mitteilungen aus dem baltischen Leben*, 2006

On vol. 17 – *История «Мёртвой воды»*: "Moroz provides one of the best available surveys of Russian neo-paganism."
Mischa Gabowitsch, *e-Extreme*, 2006

On vol. 18 – *Этническая и религиозная интолерантность в российских СМИ*: "A constructive contribution to a crucial debate about media-endorsed intolerance which has once again flared up in Russia."
Mischa Gabowitsch, *e-Extreme*, 2006

On vol. 25 – *The Ghosts in Our Classroom*: "Freyberg-Inan's well-researched and incisive monograph, balanced and informed about Romanian education in general, should be required reading for those Eurocrats who have shaped Romanian spending priorities since 2000."
Tom Gallagher, *Slavic Review*, 2006

On vol. 26 – *The 2002 Dubrovka and 2004 Beslan Hostage Crises:* "Dunlop's analysis will help to draw Western attention to the plight of those who have suffered by these terrorist acts, and the importance, for all Russians, of uncovering the truth of about what happened."
Amy Knight, *Times Literary Supplement*, 2006

On vol. 29 – *Zivilgesellschaftliche Einflüsse auf die Orange Revolution*: „Strasser's study constitutes an outstanding empirical analysis and well-grounded location of the subject within theory."
Heiko Pleines, *Osteuropa*, 2006

On vol. 34 – *Postsowjetische Feiern*: "Mühlfried's book contains not only a solid ethnographic study, but also points at some problems emerging from Georgia's prevalent understanding of culture."
Godula Kosack, *Anthropos*, 2007

On vol. 35 – *Fascism Past and Present, West and East*: "Committed students will find much of interest in these sometimes barbed exchanges."
Robert Paxton, *Journal of Global History*, 2007

Series Subscription

Please enter my subscription to the series *Soviet and Post-Soviet Politics and Society*, ISSN 1614-3515, as follows:

❐ complete series   OR   ❐ English-language titles
                                                ❐ German-language titles
                                                ❐ Russian-language titles

starting with
❐ volume # 1
❐ volume # ___
    ❐ please also include the following volumes: #___, ___, ___, ___, ___, ___, ___
❐ the next volume being published
    ❐ please also include the following volumes: #___, ___, ___, ___, ___, ___, ___

❐ 1 copy per volume   OR   ❐ ___ copies per volume

Subscription within Germany:
You will receive every volume at 1st publication at the regular bookseller's price – incl. s & h and VAT.
Payment:
❐ Please bill me for every volume.
❐ Lastschriftverfahren: Ich/wir ermächtige(n) Sie hiermit widerruflich, den Rechnungsbetrag je Band von meinem/unserem folgendem Konto einzuziehen.

Kontoinhaber: _____ Kreditinstitut: _____
Kontonummer: _____ Bankleitzahl: _____

International Subscription:
Payment (incl. s & h and VAT) in advance for
❐ 10 volumes/copies (€ 319.80)   ❐ 20 volumes/copies (€ 599.80)
❐ 40 volumes/copies (€ 1,099.80)
Please send my books to:

NAME_____ DEPARTMENT_____
ADDRESS _____
POST/ZIP CODE_____ COUNTRY _____
TELEPHONE _____ EMAIL _____

date/signature_____

A hint for librarians in the former Soviet Union: Your academic library might be eligible to receive free-of-cost scholarly literature from Germany via the German Research Foundation. For Russian-language information on this program, see
http://www.dfg.de/forschungsfoerderung/formulare/download/12_54.pdf.

Please fax to: **0511 / 262 2201 (+49 511 262 2201)**
or mail to: *ibidem*-Verlag, Julius-Leber-Weg 11, D-30457 Hannover, Germany
or send an e-mail: ibidem@ibidem-verlag.de

ibidem-Verlag
Melchiorstr. 15
D-70439 Stuttgart

info@ibidem-verlag.de

www.ibidem-verlag.de
www.edition-noema.de
www.autorenbetreuung.de